"Wondrous.... The players' humble triumphs remind us that no win is too small.... *One Goal* illustrates how sport changed the history of a small town in Maine and connected so many people. It's a relevant tale in today's political climate, where fear and bigotry can be conquered by inclusion, understanding, and the beautiful game."

—Shireen Ahmed, cohost of the Burn It All Down podcast

"The power of sports in a community is illustrated convincingly in *One Goal*."   —*The Christian Science Monitor*

"[A] relevant and rewarding narrative ... Bass's effective portrayal of Lewiston as a microcosm of America's changing culture should be required reading."   —*Publishers Weekly*

"Bass captures the essence of this unlikely band of brothers perfectly. This isn't a story about a soccer team.... More than anything, this is a story of hope. The hope that brought thousands of Africans to a remote corner of America in search of a better life. The hope that made a city finally open its arms to the children of those immigrants. The hope that our future still might be better than our past."

—Tom Caron, anchor, New England Sports Network

"On the surface, [*One Goal*] seems to be a soccer story, chronicling a high school soccer team as they try to win the state championship. But the community has a larger story to tell, and Bass does this masterfully. A touching account that is highly recommended for all readers."   —*Library Journal*

"The inspirational story of how Somali refugees and native-born white kids in Lewiston, Maine, banded together to win a state championship, helping bridge racial and cultural divides ...Bass broadens the story to show how it fits into the story of immigration, racism, Islamaphobia, and economic decline in rust belt American towns." —*The Hollywood Reporter*

"*One Goal* is *Friday Night Lights* for the twenty-first century." —Brian Phillips, author of *Impossible Owls*

MORE PRAISE FOR

ONE GOAL

"Amy Bass tells a story that encompasses many of the things people love about sports, but also epitomizes many of the reasons sports matter."   —Bob Costas

"In this noisy era of glib hot takes and childish finger-pointing, it's too easy to forget that the national character—hardworking, immigrant-fueled, optimistic—was built from the bottom up. Let Amy Bass remind you. Let her take you to our frosty upper right-hand corner, to Lewiston, Maine, where quiet heroes like Mike McGraw, Abdi H., and the magical Blue Devils show again just how it's done. This is not just a great story, deftly reported and unflinchingly told. It's not just a story of one obscure high school season. It's *the* American story, just when you feared that it might be fading fast, renewed."
                      —S. L. Price, *Sports Illustrated* senior writer and author of
         Playing Through the Whistle: Steel, Football and an American Town

"A lively, informative, and entertaining ... underdog story that skillfully blends elements of human compassion, passion for a sport, determination, and endurance with overtones of societal pressure and racism. It's an exhilarating narrative that shows how perseverance and the ability to disregard the narrow-mindedness of xenophobia can lead to victory.... An edifying and adrenaline-charged tale."   —*Kirkus Reviews* (starred review)

ONE GOAL

ONE GOAL

A COACH, A TEAM,
AND THE GAME
THAT BROUGHT
A DIVIDED TOWN TOGETHER

AMY BASS

hachette
BOOKS

NEW YORK   BOSTON

Hachette Books
Hachette Book Group
1290 Avenue of the Americas
New York, NY 10104
hachettebookgroup.com
twitter.com/hachettebooks

First Edition: February 2018

Hachette Books is a division of Hachette Book Group, Inc.

The Hachette Books name and logo are trademarks of Hachette Book Group, Inc.

The publisher is not responsible for websites (or their content) that are not owned by the publisher.

The Hachette Speakers Bureau provides a wide range of authors for speaking events. To find out more, go to www.hachettespeakersbureau.com or call (866) 376-6591.

Library of Congress Cataloging-in-Publication Data

Names: Bass, Amy, author.
Title: One goal : a coach, a team, and the game that brought a divided town together / Amy Bass.
Description: First edition. | New York : Hachette Books, 2018.
Identifiers: LCCN 2017034578 | ISBN 9780316396547 (hardback) | ISBN 9780316511018 (large print) | ISBN 9781478923794 (audio download) | ISBN 9780316396578 (ebook) Subjects: LCSH: Soccer--Maine--Lewiston--History. | Lewiston High School (Lewiston, Me.)--Soccer--History. | Somalis--Maine--Lewiston. | Race relations--Maine--Lewiston. | Lewiston (Me.)--Social conditions. | BISAC: BIOGRAPHY & AUTOBIOGRAPHY / Sports. | SPORTS & RECREATION / Soccer.Classification: LCC GV944.U6 B37 2018 | DDC 796.334/620974182--dc23 LC record available at https://lccn.loc.gov/2017034578

ISBNs: 978-0-316-39655-4 (trade paperback), 978-0-316-39657-8 (ebook), 978-0-316-51101-8 (large print)

Printed in the United States of America

LSC-C

10 9 8 7 6 5 4 3 2 1

For Sundus and Miles and Saaliha and my Hannah.

May they ensure the future welcomes all, everywhere, always.

CONTENTS

When you have a football at your feet, you are free.
                                              —Ronaldinho

INTRODUCTION

Master of the front handspring flip throw-in, Maulid Abdow held the ball and surveyed the vast field before him under the gray November sky. His teammates spread in a sea of blue across the green pitch—Karim and Moha, Nuri and Q, Maslah and Abdi H. White-shirted Scarborough defenders multiplied by the second. Scarborough's goalkeeper, Cameron Nigro, stood out among the scrambling traffic before the box, his black-and-gold adidas flame shirt mirroring his shocking blond Mohawk. He towered above the fray, a human roadblock before the net.

If Sid Vicious ever thought about playing soccer, he would've looked to Cam Nigro for style tips.

Maulid knew that his parents, Hassan Matan and Shafea Omar—neither of whom spoke much English, but both could talk soccer—were somewhere in the stadium amidst the cacophony cheering the Lewiston Blue Devils. Women, heads covered by colorful hijabs, sat next to students with faces painted blue and white. Men in *koofiyads* cheered beside those in baseball caps and ski hats.

Some 4,500 fans—the highest attendance ever for a high school soccer game in Maine—made their presence known from the stands of Portland's Fitzpatrick Stadium on November 7, 2015. They gathered to watch the undefeated Blue Devils finish their season on top, which they had failed to do just one year ago against Cheverus High School. The 113 goals that brought them to this moment didn't matter anymore. Their national ranking didn't matter anymore. The goal they had scored earlier, the one a referee took away—"offside" was the call—didn't matter anymore. All that mattered was this moment, this game, this team.

Maulid glanced at the clock: just over sixteen minutes remained. Funny and charming off the field, his deep voice often gently ribbing his friends before descending into rich laughter, he now stood deadly serious. His slim legs fidgeted back and forth, his hot-pink-and-blue cleats making dizzying patterns as his right foot pushed out in front, ready to take the lead.

"Ohhhhhh, this isn't the jungle!" he heard, followed by what he assumed were monkey noises. "Stop flipping!"

Maulid had no patience for racist trash talk, but Scarborough fans had a reputation. There'd been an incident about a year ago when Scarborough played Deering. But Coach drilled into them that putting points on the scoreboard was the best response, something he intended to do right now.

"We play," Coach McGraw said in one of his legendary pre-game speeches, "the right way. You rise above everybody else. We play hard. We play fair. Because winning without playing fair is a shallow victory. You let other people play those games. Those games take energy, energy that they waste."

Just beat 'em.

Everything the coach said corresponded to what Maulid's parents told him about living in Maine: ignore ignorance. His parents were very happy to live in Lewiston. They appreciated the schools, health care, and jobs. Those things were important. But it was more than that. They felt free in Lewiston; something his mother had realized when she traveled back to Africa on a U.S. passport for the first time to see her family. Compared to what she saw there, she could never say that life in Lewiston was hard, no matter what it threw at her.

But it wasn't perfect. She understood that no matter how long they were in Maine, not everyone would be okay with it. Her kids told her about the stuff people wrote online, in response to the many newspaper articles over the years about Somalis living in Lewiston. She heard it herself when running errands or heading to her job at Walmart or to babysit. "Why are you here?" they asked, sometimes swearing. "Why are you taking money from our government?" Worry about yourself, she told her children. Yes, it hurts, but they can't hurt you. They have no authority to do anything to you.

On the field, Maulid heard it all, especially when the game turned rough, as it often did against Lewiston. Years ago, when he first came to America, he had no idea what kids were saying to him, but he knew it wasn't good. Now he understood those kinds of words all too well.

"Get outta my side, nigger," a defender might taunt. "Go back to your country."

"I can't go back," Maulid says of such incidents, understanding that Lewiston is his home because it has to be. "And if I could, they can't make me."

Ignore them, Maulid thought as Scarborough fans continued to bait him. He didn't have it as bad as Mohamed "Moe" Khalid, who played in the backline on this side. They were relentless to Moe, but he could take it. Moe played lacrosse in the spring and was no stranger to the n-word.

At least they're watching, Maulid thought. He looked back at the bleachers and grinned just for the hell of it. They could say whatever they wanted. He wasn't going to stop.

He squeezed the white-and-black ball tighter, pressing it harder between his palms. It no longer felt slippery. He hoped a little spit on his dark fingers would be the magic glue that gave him the pinpoint precision he needed.

In a battle such as the one unfolding on the field, Maulid understood how a set piece—a moment when the ball returns to play after a stoppage, usually by a corner kick, free kick, or throw-in—could make all the difference. In the game against Bangor just a few days earlier, Maulid had made it happen. Indeed, he felt like he'd done it a million times before, but every second of this game felt like the first. At the half, McGraw had emphasized they had to find one chance, one play, to get that one goal.

"Let's see what kind of conditioning we've got," he'd said to his huddling players as they bounced on their toes. "Let's take advantage of the one break we're going to get, and we'll see what we'll see."

Watching Maulid from the sidelines, Coach Mike McGraw knew all too well that the longer Scarborough held down his offense, the more one play could make the difference. They hadn't been held scoreless for an entire half all season. This was unfamiliar territory.

No, he assured anyone who asked. He didn't *need* a state title. He *wanted* one. More than anything. In the classroom, on the field, he was a patient man. But he'd waited a long time for this chance. Thirty-three years, to be exact. One would be hard-pressed to find a more experienced high school soccer coach than McGraw, who first took Lewiston to a state soccer final in 1991. Then, his roster had names like Kevin and Steve, John and Tony. Now he coached Muktar, Maslah, Karim, and Abdi H. For many reasons, this was not the same team.

All but one on the starting varsity roster were refugees.

The meteoric rise of the Lewiston Blue Devils to the top ranks of U.S. high school soccer shows what happens when America works the way it is supposed to; the way it reads on paper. On the surface, the Blue Devils are a simple feel-good tale: refugee kids playing soccer. But theirs is more than just a great sports story. The Blue Devils made their championship run in one of the whitest states in America, in a city that didn't talk about hope for a long time. They played soccer while politicians debated Syrian refugees and American security, and the presidential campaign of Donald J. Trump generated headlines about the prospect of building a wall to keep out immigrants, illegal or otherwise.

But the world's 60 million refugees are not mere immigrants. Theirs is almost always a story of war, of people fleeing—by foot, by water, by any means necessary—a dying country toward a life of limbo. The families of these soccer players arrived in Lewiston to mixed receptions and created a community with soccer at its core, the players translating tight-knit family and community connections to success on the field. As they learned to deal with language barriers, racial slurs, and new cultural norms, they played soccer in city parks and recreational leagues. In winter, they gathered in the parking lot of the Colisée, the local hockey arena, sky-high snowbanks marking the goals. Once the boys were playing for local legend McGraw in high school, they built a team with one goal: the first state soccer championship in Lewiston history.

A small, Catholic, French-Canadian city on the banks of the Androscoggin River, Lewiston isn't the Maine of blueberry pie and lobster boils, sailboats and the Bush family. For decades, the former mill town's postwar economic downturn saw its abandoned redbrick factory buildings begin to crumble into the river and canals. By 2000, more than half of the city's families with children under five lived at or below the poverty line. Residents of Auburn, the "twin" city across the river, refer to "Dirty Lew" with a scorn usually reserved for thieves and murderers, both of which they claim Lewiston is filled with.

But in 2001, Lewiston changed. Thousands of Somali refugees knocked on the city's door, drastically altering its sense of self. In about a decade's time, the city of 36,000 welcomed approximately 7,000 African immigrants. Never in modern U.S. history had a city of this size taken in so many newcomers so quickly. The new residents shifted Lewiston's demographic landscape, halting the population decline that had plagued the city for the last three decades.

According to U.S. census data, before the Somali influx, some 96 percent of Lewiston identified as white; almost a third spoke a language other than English at home, primarily French. Within a decade, the city's non-white population surged over 800 percent, seven times higher than the state average of 1.2 percent. Nowhere is this more apparent than at the high school, one of the largest in the state. Of its 1,300 or so students, approximately 25 percent are African immigrants, the majority of whom are Somali.

The soccer team represents a coming of age for Somalis in Lewiston and a blueprint of sorts for a global future. The team's success embodies a negotiation between an immigrant community and its chosen home, an often difficult conversation about language, religion, culture, education, and family.

Soccer has been a microcosm of Lewiston's transition from former factory town to global host. These players, McGraw says to anyone who asks, are seeds that can grow into something new for Lewiston. It's not a *Hoop Dreams* story, where kids use sports to escape something. These kids aren't trying to escape—that part already happened—and they aren't problems to be solved. They are classmates, teammates, and neighbors, forging relationships for a community to emulate. Soccer is how these kids live where they landed.

CHAPTER 1

WHY NOT US?

When Lewiston lost its first state championship—a 2–0 shutout by Brunswick—in 1991, Mike McGraw didn't know when, or if, he'd get another chance. Many hoped the next year would be it, but it wasn't. Despite scoring fifty goals—the most yet in Lewiston history—players such as Dan LeClerc, Earl St. Hilaire, and Swedish exchange student Per Kiltorp did not get back to the final. But eventually, some twenty-three years later, November 8, 2014—a year before Maulid tried to figure out how to get the ball over the heads of Scarborough's defense—McGraw got another chance.

The 2014 Maine Class A Boys Soccer State Championship had all the hype of a Hollywood movie. As the *Lewiston Sun Journal* explained, the game pitted Lewiston's fairy-tale season against the Cinderella run of Cheverus High School.

Seeded seventh entering the playoffs, Cheverus was delighted just to be at the ball, filling its Twitter feeds with the hashtag "#WhyNotUs?" as it worked through the playoff bracket. Not only were the Stags there to win, they might actually have the chops to make it happen.

Why *not* them?

Lewiston's team rode into the championship game confident about the outcome. Despite some battles along the way, they had a nearly flawless record. In early October, after a hard-fought 2–1 win over Bangor, even the usually reserved McGraw admitted they could go all the way, peaking at exactly the right time, playing like a championship team. But the Blue Devils had a lot of baggage to deal with, coming up short in heartbreaking fashion year after year.

In 2012, a second-seeded Lewiston squad faced top-seeded Mt. Ararat in the regional final, the last stop before the state championship game. Even now, Lewiston Athletic Director Jason Fuller can't talk about it without grimacing.

"Still painful," he says.

With forty-six seconds of regulation play left on the clock, Lewiston tied Mt. Ararat 1–1. Excited Lewiston fans spilled onto the field, creating chaos and merriment despite Fuller's best efforts to keep them in their seats. He knew the refs weren't going to like a horde of cheering kids running over the sideline. When junior midfielder Abdullahi Shaleh ripped off his shirt, a once-popular move that FIFA outlawed in 2003, an official quickly raised a yellow card.

The call? Excessive celebration.

From the stands, Denis Wing, whose son Austin was then a freshman goalie, shook his head at the call. He wanted to be surprised that the ref had booked the kid, but knew all too well what some officials did when Lewiston was on the field. He had once played soccer for Lewiston.

Wing grew up on Chestnut Street. It's a neighborhood where many of the Somali players now live, in the rectangular triple- and quadruple-stacked apartment houses of Lewiston's "tree streets." Upperclassmen at nearby Bates College are known to warn freshmen to turn back if they ever hit Walnut, Chestnut, Ash, and so on. But Wing only knew it as his old neighborhood, bristling whenever he heard someone talk badly about Lewiston's "downtown kids," code words for Somali. *He* was once a kid who lived downtown, back when the phrase described French-Canadian kids like him. From sunrise to sunset, he played next to the Colisée parking lot in Drouin Field, kicking balls through a set of rusted goalposts.

The Wings—Denis and his wife, Kathy; Austin and his younger brother, Dalton—now live in a house with a pool on the outskirts of town. Denis and Kathy liked helping out with their sons' teams, becoming increasingly involved with soccer's Booster Club, and were sideline fixtures on game days. Denis Wing knew soccer well. But today, he was confused. He watched as Mt. Ararat's goalie talked to the official. After a quick back-and-forth, the goalie walked back to the box. The referee brought out a red card. Taunting.

Down on the field, McGraw stood stunned as Mt. Ararat fans cheered. Taunting? How could Abdullahi taunt fans who were on the other side of the bleachers? Taunting *who*, exactly?

Wing couldn't believe it, either. The red card was bad enough, but the way it happened seemed absurd. The goalie talks to a ref, and a red card comes out? The ref was going to take the word of what the goalie *said* happened? If it was excessive celebration *and* taunting, why didn't the red card come out in the first place?

For generations, Lewiston athletes knew all too well what other schools thought of them. Even before the Somalis started playing, before questions of racial bias threatened every time a ref pulled a card, Lewiston got a bum rap. When teams played Lewiston, McGraw says, they tended to "junk it up a little bit." The "Dirty Lew" has long resonated throughout the state as a city filled with broken homes, cars, and people; not the stuff of tourism brochures. McGraw remembers once, long ago, when one of his players got a yellow card in a game against Westbrook. Baffled about what the player had done, McGraw asked for clarification.

"Typical Lewiston kid!" the ref replied, an answer McGraw knew all too well.

"We didn't lose to Westbrook for a long time after that," McGraw chuckles.

Wing could never get over the kinds of calls that Lewiston stomached, or the calls other teams didn't get, especially now that Lewiston fielded a team with so many brown faces. And it wasn't only with soccer. In 2007, a man threw some kind of substance into Mohamed Noor's eyes at the New England Cross Country Championships in the wooded part of the course. Previously unbeaten, Lewiston's star runner fell from second to 124th place, running much of the race with his eyes shut. An ambulance crew later treated him for extreme nausea; the perpetrator was never caught.

Wing knew the game he was watching was no exception. *What about Mt. Ararat stepping over the line on every throw-in?* he thought. But no. Instead, Lewiston got a red card for taunting, the refs visibly irritated that fans stormed the field, and went into overtime a man down.

Lewiston's offense dominated overtime but couldn't find the back of the net. Two minutes into the second overtime, Mt. Ararat did, redirecting a long throw-in. The Blue Devils collapsed on the field as the Eagles ran screaming to the cheers of the home crowd.

"The kid's foot was over the line again," a parent near Wing said, staring at the field. "His foot was *definitely* over the line."

Coach McGraw felt the loss. It hurt. Years later, he can pull out an instant replay of that game as if it was yesterday.

"I kicked myself in the hind end because instead of taking a player out of the attacking zone and putting him defensively, I should've taken a midfielder and put him up in the attacking end," he says of the lesson he learned that day. "Then, instead of attacking with four midfielders like we do, attack with three and still have five extra guys—our defenders can hold their own. Or even take an extra defender off and put him up front, because we were that good."

McGraw knows that hindsight is twenty-twenty. But the loss to Mt. Ararat was a wake-up call. Never again would he panic when playing a man down.

A year later, in 2013, Lewiston returned to the regional final, this time against Hampden Academy. The Blue Devils trailed by a goal at halftime, their fast-paced offense slowed by a strong Bronco defense. With Austin Wing, now a sophomore, in goal, Lewiston launched an uncompromising comeback in the second half that forced the game into overtime. But it ended in heartbreak: a Hampden header happened so fast Austin barely had time to think about warding it off. Reaching the state championship game had become Lewiston's ultima Thule, seemingly in reach yet unattainable.

"You guys have been so snakebitten!" other coaches said to McGraw, reeling off snapshots from Lewiston's greatest defeats: last-second throw-ins going in, balls hitting off the back. Losing big games became Lewiston's calling card.

The 2014 season changed that.

The team emblazoned its new attitude on the back of a t-shirt senior midfielder Mike Wong designed. "Our Turn," it announced above the outline of a player on his knees, arms outstretched overhead in victory. The boys were confident, in sync. They dominated opponents, playing a fierce offense that paid little heed to anyone's defense. Their backline, composed of a mix of Wong, Zak Abdulle, Aden "Biwe" Mohamed, and Ibrahim Hussein, protected what the fleet feet of the offense put into the net, offensive energy feeding defensive determination.

At the end of the regular season, twin city rival Edward Little High School, which sits atop Goff Hill in Auburn just across the Androscoggin River, forced the Blue Devils to play from behind for the first time that fall. But they made up for it in the second half, scoring three times in the last twelve minutes of the game. Karim Abdulle and Abdi Shariff-Hassan—Abdi H.— converted penalty kicks. Senior Gage Cote met a cross from Hassan "Speedy" Mohamed, a kid whose nickname fit so well even his mother adopted it, and lasered it into the net.

Speedy was the kind of kid McGraw liked to spring on other teams. He wasn't the prettiest of soccer players, but the champion sprinter moved faster than anyone McGraw had ever seen, from midfield to the box and back again in a flash. If the opposition's defense tried to chase him down, which was almost impossible, more opportunities opened for his teammates. If the opposition decided he couldn't be defended, he could get the ball in front of someone for a shot, as he did with Gage.

McGraw was thrilled that his team successfully came from behind, knowing it was good preparation for the playoffs. The Blue Devils ended the regular season 13–0–1, marking only the third time the team finished undefeated, and the first time since 1981. Finally, they were the top seed heading into the playoffs.

As the t-shirt said, it was their turn.

After handily making their way through the postseason bracket, the Blue Devils knew they had the chops to beat Brunswick in the regional final. Lewiston's front line netted sixty-six goals that season, while the defense allowed only twelve. They'd won four of their last seven games in shutouts.

But the team had to make some adjustments when two key defenders were benched after getting caught at a party with alcohol. Photographs rapidly circulated through social media, ensuring that everyone knew about it. Mike McGraw believed in rules and consequences, playoffs or not. More than winning, he wanted his players to learn. But it was a tough lesson.

The Blue Devils had a deep squad and could work around missing players. McGraw moved Moe Khalid, who played midfield off the bench, to the backline. Midfielders play between the offensive forwards and the defenders, connecting the two lines. Depending on a team's strategic formation on any given day, midfielders have to be versatile. Some lean toward defense, breaking up opponents' attacks. Others swing between offensive and defensive roles, using good passing skills, stamina, and speed to work the ball box-to-box. Still others, the most creative and adept, are playmakers, more attack-minded. They control possession and pick out the perfect killer pass, doing less defensive work than their teammates.

Strong and with some size, Moe tended to play more defensively, but he was able to switch gears and turn strength into speed when needed.

"I can attack," he says of his versatility. "Wherever I am, I always attack."

Moe liked the move to defense. It suited his competitive temperament, which could be aggressive. While he's charming and handsome, Moe's moods swing dramatically, changing from amiable to ferocious in a flash. He has always been this way, fiercely strong-willed, sometimes abrasive, extremely independent, and very outspoken. The loyalty he shows friends, the sweet demeanor he reserves for family—especially younger brother Sharmarke— can morph into fury. He is, he admits, no stranger to trouble.

Moe grew up in Hagadera, one of five refugee camps in Dadaab, Kenya. Run by the United Nations High Commissioner for Refugees (UNHCR), Dadaab is the world's largest refugee camp, overcrowded and underfunded. Located in Kenya's Garissa County, the UN estimates that some 350,000 refugees inhabit the rows of dwellings made of varying combinations of tarp, plastic, and mud. Others estimate that the population approaches half a million. If considered a city, Dadaab would be Kenya's third largest. The hotels, shopping centers, taxis, buses, and schools are largely run by refugees, and stimulate the regional economy. According to a recent World Bank report, Dadaab generates approximately $14 million within the Kenyan economy each year. Other analysts claim the figure could be twice that.

From the air, Dadaab would resemble the tract housing found in many American suburbs. Homes are lined up on square partitions of land. Dusty, straight roads in right angles connect them. But on the ground, the view is very different. Families scramble to get water, wood, and food during daylight hours, standing in long lines for rations while keeping a watchful eye on encroaching darkness, wary of the crime that escalates once the sun goes down.

The camp was established in 1991 as a stopgap measure to house those fleeing the bloodshed that accompanied the ouster of Somali president Mohamed Siad Barre. But recently the Kenyan government has made clear that it wants out of the refugee business, claiming—accurately, it seems—that the camps harbor members of the Al-Shabaab terrorist group. In 2013, Kenyan and Somali leaders signed an agreement to begin the repatriation of Dadaab's residents. In the wake of the Al-Shabaab attack on Garissa University College in 2015 that left 147 dead, efforts to close Dadaab gained momentum, despite the fact that the attackers were Kenyan, not Somali.

Unlike some of his teammates, who simply say "nice"—a word they use often in response to a question they don't want to answer—when asked about growing up in a refugee camp, Moe speaks freely, vividly, about his time in Hagadera. He remembers the day the grocery store burned down. The robberies. The daily demand to get fresh water before the well shut down during Asr, the third of the five daily prayers, around four o'clock in the afternoon. He remembers his mother, Habibo Farah, a small, shy woman he describes as "the strongest person I know," walking to different houses at night, searching for leftovers his family could have for dinner. He remembers nights with no dinner at all. His father wasn't around much, there was little money, and hunger threatened constantly.

When he was just three years old, he saw one of his best friends digging through his own excrement to find something, anything, to eat.

Moe still has mixed emotions about leaving Kenya. Just six years old, he was excited about living in America. But his two teenage sisters, Halima and Marwa, had to stay behind because they were older, and the system didn't recognize them as immediate family. Farah remembers being too afraid to ask questions, worried that she would lose her window to the United States. It was an agonizing decision, but the need to feed and educate her younger children won out.

Moe came to Lewiston in November 2005 via Elizabeth, New Jersey. The five months in New Jersey remain etched in his mind. He recalls neighborhood kids making fun of the way his mother talked, and hearing Farah crying at night. She couldn't speak English and didn't know anyone. She worried about her girls still in Africa. He remembers his first day of school, third grade, when he had to share a desk because there weren't enough. A little girl with dark hair and tan skin called out to him, beckoning with her hands. He didn't understand a word she said but understood she wanted him to sit with her. Relieved, he went to her desk and sat, not knowing what to do next. The girl continued to talk to him, putting her arm around him in a sort of half-hug. Terrified, Moe froze. What was she doing? It was the first of many things he didn't understand.

But when his family arrived in Maine, they found people who

understood. They settled in a ground-floor apartment just off Kennedy Park across from Country Kitchen, a giant baked goods factory. During Ramadan, the smell of baking bread that permeates the street all day makes fasting even harder than usual. In the apartment's small kitchen, her bare feet moving quickly on the yellow linoleum floor, Farah prepares stews and fried dough for her children to eat with *sambusa* for *iftar*, the meal that breaks the fast after sundown. A cooler of tea with milk sits on the small table in the middle of the room next to a stack of fresh *malawah* or *sabaayad*, the family's cat eyeing everything warily.

There were occasional gaffes in Lewiston, like the time Sharmarke ordered mac and cheese at Applebee's and didn't know there was bacon in it. In school, cafeteria workers knew to prevent Somali kids from grabbing a slice of pepperoni pizza, but restaurants were different. Pork is *haram*, or forbidden, in Islam, as pigs are considered unclean. Observant Muslims do not eat or touch them. That night, Sharmarke dreamed he was turning into a pig, something big sister Safiya still laughs about.

There were other things, too. While school was tolerable, Moe soon learned that people in cars could be, in his words, "pretty racist," often yelling, "Go back to *your* country!" as they drove by. His neighbor, too, an older, white veteran, seemed none too happy they were there. Moe would overhear him complaining about his family. "Those black kids are all just a bunch of thieves," he'd say. "They benefit off the government, and they don't work for shit."

Moe's mother, who finds strength in her daily readings of the Koran, didn't care about such blather, but she worried about her son's temper. "There's a lot of idiots out there," she told him, encouraging him to be strong. "Ignore them."

For the most part, though, Lewiston was okay, especially on the soccer field. Moe found soccer in Lewiston almost immediately, playing in a small downtown field with a bunch of older kids. They created their own leagues—red, yellow, and blue—and played mini-tournaments. When he was eleven, he scored against one of the best players in the neighborhood, making his older mentors proud. They taught him to play tough, and he learned to never be intimidated.

Moe doesn't remember a time when he didn't play soccer. It's his much-needed outlet, his escape. Soccer channels the anger that sometimes boils over. In Hagadera, he often skipped school to play, preferring a friendly game in the streets to the beatings he often received from teachers.

Coach McGraw knew Moe could concentrate his energy to clear the ball as well as anybody, twisting his body to get the most force he could out of a kick, leaning back and watching it sail away with precision. Moe was one of the reasons McGraw wasn't worried about making changes to the team's defense before the 2014 regional final against Brunswick. His guys played every day. They were as familiar with each other as with their own families. It was an essential part of their winning formula.

After a scoreless first half, McGraw encouraged Karim to shoot more, noting that Brunswick's goalie wasn't very tall. As always, Karim obeyed. Early in the second half, his back to the goal, he faked direction, twirled around, and rocketed the ball into the net with his left foot. Less than half a minute later, he knocked in another one. It was done: Lewiston 2, Brunswick 1. After two years of playoff catastrophes, Lewiston eradicated its anguish to become the 2014 Eastern Class A Regional Champions. For the first time since 1991, and only the second time ever, the Blue Devils headed to the state final. McGraw was ecstatic as he watched the team celebrate. But there was still one game left to play, and it was a game Lewiston had never won.

McGraw's caution was justified. If the undefeated Blue Devils were the closest thing Maine high school soccer had to a Goliath, the Cheverus Stags were about to become their David.

Founded in 1917, Cheverus is a private co-educational Catholic school overlooking Portland's scenic Back Cove district. The school has bucketsful of state sports titles, especially cross-country running and indoor track, but only one soccer championship, a 2–1 victory over Mt. Ararat in 2001. Going into the playoffs in 2014, Cheverus posted a dismal record in its last regular season games, 1–1–4. However, it quickly became an unlikely contender for the state title as it shocked second-seeded Falmouth in the quarters and top-ranked Scarborough in the regional final.

Why not them?

From Indiana's Milan High School—the Hoosiers story—to the Miracle on Ice at the Lake Placid Winter Olympics in 1980, sports thrive on Cinderella stories. In 2014, Cheverus wanted to claim a glass slipper by vanquishing top-seeded Lewiston.

The Stags, especially their keeper, peaked at exactly the right time. Jacob Tomkinson was nothing short of a miracle worker in goal, warding off Lewiston's overwhelmingly dominant advantage in shots. From the get-go, Abdi H. felt something was a little off. He tried to outshoot his nervousness in the early minutes, but hit the woodwork over and over again.

"Keep going," he chanted. "Stay positive."

At the half, down 1–0, Moe was worried, his handsome face crinkled as he listened to McGraw. Like Abdi H., he felt something was off, something more than nerves. It was like they had started to give up. But McGraw told them he didn't care about the one-goal deficit; the game was going exactly as he imagined. He knew Cheverus would try to weather Lewiston's offensive storm, squeak in a goal, and hold tight. But he was confident they would attack in the second half while the Stags held on for dear life in a defensive shell.

But expect the unexpected, McGraw warned. It's what he always said.

"They got one opportunity," he remembers of that second half.
"The shot deflected off one of our players and just slid into the
goal, two to nothing."

He refused to panic, but he decided it might be time to worry.

"Then we're in a scramble," McGraw recalls. "At that point, my
kids are playing their brains out. And we're in the box. They've
got everybody back in the box and we're just pounding and
pounding, and finally get a goal."

After the Blue Devils scored, they got a penalty kick because
of a handball in the box. The day before, they endlessly practiced
kicks, over and over, in hope of just this kind of gift. With a tie,
they could ride into overtime and finish it. All Abdi H. had to do
was put it in the net.

There is an almost regal quality about Abdirahman Shariff
Hassan, or Abdi H., as Coach—and most everyone else—called
him, something he inherited from his father, Omar Mohamed,
who'd been a religious teacher in Somalia. It was how his parents
had met: his mother's younger siblings went to his dad to learn
the Koran. People still came to his father to study, gathering in the
family's Lewiston apartment for lessons.

Abdi H. has a quiet, slight presence, standing about five foot
eight. He is polite, humble, and offers a timid but warm hand-
shake that belies his strength. His beautiful face looks like someone
drew him, except he is standing right there, his skin almost
translucent with a tan sheen that glows around his chiseled fea-
tures. His profile is distinguished, powerful, intense.

On the soccer field, Abdi H. leaves no question regarding his
command of the game, his concern for his teammates, and his
desire to win. His eyes are everywhere, working the field like a
chess game to stay two, three, four strategic steps ahead of his

opponent. He sees things no one else does. But off the field, he is soft-spoken, thoughtful. When he smiles, his mouth barely moves, the corners turning up only slightly, yet somehow consuming his entire face. It is a rare occurrence, something usually reserved for family or closest friends. But when he does smile, you feel like you've won something.

Abdi H.'s family came to Maine via Kentucky. Like so many of his teammates' families, his parents fled Somalia during the civil war. They landed in Ifo, another of Dadaab's camps, where he was born.

Like Moe, Abdi H. remembers many details of refugee camp life. He recalls his mother "farming" a small garden, helping her when he was just three years old. He remembers the tiny clothing shop his father worked in, where the child helped his father fold items after customers came through. He also remembers the violence of the camps, the assaults, the fear, and the danger. But most of all, he remembers playing soccer.

To his parents, nothing was more important than school. They saved money to hire a private teacher, but the lure of soccer often won out. He remembers going with his older brother to find games, matches staged between buildings to stay out of sight from the police. When the police would finally come to send them all to school, they simply moved their game to another alley.

In 2005, Abdi H.'s family made it to the United States. They were lucky, managing to stay intact and move together. Others spend years waiting for resettlement authorization. Many, like Moe's sisters, are separated.

Louisville was, he recalls, a "rough" time for them, an overwhelming experience. "I was little," he says. "And it was the first time I saw white people, too, so I was just scared."

Thrown into second grade at age eight, he didn't understand anything anyone said to him. He remembers looking out the win-

dow at kids playing, asking his mother, Adey Amin, why they left
Kenya. "It will get better," she patiently told him each time, thinking about the violence of the camp, the beatings, the stuff Abdi
H. didn't yet know about. When she and his father escaped Somalia with his three older siblings during the war, she said, it took
them a long time to get used to Kenya. But they did. And now he
would get used to America.

However, life in the refugee camp was all Abdi H. had ever
known. Every morning, he had walked five miles to a well with
his mother to get water—it was so heavy, he remembers—for the
family. His father walked with them before heading to the market, where he would try to sell things. One morning, the routine
changed.

"*Soo baax,* Abdirahman," his mother said to him. "Let's go." He
was sad to leave behind his things and his friends, yet he was excited. But once in Kentucky, his new life just didn't feel right.

"We didn't speak English and our parents didn't speak English,
and it was just so hard to get around and communicate with other
people," he recollects. "And the Somali population in Kentucky is
not as large as Lewiston—we didn't have the community, and my
parents said we had to move to Maine so we can have people help
us out."

They had family in Portland who'd been in the United States
for a while. These relatives knew the language—their English was
very good. They understood American culture. Abdi H.'s parents
uprooted the family again in hope of finding a better quality of
life.

When Abdi H. was in fourth grade, the family arrived in
Lewiston, where they found the Somali community they'd been
looking for. It wasn't about geography; it was about people. The
scars of Somalia's civil war went deep, but could not diminish the
importance of keeping their culture, language, and customs alive.

Finally, it seemed, they'd found a place that felt as close to home as could ever be in the United States. His father found a job at a local pizza company; his mother started babysitting. Abdi H. learned English, becoming his parents' translator and his younger siblings' homework helper.

Even with the added responsibilities, Lewiston felt better than Louisville to the new student at Montello Elementary School because of the community that welcomed them. He had peers who spoke Somali, who understood the ways of Islam, and who liked the same foods that he did. And, most important, they loved soccer.

"The game," he says, "just comes with the culture."

To say that Abdi H. is obsessed with soccer is an understatement. He fills his Twitter feed with games he watches; not just as a fan but rather, according to McGraw, as a student of the game. A snapshot of Amel Majri training. A match between Liverpool and Dortmund. Barça. Ronaldo.

"I do not want any C. Ronaldo haters to speak today," he tweeted after a hat trick by the Real Madrid star.

Abdi H. would watch the English Premier League (EPL) all day, every day, seven days a week. While many immigrants in the United States follow their homeland's national team, he is a Manchester United fan because he's never had a home team to cheer.

But his eyes light up at the prospect of Somalia playing soccer internationally. Because of civil war, FIFA prohibited sanctioned matches from taking place in Somalia. However, the country continued to harbor a passion for the game, whether it could be played in Mogadishu Stadium or not. While the national team, the Ocean Stars, has never qualified for the World Cup, soccer remains Somalia's most popular sport. Somali teams first emerged in the 1940s, created by the Somali Youth League, the country's first political party and a key player in its campaign for independence from colonial chains. The SYL put together a team—the Bondhere—to play against Italian expats, giving soccer a strong anti-colonial thread. The Somali Football Federation followed a decade later.

Soccer stadiums are among the few structures in Somalia relatively untouched by years of war and more recent violence by Al-Shabaab. While Al-Shabaab banned sport in 2008, today the 35,000-seat Mogadishu Stadium plays a central role in the country's tentative recovery plan.

But for kids like Abdi H., who spent the first years of their lives playing in Kenyan refugee camps, soccer doesn't need a stadium or uniforms or cleats. Soccer happens, he says, when there's a ball and a passion.

"The second you're done watching, you just want to go out there and start playing," he says of his obsession with the EPL.

When Abdi H. talks about soccer, he gets louder as he describes games and teams, especially his beloved Manchester United. He is animated, happy, loose. But on the field facing Cheverus that day in 2014, he was all business, feeling the pressure with every minute that passed on the clock.

In his final preparations for his penalty kick, Abdi H. bent over and touched the ball one last time, looking at it resting before his neon green-and-black cleats. He was cold. He wore leggings underneath his shorts and gloves on his hands, but for the first time during the game, he felt cold. He turned his head, his spray-painted blue hair in stark contrast to his white uniform, and waited for the ref to blow the whistle. As the ref raised his left hand, Tomkinson began to jump in the goal, opening his arms as Abdi H. took a small step back. Hearing the whistle, he moved back to make room for a short run while Tomkinson crouched, arms still outstretched. Abdi H. fired his shot as Tomkinson threw his body to the left, diving sideways.

The team believed the ball was going in. The fans believed the ball was going in. They had no question as to what would happen because Abdi H. hadn't missed a penalty kick all year. That's right: not one. All year. Until now.

Tomkinson embraced the ball, hugging it to his chest, and quickly leaped up as his team roared, a swarm of celebration. Abdi H. stood, dumbfounded, his hands gripping his head in disbelief. He turned and slowly started to walk back to midfield as Tomkinson booted the ball. It felt impossible to get back into the game, but he knew he had to.

"When you take a penalty, you just try to pick one side and place it, and hopefully you can beat the keeper," Abdi H. says of what had been his fail-safe move. "And I think from the get-go, from the beginning, the keeper picked his side and he just happened to go to the same side as me."

After the game, Abdi H. told McGraw his timing had been off because Tomkinson had moved into the middle just before the whistle. His kick went exactly where he wanted it to go, but without the kind of pace it should have had. Tomkinson devoured the low, left-leaning shot as if Abdi H. had told him where it was going to go.

"He played an awesome game," McGraw says of the Cheverus goalie. "A hot goalkeeper can mean the difference in a game."

Abdi H. tried to regroup, digging deep, but it was hard with the clock ticking.

"All right, what now?" he yelled, doubt creeping in, gnawing at him. "We can score one more! SCORE. ONE. MORE."

But as darkness descended on the field, Cheverus took its one-goal lead and did exactly what McGraw expected, putting in a defensive shell that didn't let anyone or anything through. The Stags were happy to just wait out the clock.

Within the local sports scene, Cheverus's 2–1 victory was an upset of enormous proportions. It was like Aston Villa's 1–0 victory over Bayern Munich in 1982 for the European Cup, or Denmark winning Euro '92, a tournament they qualified for only after Yugoslavia bowed out because of geopolitical instability.

It took only a moment for Mike Wong to realize he'd just played his last game. He fell to the ground, his face twisted in agony. He couldn't get up because when he did, it would really be over. Karim stood over him, his hand on his teammate's head as he waited for him to stand up.

"It's a cruel game," McGraw told reporters afterward. He praised his team, how they worked hard, kept their heads on straight. He acknowledged the chances they hadn't capitalized on. It was the same old story: It wasn't the right time. Maybe next year, maybe never.

His public face good-natured as ever, inside McGraw was angry.

"We played right into Cheverus's hands," he remembers, his face reddening at the thought of it. "We should've won it, and we did everything right."

But when he thinks about it, McGraw admits that isn't true.

"Not only were my players impatient, I was, too," he says. "I didn't settle them down and tell them to move the ball back, stretch them out, play the game, because we were..." He pauses, frustrated. "We were *so used* to dominating!"

And they did, at least on paper. The Blue Devils outshot the newly crowned state champion 21–7. But they didn't finish their shots, so they didn't finish what they set out to do. The 2015 season started, knew McGraw, right then and there.

"There was no way we were not going back."

CHAPTER 2

WE HAVE TO GO BACK

The bus ride to Lewiston from the Cheverus game was far different from the one that got them there. On their way to the game, the team proudly carried its winning season on the sleeves of their blue warm-up jackets. They were soaring; hair sprayed blue, wearing game-day Mohawks with mixed results. But now they sat in sweaty, suffocating, smothering silence, rehashing all that had happened.

"It was," remembers McGraw, "a pretty quiet ride."

The walk to the bus from the field felt interminable. Parents dotted the route, gently offering consoling remarks. The team kept its collective head down, barely acknowledging them.

Where was the bus, anyway? Why was it taking so long to find it?

On the bus, their misery only grew. They were hungry and wondered if they'd stop at Subway. In the old days, it was McDonald's, where both coach and bus driver ate for free. Now they couldn't do that because most of the players had no money for such things. But Kim Wettlaufer, a Lewiston businessman with deep connections to the Somali community, owned a bunch of Subway franchises and kept the team fed.

Maulid was hungry—he was always hungry—but he hated ordering. It made him nervous. He usually asked his dad to do it, even though his English wasn't all there either. Maulid never remembered what he liked. Besides, it was just food. It wasn't going to make anything better.

While the players stewed, McGraw had trouble sitting still at the front of the bus next to assistant coach Dan Gish. Gish felt terrible. He kept replaying the game in his head, growing more frustrated by the minute. *If we'd just put that first one in*, he thought, *the game would've been over because the offensive floodgates would've opened. Cheverus wouldn't have known what . . .*

Gish stopped. Would've. Should've. None of that had happened. Instead, they hit the crossbar. The post. Then Cheverus scored, not once but twice. Hustle goals; nothing they couldn't handle. But the pressure, the second-guessing, the hesitation—it just killed them. He could actually *feel* the kids thinking, *Uh-oh, here we go again.* Gish shook his head. He had to stop doing this. He needed to figure out something to say, anything to break the silence, fill the bus with its usual energy. But he had no words. He could only think they'd blown their chance. They finally got to a state championship game, and now it was over. Would they ever get back?

Gish turned to the man sitting next to him, a man he respected and loved. A man who'd waited so long for this chance, worked so hard, only to see it disappear.

"Coach, I'm so sorry," Gish whispered. "I don't know what to say."

The two briefly embraced, a tentative side-hug. After looking at Gish a moment, McGraw hoisted himself up and walked back to the middle of the bus, gripping each seat as he moved, his white hair making his cobalt blue eyes pop vividly. Hip and knee surgeries had taken a toll on this man who once played on a championship high school football team. He started to pace the aisle, talking, something he'd never in four decades of teaching and coaching had trouble doing. "We're coming back," he announced to the rows of defeated faces, his end-of-season hoarseness more strained than usual.

He surveyed the tops of their heads, waiting for them to look up, which they did when they heard his voice. He was Coach. When he spoke, they listened, staring at him directly. Eye contact was something many of them had had to learn. The Somali Bantu Youth Association gave workshops on such things. Their parents had raised them to look down as a sign of respect, to avoid looking directly into someone's eyes. But in the United States, whether it was a teacher, a cop, or a coach, eye contact was important.

"When we get off this bus, we train from day one, because we are gonna get there."

McGraw realized he'd just violated one of his own rules. He'd committed to the next season without his usual two-week waiting period. He'd tried to quit once. It was early in his career after a devastating loss. He went home and told Rita, his wife, that he didn't want to do it anymore.

"Look, you lost, you feel awful," Rita said. "Why don't you give it two weeks, and if you still feel the same way, resign."

So he waited, and then everything was fine. It was like coaching had become a bad habit, something that just kept coming back. Usually by December, he started thinking about what he had to do next, which teams he wanted to play over the summer, getting things ready. It was routine.

This time, he didn't need two weeks.

McGraw kept talking to the players, barely thinking about the words coming out of his mouth, knowing he was talking more for himself than for them. He wanted them to look ahead because what lay in the rearview mirror had crushed their souls. They were just kids. They were *his* kids.

"There is no denying we are gonna get back into this game," he repeated, "and we are going to *win* the game."

"Yep, *naäam,* yuh Coach, *haa,* yes, *ndiyo,* we are," the players muttered in their usual mix of Somali and Arabic, English and Swahili, nodding in agreement. They just wanted to sit. But they dutifully listened, earbuds and Beats hanging loosely around their necks, waiting to fill their heads with African music, rap, and pop.

McGraw continued his impromptu speech, feeling his blood pressure going up. Losing was not good for his health. His team's string of postseason tragedies, year after year, took a toll. The veins in his neck pulsed. He could hear his heartbeat in his head. His face got hot, and there was a slight ringing in his ears. He felt like what he wasn't saying was going to kill him: they should have won that game.

Instead, they played right into Cheverus's hands. *Cheverus,* for God's sake. The seventh seed. The word kept echoing in his head. The more he thought about it, the hotter he got. He thought it would be Scarborough. He was ready for Scarborough. How in God's name did Cheverus beat Scarborough to get into the final?

"In no uncertain terms," he said, his voice breaking, "we are going to be back. You'll go to school and hold your heads up, because your friends are still your friends and the people who love you still love you. It can be a cruel game that has been pretty beautiful for us, so go to bed and don't think too much. Tomorrow will be tough, and then it will get a little easier."

He felt bad for the seniors who couldn't go back, he said, players like Ibrahim and Mike and Speedy.

"We have to go back," McGraw said one last time. This was not the right ending to their season.

A few rows back, Austin Wing sat dejected and quiet. The quiet part wasn't unusual—he'd never been a loud kid. But the team bus was where he left that part of himself behind, joining his teammates' raucous chants and songs. He usually had no idea what language he was singing in, never mind what anything meant, but he didn't care. He loved joining in, getting loud, and clapping until his hands hurt.

Austin was glad that Coach was talking. The first ten minutes of the ride were silent, which he found unbearable, heartbreaking. But his heart wasn't the only thing that hurt. He'd been dealing with a pilonidal cyst that made even walking difficult on some days. In another week's time, he had basketball tryouts. How was he supposed to run? His doctor didn't even want him to try out for basketball, never mind play.

How had they lost to Cheverus? Austin asked himself. He knew it hurt them to play with two key defenders on the bench because of that party. Their suspension was scheduled to end on Monday, but the administration wouldn't budge. Rules were rules. Moe had moved from midfield to defense, and had the strength and attitude to make it work. But today...

Austin shook his head. Today was about more than missing players. They'd been too confident against a number-seven seed. Thought it would be a blowout. Some blowout. Cheverus played hard. Physical. And that goalie! Austin had heard the goalie had been hot throughout the playoffs, but what a game that kid had. After Cheverus beat Scarborough, Austin knew Scarborough's coach, Mark Diaz, had told McGraw about the kid's amazing saves. They'd done some role-playing in practice to prepare, working on ways to attack, break through. They had reviewed strategy for two days in McGraw's classroom, going over each player, figuring out who to mark and how to get to goal. But still, Austin hadn't realized the goalie was *that* good.

Austin thought about last night, the team dinner at the Trinity Jubilee Center in downtown Lewiston. He loved those dinners. His mom and grandmother made vats of pasta and meatballs, some of his teammates brought *sambusa*, and they'd eat and laugh and, sometimes, dance. "Gish the Fish!" some chanted, trying to get the assistant coach on the floor.

The highlight was when Abdi H. took a water bottle and pretended it was a microphone so he could "interview" Austin's grandmother. Austin, like many in Lewiston, called his grandmother *Mémé*. It was a French-Canadian thing.

"Season ticket holder for three years in a row, are you prepared for tomorrow's game?" Abdi H. asked Mémé, who wore a red sweater, a delicate gold cross around her neck. Not terribly tall himself, Abdi H. towered over her small frame.

"Yes, I am," she answered. She got stern. "You guys better win, or you're in trouble!"

The team hooted and hollered, loving every second as Abdi H. put the water bottle down to join the fun. They'd thought they were so ready.

Abdi H. sat just behind Austin on the bus, the spirit of last night's fun replaced by the misery of losing. He, too, listened to McGraw preach, all the while replaying the game in his head. *If only I hadn't missed... Stop it,* he thought. *This isn't about you. You're a captain. You're only a junior, and you're a captain. Think about the team.*

The ride felt strange to him. Usually the bus was filled with the sounds of victory, dancing, and fist bumps, the white kids clapping just so they could take part, chiming in whenever they could. Abdi H. smiled for a moment, thinking about it. But now McGraw was the only one making noise.

He thought about what McGraw was saying; how they could come back next year and finish it. Despite their dominant record, they'd never been a great finishing team, shots hitting the crossbar or flying over the goal more often than not.

Abdi H. had started playing for McGraw during the summer

season when he was still in middle school, before he was supposed to, everyone looking the other way so he could build experience. He made varsity his freshman year and scored sixteen goals, making him the top offensive player on the team and throwing him into a leadership role at an early age.

As McGraw paced, his face reddening, his blue eyes barely blinking, Abdi H. decided he believed Coach. He was a junior now, forty-six goals under his belt—twenty-four just this season. He thought about his time line playing for McGraw. They had just lost the state final. Last year, when he was a sophomore, they went out in the regional final. Freshman year? The same.

It made sense, Abdi H. decided. Every year he played for McGraw, the team got a step closer to winning a state championship. Of course they'd be back next year. It just made sense. And according to his time line, he reasoned, they could win. He relaxed a bit in his seat and put his headphones on, looking down at the phone in his hand. He looked at the texts coming in, some from teammates sitting just a few feet away. He was okay.

From the front, Gish was having a hard time listening to his colleague. Like Austin, it felt like his heart had broken. It was going to be a long time before he could shake the image of Mike Wong collapsing to his knees in the middle of the field at the end, his yellow cleats sticking out behind his white shorts, head down, inconsolable, while Karim stood over him, his hand on Mike's head in a futile attempt to provide comfort. *That was typical Karim,* thought Gish. Even high-scoring Abdi H. deferred to Karim. The most versatile player on the field, a true all-rounder, elegant, he had an all-knowing way about him, as if he was the team's very own Somali elder. He possessed the same qualities people said made some of the older men in Lewiston's Somali community elders. Experienced. Wise. Trustworthy. Knowledgeable. Respected. It was as if he was saying to Mike, "It's all right, son."

But it wasn't all right. *They deserved a championship*, Gish thought. They deserved it just as much as the man who was now trying to help them cope.

Gish's eyes shifted to Austin and then to Abdi H. *Huh*, he thought. *Look at that*. They knew. They got it. They accepted the mission McGraw laid out. Gish smiled for the first time in hours, knowing what was coming next. *When these guys get off the bus*, he thought, *they're going to go play soccer*.

That night, Gish couldn't sleep, unable to forget the sight of twenty-five hearts breaking before his eyes. He thought about his daughter, Lilly, nine years old, sitting in the stands. She loved the team. Austin and Abdi H. often helped at her soccer practices. She knew her father considered them family. It wasn't about the money; he would have coached for free. It was about the players, the fans, the school, and McGraw.

When Gish got home after the game, Lilly greeted him at the door, tears streaming down her face. He embraced her and his fifteen-year-old son, Hunter. He tried to keep his own emotions in check as he held his kids, his wife, Cindy, looking on.

"Why'd they lose, Daddy?" Lilly finally asked, her eyes red and swollen.

He gave her the speech that a coach gives to his players after such a day. Sometimes, he said, it doesn't always go your way. You might be the better team, but you've got to play the game. You can't ever assume you're going to win. It's hard.

"We're just going to keep trying," he promised, looking into her deep blue eyes so much like his own. "We're going to keep trying."

But it was hard to think ahead. He wasn't like McGraw, who could shake off a loss with a "the sun is going to come up tomorrow" attitude. McGraw usually cracked a joke about a player, made his team laugh, and moved on. Yet this was different. How could they shed a loss of this magnitude? He kept thinking about how they could have prepared differently to finish better in the game. Balls needed to go into the net. The number of shots didn't matter if they didn't go in.

Gish didn't want to dwell on the past anymore. He tried to think about the comeback McGraw had promised on the bus. It was actually less than a year away, he reasoned. Summer soccer. Tryouts. Preseason. The end-of-summer jamboree. He picked up his phone and started to text McGraw some of his ideas, plotting their road back to the state final. Just as the players headed to the park to play a pickup game when they got home, he, too, had to get back to work.

A few miles away, Shobow Saban was having trouble finding light in the loss. He hadn't planned on spending the night at his mother's apartment in downtown Lewiston. He drove up from Worcester just to see the game. The senior biology major at Assumption College had played for McGraw for four years. He still spent summers working with Somali youth at a local community center, teaching them about citizenship and the juvenile justice system. He'd been excited to drive the nearly two hundred miles to see his old team finally win its first soccer championship. He'd made plans with a former teammate, Abdi Abdi, to meet at the game, but intended to drive back to school right after to finish a lab report.

When Shobow arrived at the game, he was full of enthusiasm, excited to see players like Abdi H. in action. For years McGraw had told them a championship would eventually happen. But watching the game was excruciating. With each minute that went by, Shobow deflated a bit more as Lewiston tried to dig itself out of a hole.

As Abdi H. lined up to take his penalty kick, Shobow finally felt hopeful. Lewiston didn't miss penalty kicks, he thought. Somalis, especially, didn't miss penalty kicks. This was it. Abdi H. would score, the game would turn around, and they would be state champions.

"WHAAAT?" Shobow screamed when Abdi H. missed. "What are you DOING?"

He sat there in disbelief. That was it; that was the state championship. The clock didn't matter anymore. It was not their year. *Allah did not want it so,* he thought after the game. How could he have been so wrong? He said good-bye to Abdi Abdi and got into his car, sitting for a moment, thinking about his lab report. He couldn't do it. He couldn't drive back to Worcester. He headed toward Lewiston.

The next morning, as Shobow contemplated his drive back to college, Abdi H. woke up not quite knowing what to do. He thought about McGraw's words from the day before. He still believed him—they *would* be back next year—but he hadn't fully processed the loss and didn't know where to start.

He decided to go for a walk. The apartment was a comfortable place: the lace-covered table; the dark wood hutch with his family's few treasures gleaming through its glass doors; the decorative rugs; the leather-like couches they crowded onto. Abdi H. was one of eleven kids ranging in age over a twenty-four-year span. "Our own starting eleven," he often said with a smile when talking about his siblings. But this morning the apartment suffocated him. He needed to get outside.

The door to the apartment building often sticks, so residents keep a large stick nearby to wedge it open. The building is one of the larger ones downtown, four floors tall. Most apartment houses in Lewiston are triple-deckers, adorned with tired, chipped remnants of Italianate-style architecture and a few "For Rent" signs in the windows. Standing on the creaking front steps, Abdi H. could see the Colisée to his right, its parking lot a familiar playground, and the spires of the Basilica of Saints Peter and Paul in front of him.

Downtown Lewiston has been among the poorest neighborhoods in Maine for a long time. Variety stores and halal markets dot many corners, Somali women popping in and out, *jilbabs* flowing behind them, children in tow. Poor white families who have lived in the tired apartments for generations now reside next to the city's newcomers.

Abdi H. had no real destination in mind; he just wanted to walk. He constantly shooed his younger siblings outside, shutting off the television and telling them to go play. He liked being outside. He wasn't much for television, unless a soccer game was on.

As he started walking, he pretty much had the city to himself. Lewiston wore a Sunday morning quiet, church bells occasionally interrupting his thoughts. He was glad for the solitude. It was rare someone didn't stop to talk to him, to ask about soccer and school. The little kids he helped coach for various youth leagues in his spare time, from Gish's daughter's team to the Somali youth teams, were forever running over to say hello. His father, who prioritized school above sports, always seemed puzzled when people asked about soccer. He wasn't a typical so-called soccer dad—few of the Somalis were—who wore his son's goal tally on his sleeve, but he was proud of the role Abdi H. had come to play in the community. Modest to a fault, Abdi H. has a hard time talking about his reputation. But it was something he took very seriously.

He slowed for a moment when he saw some of his teammates ahead: Karim, Moe, Zak, Q, Nuri. He called out to the group, running to catch up with them. They were getting Chinese food, they said. He decided to join them, and the group headed to the buffet place just around the corner. They were somber. Nuri, especially, had had a rough night, waiting until he got home to release his grief over losing. He didn't want to cry in front of his friends, but it was the worst day he'd ever had. He'd heard his mother cried the whole way home from the game.

Although Noralddin "Nuri" Othman hadn't been in Lewiston very long, he lived within blocks of Moe, the Abdulle brothers, and Q, just off Kennedy Park, and they'd become close friends. He arrived in Lewiston on March 18, 2014, from Turkey, a long trip that included a stopover in Germany. Born in Jeddah, Saudi Arabia, to Somali parents, he'd been traveling ever since he could remember, his family always searching for a home. They'd fled Somalia through the north, where the narrow waters between the Red Sea and the Gulf of Aden lead to Yemen and Saudi Arabia. But both Yemen's escalating civil war and Saudi Arabia's escalating intolerance of refugees pushed many over the border. After a brief return to Somalia, Nuri's family headed to Turkey, where they spent four years before coming to Maine.

Nuri kept playing with the crown of hair that rose large and bushy over his head. He was proud of his Afro. His teammates loved teasing him about it. *What a season,* he thought, wondering what to order when they got to the restaurant. He'd swung between the JV and varsity squads until midseason, when Coach wanted to shake things up a bit.

"We have to give you a chance," McGraw had said to him, his arm across his shoulders. He stared at Nuri for a moment, his steely blue eyes conveying just how serious he was.

Coach believes in me, Nuri thought. *He trusts me. He wants me to do well.* It had taken him a while to believe all that. But once he did, it changed everything. By the first game of the playoffs, Nuri joined the starting lineup and never looked back.

"When he gave me a chance," Nuri remembers, "I was so nervous, but I did so good."

But Nuri's best wasn't enough, and now he was trying to make it better by ordering a lot of Chinese food. Moe, especially, just kept ordering more and more. But they couldn't eat. Such a waste of money that they really didn't have. As they pushed chicken lo mein around their plates, they tried to talk about the game. Karim couldn't stand it.

"Shut up," he said to them in frustration. "Cut it, cut it, I don't want to hear it."

They did. They always listened to Karim. But five minutes later, like everyone else, he started talking about it.

"Why did the clock go by so fast?" someone asked, causing laughter.

They felt that the clock had worked double-time to ensure that Cheverus was on top at the end. They started to trade stories, but Moe, always on edge, couldn't take it any longer. He got up from his seat and lay down on the floor. He did this sometimes; just shut down when he couldn't deal with his feelings. It was better than lashing out. His friends were sad, disappointed, but he was angry. This was supposed to have been their year. They were going to be the ones to do it for McGraw after no one else could.

Giving up on food, the group decided to head over to the woods near the high school. *I can't think about soccer anymore,* Nuri thought as they walked, taking selfies along the way. Everything felt dark. Coach had said it would happen next year, but he couldn't find his way back just yet.

For Abdi H., Chinese food and his teammates helped the loss fade a bit more. By the time he headed home, the sun waning over the river, he again felt reassured about what McGraw had said the day before. The next season started now, and it was going to have a different ending. His family did not come to Maine for a soccer championship, but now it was part of the journey.

CHAPTER 3

WELCOME TO
VACATIONLAND

As one heads north into Maine from New Hampshire, the Piscataqua River Bridge materializes, a dull green arch separating Portsmouth from Kittery. At the halfway point on the bridge, high over the tree line, a small green sign matter-of-factly announces: "STATE LINE—MAINE—VACATIONLAND." Once across, the change of scene feels immediate. The trees lining the interstate grow taller, keeping watch on all who enter. The seventy-mile-per-hour speed limit favors the never-ending road ahead, gentle, rolling dips breaking up the increasingly stark landscape.

"Welcome to Maine," a blue sign announces. "The way life should be."

The highway is littered with warnings about moose and large fines for boaters who don't properly clean their vessels before setting sail in Maine's pristine waters. Cars with the signature VACATIONLAND license plate, a lobster or pine branch indicating a local's identity, dot the road. In the off-season, traffic is light, an eerie sense of solitude permeating the highway. But between Memorial and Labor Days, the turnpike becomes unbearable, cars sitting for long stretches between exits as tourists try to get to a beach or a lake, a mountain or a forest.

A Howard Johnson's once greeted weary visitors at exit 25, Kennebunk. Now a giant sculpture of a moose welcomes those who need coffee, a bathroom, or a bite of fast food. There are also, according to a sign, "live lobsters to go."

Venturing farther north, another sign reassures drivers their long journey will not be for naught. "Maine," it says. "Worth a Visit, Worth a Lifetime."

This slogan is one that African refugees have taken to heart.

Within months of the first Somali families settling in Lewiston in 2001, a busful rolled up the turnpike. The deeper they drove into Maine, markers extolling the virtues of "Vacationland"—Beaches! Lakes! Skiing!—were fewer and farther between. As the turnpike took an inland curve west, it shrank to two lanes on each side, more popular tourist destinations in the rearview mirror.

For Somali refugees, the turnpike represented the final stage of a long trip to a new life. For some, like Abdi H. and his teammates, the journey from Africa at such a young age is a cloudy combination of memories in many languages. Their parents guard their refugee stories. The memories are painful, filled with the violence of displacement. Starving themselves so their families could eat. Carrying their children when they themselves could barely walk. Losing everything, from their homeland to their family to their way of life. To share these tales is to relive them, to experience the trauma again, to engage with the nightmares. They don't need or want their children to know the specifics of what they went through; only that they respect their parents' quest to survive and the need to move on.

"We moved past it," one mother says of their long journey from Somalia to Maine. "We went by."

For Abdikadir Negeye, each part of that journey remains all

too vivid. Negeye fled Somalia with his parents when he was five years old. Thousands took the journey; days of walking toward the Kenyan border, losing older and weaker family and friends along the way. Hiding from animals and rogue armed militia. Little food, and even less water.

Negeye barely remembers Somalia, but the Kenyan refugee camps where he lived for fourteen years remain rooted deeply in his mind. His family of twelve lived in a one-room hut with a plastic-covered roof. He remembers the long lines for grain rations, and the cries of hungry children with a constant burning in their bellies. On the days that they had breakfast, there was no lunch or dinner. Thieves preyed upon their rations. It was dark at night, and with darkness came danger.

Negeye took classes, trying to learn English as best he could, hoping if they ever were resettled in the United States, he would be able to speak the language and help his family. And he played soccer to help pass the long days of waiting for life to begin.

After ten years in Dadaab, Negeye's family moved to Kakuma, a standard procedure in Bantu resettlement. According to Colby College anthropologist Catherine Besteman, who studied the Bantu in Somalia and then reunited with many of them in Lewiston years later, the identity "Bantu" formed in the camps, marking Somalis who came from the agrarian villages of the Jubba Valley. The UNHRC classified them as especially victimized, with few resources to expedite their resettlement. The persecution of the Bantu, historically poor and without formal education, from villages without schools or electricity, was centuries old, rooted in the days of the Arab slave trade. When civil war spread throughout Somalia in the 1990s, warring parties violently drove them from their lands. Once in the refugee camps, Besteman writes, those identified as Bantu learned how to highlight the right stories to warrant passage to the United States.

After four years in Kakuma, Negeye's family headed for Georgia, where everything from the bright lights to the language seemed strange. Despite his English lessons, Negeye couldn't navigate the southern accent. His first day in Decatur, he tried running errands for his parents. He couldn't understand the woman at the grocery. Her words didn't sound like the ones he knew.

In April of 2006, the family decided to move to Lewiston. They'd been in Decatur only a few months when his older sister, who'd left Georgia to find them a better place to live, called. Lewiston, she told them, was the place. They'd have Somali neighbors, she said. Come.

The family was unprepared for how long the journey to Lewiston would take. Negeye remembers looking out the window of the bus as it wound northward. The then-nineteen-year-old found the view constantly startling. His mother, brothers, and sisters, just a few packed bags among them, only knew to listen for "Lewiston" on the thirty-plus-hour ride. But when they finally got off the bus, Somali friends were waiting, as was most always the case.

"We had welcome," he recalls of the many Somalis who offered them food and housing. "It was a very big relief."

Once in Lewiston, the clan identifications that could create conflict in Somalia and the camps often took a back seat to national and religious identities, the emphasis on communality providing support for newcomers. Lewiston's burgeoning Somali community helped new families settle in quickly. Women shopped together to purchase groceries in bulk to maximize pooled resources and shared big-ticket items like cars. The Somali saying, *Ilko wada jir bey wax ku gooyaan*—Together the teeth can cut—was central to settling into this new life.

Education was foremost in Negeye's mind. He wanted a high school diploma; maybe even a college degree. He talked to one of his friends from the refugee camp, Rilwan Osman, who had also moved to Lewiston. Osman fled Somalia with his mother in 1996 when he was twelve years old. They escaped as soldiers forced his father and others into a river, trying to distract a crocodile that had attacked one of the soldiers' women. The family never saw him again.

Osman told Negeye about Loring Jobs Corps at the former Loring Air Force Base in Maine's northernmost region, Aroostook County. The base closed in 1994, and now offered free residential education and training to low-income students. Its high school equivalency program appealed to Negeye. Within a few months of arriving in Lewiston, he left his family for Loring, where he would live for almost two years. He promised to return. With the years of instability, violence, and war behind him, he hoped, he had ideas for helping his people in their new community.

Some of those ideas involved soccer.

The global Somali diaspora began long before the first families came to Lewiston, the product of the country's longtime political and environmental instability. Located at the easternmost point of Africa—the Horn—Somalia's landline borders Djibouti, Ethiopia, and Kenya, with the Gulf of Aden and the Indian Ocean on its eastern coastlines and perpetually unstable Yemen just a short boat ride away. Like much of Africa, twentieth-century Somalia experienced the effects of decolonization and the Cold War, but elections and assassinations toward the end of the century greatly weakened leadership. As borders were drawn and redrawn, catastrophic drought over half the landscape brought famine and reinforced poverty.

While an internationally backed government installed in 2012 renewed some hope in Somalia, the country remains under the heavy shadow of its history and the perfect storm of events that led to the failed state. Guerrillas sowed the seeds of civil war in the 1980s as they organized to overthrow the military regime of Siad Barre, who had been in power since 1969. In the heat of the Cold War, the United States contributed millions to making Somalia armed and dangerous.

In the wake of increasingly violent political instability, the first waves of Somalis bolted the country. In 1991, rebels threw Siad Barre out of Mogadishu and full-scale civil war broke out, creating an even larger exodus, particularly from the southern regions. The UN created Kakuma and Dadaab to accommodate those flooding over the border. Somalis who stayed behind faced an almost indescribable humanitarian disaster.

As Somalia's civil war raged for decades, increasingly radical Islamist-led rebellions emerged, intensifying the violence. With this, the refugee crisis only grew. In 2007, the UN declared Somalia Africa's worst humanitarian crisis—a completely failed state.

"If this were happening in Darfur, there would be a big fuss," Eric Laroche, the head of UN humanitarian operations in Somalia, told the *New York Times*. "But Somalia has been a forgotten emergency for years."

American perceptions of Somalia rely on a mixture of headlines about piracy and civil war, with Hollywood's versions of both. Ridley Scott's *Black Hawk Down,* a Jerry Bruckheimer–produced action film based on journalist Mark Bowden's account of the Battle of Mogadishu, met with enormous international criticism. The film's portrayal of Somalia as a place so dangerous that even U.S. special forces couldn't go in without facing insurmountable violence underscored America's already frightening perception of the country. Paul Greengrass's *Captain Phillips,* which posed Tom Hanks against first-time Somali actor Barkhad Abdi, fared a bit better. The story of the hijacking of a merchant marine vessel in the Indian Ocean in 2009 by Somali pirates warranted an Oscar nod for Abdi, whose family had landed in the large Somali community in Minneapolis after fleeing the civil war.

While Minnesota's Somali population is in the tens of thousands, Lewiston's is larger per capita. Of the approximately one million Somali refugees in the world, thousands call Maine home. The vast majority landed somewhere else, like Atlanta, Georgia, or Columbus, Ohio, before making the move to Maine on their own.

Refugee resettlement is complicated. After the UNHCR accepts a family into a camp, the wait begins for a match between a UNHCR request and a country willing to find resettlement sites. Once they get through the UN side of things, the process to gain entry to the United States is a whole other bureaucratic nightmare. The tenuous process is susceptible to the politics of the time. A few months after the first Somali families settled in Lewiston, for example, the terrorist attacks of September 11, 2001, stalled people in the middle of the process and created much greater anti-Muslim and anti-immigrant sentiment among many Americans.

Once in the United States, many Somali families continue their nomadic ways to find a stable community. At first glance, the secondary migration of Somali refugees into one of America's whitest, coldest states seems odd. Maine's refugee community began in Portland, the state's urban cultural center. But as the twentieth century came to a close, Portland's housing market got tighter and more expensive. The historic Old Port district appealed to upwardly mobile professionals and artists who enjoyed its bountiful boutiques and restaurants, picturesque views of Casco Bay, and quirky neighborhoods. Options to house refugees became increasingly limited. Simultaneously, Lewiston, just forty minutes away, hit historically low population numbers, leaving many of its downtown apartments vacant.

In February 2001, a handful of Somalis that Portland couldn't accommodate moved to Lewiston. According to Phil Nadeau, Lewiston's assistant city administrator, those few opened the floodgates. Based largely on word of mouth about Lewiston's relatively low crime rates and decent schools, busloads of ethnic Somalis made their way there. The Bantu were not far behind. Within a few years, Lewiston's vacancy rate fell from 20 to 7 percent as the city's population rate stabilized. Refugees, it seems, had reversed the direction people traveled on the Maine turnpike.

Nadeau has become a go-to guy in the world of secondary refugee migration, publishing widely about Lewiston's experience and serving as a consultant to other cities. His grandparents came to Lewiston from Quebec, opening first a restaurant and then a general store. His father took over the business in 1969 and turned it into Friends Deli, a successful catering venture. Working for his father from a young age, Nadeau had a front-row seat to Lewiston's then-vibrant downtown. His family owned some one hundred apartments amid the lively social clubs and raucous watering holes frequented by French-speaking mill workers.

When the first bus arrived from Georgia just two months after the initial Somali relocation to Lewiston, city officials were taken aback. "Who are you?" social services staffers in City Hall asked those who showed up at their door, Lewiston city maps in hand. "Portland didn't tell us you were coming!"

But they weren't from Portland.

By the end of the year, the Somali population reached between four hundred and five hundred, a relatively small group. However, just one family walking down Lisbon Street was enough to raise the eyebrows of longtime residents. Many of the men blended in as well as anyone with a brown face could, often wearing a more Westernized style of dress. Somali women stuck out even from a distance because of their headscarves and long dresses, which critics interpreted as a repudiation of American style. Something as simple as walking down the street became an arduous task for the women, always wondering what people assumed because of the way they dressed, and what kinds of words might be whispered as they went by.

Inflammatory, bigoted accusations circulated: dirty, uncivilized Somalis were turning kitchen cabinets into chicken coops to keep live fowl in their apartments. Their kids were washing their feet in the school drinking fountains. People remembered that twenty-five-year-old Staff Sergeant Thomas Field, from nearby Lisbon, Maine, was crew chief on the Black Hawk shot down over Mogadishu in 1993. They also recalled the famous images of a dead U.S. soldier being dragged through the streets. Refugee Resettlement Watch, the blog created by white supremacist Ann Corcoran, kept Lewiston in its crosshairs, with post after erroneous post about rising crime rates, parks infested with Somali drug dealers, and a refugee population who didn't try to get jobs or speak English.

City Hall started getting what Nadeau characterizes as the "Who authorized this?" and "Why are they here?" phone calls, some coming from indignant people in other towns who assumed Lewiston's refugees were sucking up all the state's funds. Many were outraged by rumors that illegal Somali families were getting $10,000 handouts upon arrival in Lewiston. "They are here legally," Nadeau assured everyone. "They can move here, and when they do, they have the same rights and the same access as anyone else."

"We work with them," he told callers, "just like I'm working with you."

Lewiston's city leaders didn't have time to answer questions. As they scrambled to wrap their heads around Somali culture and customs, it didn't matter to them why anyone was in Lewiston. They needed to figure out what kinds of supports the new residents needed, and how to fund them. As secondary migrants, most Somalis became ineligible for federal refugee funds when they left their initial landing spots, Georgia or otherwise.

Catholic Charities, a faith-based nonprofit community outreach group that oversees Maine's refugee resettlement program, helped with what Nadeau called "Refugee 101." The group opened an office in City Hall—a national first—to make things more efficient for new arrivals, with signs in English, French, Arabic, and Somali. The Portland-Lewiston Collaborative formed to share resources and knowledge, eventually receiving an Unanticipated Arrivals grant from the U.S. Office of Refugee Resettlement. St. Mary's Hospital played a vital role in the health and well-being of new arrivals, while the Trinity Jubilee Center, the B Street Community Center, Bates College, and Tree Street Youth, which offers after-school and summer programming, as well as precollege seminars, for downtown kids, eventually filled in remaining gaps.

Those who balked at the arrival of the Somalis were forgetting the city's long immigrant history. While an entirely different set of circumstances drove the Québécois to Lewiston, they, too, introduced a new language, culture, and religion upon arrival, dramatically changing Lewiston's demographic landscape a century or more earlier.

It is a history inscribed in Lewiston's very skyline. From the top of Mount David, a glorified pile of rocks, or "granite outcropping," located in a wooded area on the far corner of the Bates College campus, there is an impressive view for a short climb. To the east lies the college campus, its redbrick buildings outlined in bright white trim, architectural exemplars of the colonial revival style with Georgian touches thrown in.

Pivoting away from Bates, the orange mass of a Home Depot runs into the small city sprawl of houses and office buildings, the old factories dotting the canals, the giant smokestack of the Bates

Mill towering above. The needle-like spire of St. Mary's Church, now the Franco-American Heritage Center, stands in stark contrast to the gothic façade of the Basilica of Saints Peter and Paul. Reminiscent of Notre-Dame de Paris, its rose window suggests the famed one in Chartres.

Sitting grandly on Ash Street, the basilica holds the last remaining French-language mass in Maine, an aide-mémoire of the workforce who saturated the city in its industrial heyday. Built at the turn of the twentieth century, it was the religious and social center for French-speaking Canadians who came to Lewiston to work and live.

Lewiston is Maine's second-largest city. When paired with Auburn, its so-called twin city across the Androscoggin, the metropolitan area comes close to sixty thousand people, making L/A, as locals call it, an urban center within south-central Maine. While equidistant from Maine's mountains and its coast, about an hour to each, Lewiston is an unlikely stopping point for anyone seeking "Vacationland."

The Arosaguntacook tribe, a member of the Abenaki nation, first inhabited what is now Lewiston. As English settlers and their infectious diseases came to the area in the seventeenth century, the tribe migrated to Quebec. In the late eighteenth century, a group of New England land merchants, the Pejepscot Proprietors, named the area Lewiston. By the end of the century, it was fully incorporated as a town.

In its early days of settlement, Lewiston, like most of inland New England, worked an agrarian economy. But as hydropower developed in the nineteenth century, its location on the Androscoggin's Great Falls assured change was on the horizon. In 1809, Dartmouth graduate Michael Little of the Home Manufacturing Company built a sawmill next to the raging water, hoping to harness its power. Within a few years, a group of Boston investors formed the Franklin Company and created a series of canals and a railroad to exploit the site's industrial potential. Very quickly, Lewiston became "Spindle City," a textile hub filled with jobs that paid a low but living wage.

Benjamin E. Bates, for whom the college is named, is one of many who climbed on board. Founded in 1850, the Bates Mill fast became the state's largest employer, the river providing ample power to run its voluminous spinning and weaving looms. According to Mary Rice-DeFosse and James Myall in *The Franco-Americans of Lewiston-Auburn*, Bates's entrepreneurial foresight led him to purchase large stocks of southern cotton before the outbreak of the Civil War. When cotton's price went through the roof as the North and South squared off, Lewiston's mills thrived. The Androscoggin Mill, the Cowan Woolen Mill, the Lincoln Mill, Lewiston Bleachery and Dye Works, and the Lewiston Gas-Light Company joined Bates alongside the tree-lined canals. Across the river, Auburn reaped benefits from the whirlwind, becoming a leader in shoe manufacturing.

While the canals were built largely on the backs of Irish laborers who followed the Boston capitalists north, others trailed not far behind. Some southern and eastern Europeans, those who dominate turn-of-the-century U.S. immigration history, found their way to Lewiston. But the largest group came from the north, French-Canadians seeking the booming textile industry's wages. For decades, industry chipped away at the livelihoods of farming families, forcing them into increasingly itinerant ways of life. In 1874, the building of a railroad line between Lewiston and Canada's Grand Trunk Railway amplified the movement of both goods and people, securing an accessible path to steady pay. Mill managers hired French-Canadians because of their willingness to work for less. In about ten years' time, the mill workers nearly doubled Lewiston's population.

"The Lewiston Grand Trunk station," according to Rice-DeFosse and Myall, "became the Ellis Island of the Twin Cities."

No one needs to tell Florence Rivard McGraw, Mike McGraw's mother, about the area's immigration patterns. Born in Lewiston in 1928, she's lived through many of its transitions, from her own French-speaking childhood to watching African refugees play soccer for her eldest child.

Her father, Oscar Rivard, worked as a weaver at the Libby Mill. Born in Lewiston in 1893, his parents, Octave Rivard and Marie Caron, ran a boardinghouse on Lisbon Street. Oscar married Lydia Galarneau on November 13, 1916. Born in Victoriaville, Quebec, in 1894, Lydia moved to Lewiston from New Hampshire, where her parents, Jeffrey and Cezarine, first settled.

Nestled in her understated home in the outskirts of the city, Florence McGraw likes to sit at her dining room table, the television droning in the background to keep her company. It is the brightest spot in the house because of the large window looking out at her lilacs. Her late husband, Gordon, loved the backyard. He grew up living off the land in nearby Sabattus, the son of Scottish immigrants who came to Maine via Quebec. Any outdoor space provided a respite from the long hours he worked on second shift at the Bates Mill.

Some thirty family albums, all in various states of completion, surround her, documenting a story typical of so many who came to Lewiston at the turn of the twentieth century. After working for fifty years in the purchasing department of Central Maine Hospital, Florence is now retired. At her farewell party, her co-workers gave her a Caribbean cruise, really the only time she and Gordon traveled anywhere together. She found the ship intimidating—"I'm not brave for water"—but her husband, who left high school for the Navy, "was in his glory."

Florence started at the hospital when she was still in high school, hoping to avoid the family tradition of factory work.

"I refused," she says, remembering how hot the mill was, pipes everywhere, when she brought her father lunch.

"My mother didn't speak English until I brought Gordon home," Florence continues, looking at her mother's certificate of citizenship, dated July 18, 1957, more than ten years after Oscar died of cardiovascular disease at just fifty years old. Gordon McGraw only knew the French spoken at the mills, none of which fit polite conversation, and her kids struggled with it in their parochial school classrooms.

"Either I would laugh my head off or cry," she says of helping them with their homework. "I went to St. Peter's, so I had French and English all my life, but when you don't speak it, it's very hard to get it back. I can pull it out, but it would be hard for a conversation."

The eldest of five, Mike McGraw helped care for his two youngest sisters while his parents balanced their work schedules— as well as their bowling leagues—with a stable of babysitters. Like so many in Lewiston, his family often moved, living on the same streets where so many of his soccer players live today. The family albums include photographs of downtown VJ Day celebrations, right near Abdi H.'s front door, and of an uncle who lived on Walnut, just a few doors down from Maulid. Then there was the house on Oak Street that Gordon rented without telling her.

"I didn't even see the house," she says of the day she came home to find that her husband had moved their stuff into a new place. "I had no decision in it at all."

Seeing Lewiston through his mother's eyes helped Mike McGraw understand the changes that occurred on his team. He knows that people rebuked his grandparents for speaking French and accused them of taking jobs not rightfully theirs. Backlash against Francos, already stereotyped as backwards and unpatriotic, intensified during World War I, a period marked by isolationist nationalism. Maine's chapter of the Ku Klux Klan, the largest outside of the South, had a hateful focus on French-speaking Catholics. In 1919, Maine outlawed French in public schools. The language became a stigma, with teachers punishing children for uttering *oui* or *non*, and making them write "I will not speak French" repeatedly on the blackboard. When the mills began to close, sending its French-speaking workers to find other jobs, signs declaring "No French Need Apply" became a familiar sight.

"Things are different but the same," McGraw says of the Somalis coming to Lewiston. It is an old story; there are just new people living it.

Despite facing animosity, the Québécois made their mark on the city. They transformed the neighborhood wedged between the industrial canals and the river, insular and isolated both ethnically and geographically. This "Petit Canada," a French-speaking enclave composed of crowded, hastily built tenement housing, felt—and smelled—more like the Lower East Side of New York than south-central Maine. Money was scarce, winters were cold, and the work was hard. While conditions did not much improve, their roots into the city grew.

The average family size of the Catholic French-Canadian workers hovered around six or more children, which caused the so-called reformers of the era to issue eugenic cries of "race suicide." But rather than worry about what reformers thought of them, French-speaking mill workers clashed more often with Lewiston's Irish population.

Having a generation or more of a jump on the Québécois, as well as a good grasp of English, some of the Irish who helped build the mills moved into managerial positions when the French-speaking workforce showed up. Others lost their jobs to

Québécois workers who were willing to do more for less. Territorial clashes between Irish and Québécois children broke out after school each day, mirroring the ethnic conflicts of far bigger cities.

Religion was one of few common denominators, although they did not necessarily worship together. St. Joseph's, for example, held a basement mass in French to accommodate the new residents, but soon their numbers burst out of such temporary arrangements. With approximately ten thousand French-speaking worshippers by the end of the nineteenth century, construction on a new church began, and parishioners prioritized its completion over their own homes. Finally finished in 1936 at the height of the Great Depression, Saints Peter and Paul stands today as one of the largest churches in New England, and one of the few designated the status of basilica.

Being able to hold mass regularly in French, as opposed to English or Latin, became a key ingredient to Franco-American identity in Lewiston, particularly when the city banned the language. The Québécois also founded French-speaking parochial schools to further preserve their culture, strongly believing that *Qui perd sa langue, perd sa foi.*

Whoever loses language, loses faith.

But as Lewiston's Franco-American culture flourished, its mills began to decline. In the interwar era, New England's textile industry took a hit as factories moved south, where everything from transportation to labor was cheaper. After World War II, mills began to close, igniting an economic downturn that hit downtown Lewiston hardest. Shuttered stores, such as Sears and Woolworth's, dotted the once-thriving retail landscape.

Lewiston's factories crumbled for decades, although unlike many New England mill towns, they did not fall down. In 1982, B. Peck & Co., Lewiston's flagship department store for more than a century, gave in, closing its doors. Fewer factories meant fewer jobs, which meant fewer customers. With high rates of un-employment and a declining population, Lewiston hit bottom. But the core of its Franco-American community, which once endured hostility to their customs and their language, still called Petit Canada home.

They would not be the last wave of immigrants to do so.

CHAPTER 4

MANY AND ONE

On Lincoln Street across from the vast Bates Mill complex sits Labadie's Bakery, a Lewiston institution since 1925.

"Old people come in," says the girl behind a counter filled with an extraordinary arrangement of doughnuts, pastries, and whoopie pies. "'I used to live over there,' they'll say." She points to the multilevel parking garage that the bakery faces, where tenements constructed for factory workers once stood. The garage supports the urban renewal projects of the mill complex—the restaurants, brewery, and small businesses filling the massive red-brick buildings that once housed a significant portion of America's textile industry.

Next door to the bakery, a shuttered halal grocery represents someone's vanquished business dream, a "For Rent" sign in the dirty window. But a few blocks over on Lisbon Street, similar entrepreneurial endeavors thrive, indicative of the transformations in Maine's second-largest city. Once ghost-like with a few pawnshops sprinkled among vacant storefronts, Lisbon Street now reveals seeds planted by Lewiston's newer residents. Lewiston used to be the largest downtown retail landscape in New England outside of Boston, but it fell hard and fast as the mills closed and retail shopping malls, like the one in Auburn, took over.

Today, the Somalis see themselves as very much a part of Lewiston's recovering economy. "They want to stay," one longtime Lewiston resident says. "Unlike a lot of people, they want to be here." A storefront mosque discreetly occupies space beside stores selling Somali food and clothing, vibrant hijabs and *chadors* and *khimars* hanging in shop windows next to soccer jerseys. The Islamic Center, a nondescript three-story row house with entrances on both Lisbon and Canal Streets, is packed on Fridays for midday prayers. Women pray in the basement while men fill the upper levels. On weekends, there is *dugsi*—Koran study for children.

The greatest concentration of Somali businesses on Lisbon sits between Chestnut and Pine: Banadir Café, Dayah Store, Al Madina Variety and Halal Store, Maskali Café, and Al Fatah Variety. While clan identification lost much of its meaning in Lewiston, people often shop along clan lines, making for a crowded marketplace.

Most of the customers on Lisbon Street are Somali, although some hail from Congo, Sudan, Uganda, and Angola. All are welcome—*as-salaam alaikum*—that's just good business. The stores offer a variety of goods and services, including wire transfers to send money to relatives still in Africa. Advertisements for phone cards and Boost mobile are everywhere—"Lycamobile $29/month 3 hours to Somalia!" Photographs of Somali delicacies like *sambusa* line store windows, while inside, spices, teas, and mixes for guava and mango juice sit on shelves next to boxes of Tropiway Plantain Fufu flour, bags of Maggi seasoning cubes, jars of Egusi, and bottles of Praise African Red Palm Oil, perfect for stewing goat. Forty-pound bags of rice are everywhere; some families go through two per month. Boxes of halal meat—camel, chicken, goat, beef—are stored in coolers or freezer cases, labeled in Arabic.

Bananas, a staple of Somali cuisine, are offered on the green side, considered better to cook with meat and slice into rice.

One of the most successful stores on the street is the Mogadishu Store, owned and run by "Mama" Shukri Abasheikh. Her family lost its home and business when violence escalated in Somalia in the late 1980s. After almost a decade in Dadaab, she arrived in Atlanta in 1999, but hated big-city life. In 2002, she moved to Lewiston. Four years later, she opened the store, many of her eight children helping her. Her sign promises much—"Grocery Store, Restaurant, Money Transmitter, Seamstress, Tax Preparer, Halal Meat, Cleaning Services." Inside the large space, divided by a row of locker freezers, there is little a customer can't find, from colorful scarves hanging in the back to the hot food resting on small heating units. Out in front, women pile their plastic bags of goods together on spreads of colorful fabric, tying it together to loop around their heads and carry back home. Petit Canada is now Little Mogadishu.

For decades, Lewiston hoped for a revitalized downtown, a reawakening. But when it happened, it was not the way anyone envisioned. A small-town vibe permeates Lisbon Street. Somali women greet each other by name as they shop; men gather on the corner to share news. Alongside the Somali businesses, Forage Market offers organic sandwiches, frothy lattes, and what *Saveur* magazine has dubbed the country's best bagel. A few doors down, a couple of wine bars bring in the hipster after-work crowd.

The Abdulle brothers, Abdulkarim and Zakariya, or Karim and Zak, spend a lot of time on Lisbon Street. Their family's store, Bakaaraha Halal Market, is a quick walk from the apartment building they own just off Kennedy Park. The store is tucked under one of the green awnings that dot the block between Spruce and Chestnut, across from Paul's Clothing and Shoe Store, which carries Carhartt clothing and Red Wing shoes—everything a construction worker might need. Karim and Zak's father, Abdullahi Abdulle, came to Lewiston long before his sons did. Their teammates speak of him with a sense of awe. He was one of the first ones here, they say. Indeed, Abdulle was one of the first Somali interpreters in Lewiston, working with public health nurses. In 2011, he ran for school committee, wanting to bridge the disconnects of language and culture in Lewiston, but didn't win.

Karim and Zak and their friends spend a lot of time in their father's shop, where there is usually a soccer ball on one of the shelves. It is a simple space. A laptop sits on the small glass counter, a few folding chairs scattered about, while the obligatory bags of rice fill the floor. A few freezers offer a variety of meats, and women's clothing is haphazardly displayed throughout. Abdulle runs his other business, Smart Interpreters, from here as well. In addition to translation services in Somali, Arabic, and Swahili, he is a certified enrolled agent, a go-to taxman for Somalis in Lewiston.

Born in Mogadishu, Karim and Zak came to Lewiston in February 2012 after living in Nairobi for several years. They remember the war in Somalia, but also a "normal" life where they played and went to school. Although Karim is older than Zak, the boys were placed in school together in Lewiston. Their English was okay. They practiced in Nairobi by watching American movies and television, but still found the transition scary. The shows they watched tended to be about California, but Maine was nothing like California.

Inseparable friends, the brothers are quite different from each other. Karim is tall, deeply religious, and very quiet. When he does speak, his deep voice has an African lilt. Conversely, Zak is quick and witty, his pencil-thin mustache in constant motion as he laughs, weaving stories, frequently talking over Karim with little accent.

"Yeahhhhhh," Karim often intones, punctuating whatever Zak says.

They are regulars at the Safari Coffee Shop, which sits next to their father's store. Zak likes to buy sodas and charge them to "his tab." Every once in a while, his father comes in to pay, telling his prankster son never to buy anything again. When he leaves, Zak will grab another Coke.

Opened by Sharmarke Farah in 2008, the Safari is easy to miss, with only a small paper sign in the window; "ROBO'S VARIETY" still hangs over the entrance. A few photographs of Somali dishes and a list of international coffees are taped to the window, something the Chamber of Commerce requested Somali businesses do to quell rumors of terrorist activities.

The Abdulle brothers, like many of their teammates, watch soccer at the Safari alongside their neighbors, fathers, and uncles. The décor is simple; folding chairs and small tables, community notices and a clock on the wall. The window shades are usually drawn to make the screen images more vivid, although the Chamber has asked Somali business owners to rethink that, too. Karim is a Chelsea fan, something he is teased about, while Zak proclaims allegiance to Arsenal. But Zak is known to be fickle, rooting for any team that's winning.

More than watching soccer, the brothers love playing soccer, including fanatical, competitive video game sessions of FIFA Football that seemingly never end, someone yelling "rematch" at the end of each game. But when the sun is up and the grass is green, they head outside to find a game.

"We don't have enough soccer fields now," assistant city administrator Phil Nadeau says, shaking his head. "These kids live, eat, and breathe soccer practically from birth, like other kids in Lewiston who live, eat, and drink hockey."

Most often, the Abdulle brothers head a few blocks over to

Simard-Payne Memorial Railroad Park, the site of the former Grand Trunk rail yard. Set alongside the Androscoggin, the peaceful park sits in the shadow of the Bates Mill smokestack, a marker of the city's past. In recent years, a range of businesses, including the offices of Androscoggin Savings Bank, have moved into the renovated redbrick buildings, ending the stagnant vacancies of past decades. The city took over the compound, totaling seven buildings and 1.5 million square feet, in 1992, working it into strategies for economic rebirth that predated the Somali surge. According to Nadeau, the mill complex, along with Lisbon Street's rejuvenation, diversified Lewiston's economy enough to survive the global economic recession of 2008 with little impact on unemployment rates.

Simard-Payne Park is another sign of Lewiston's future, a grassy space that sits just behind Lewiston Pizza House, a veritable institution on busy Lincoln Avenue. A paved walking trail meanders along the river before crossing the old railroad bridge into Bonney Park in Auburn, which circles back to the Great Falls. A small stage hosts many community events, including Lewiston's signature Great Falls Balloon Festival.

Karim and Zak call the park Sheikh Hassan Stadium; it is a place for pickup games and leagues of their own devising. The kids named it for an old man, Hassan (they don't know his last name), who waits for them with a ball and some orange cones for goals. If he forgets the cones, they use their shoes, making piles of slides and sandals and sneakers. Hassan lives downtown in an apartment on Park Street overlooking the Kennedy Park basketball courts. In awe of his soccer skills and his devotion to the game, the kids call him "Sheikh" as a sign of respect. Outsiders call the park "Somali Stadium."

Every evening, in the months without snow, a parade of players heads through the sloping triple-decker apartments, cleats in hand, toward the river. Hassan drives there, sometimes stuffing as many as ten kids into his old Toyota. The games, often two or three at a time, are loud and raucous, with no refs blowing whistles or coaches yelling strategy. This is where Maslah Hassan, skinny and tall, his goatee giving him a tough look, dribbles the ball through twenty others, weaving and dodging, rolling his feet inside and out with step overs, scissors, feints, and drags. He runs full-tilt, throwing other players off-balance as he steps over the ball in a counterclockwise fashion, winding up as if he's going to release it. But it's not real. A small smile on his face, he fakes a cross before cutting inside and continuing across the grass, leaving the others behind. When he hits another wall of defenders, he uses the inside of his foot to take the ball back through his legs, a Cruyff turn, changing directions and continuing his race to the orange cones. Once there, he gently taps the ball through, making it look like it was easy to get there. The thirty or so people chasing him collapse, laughing.

When someone scores at Sheikh Hassan Stadium, players celebrate with wild abandon, not a word of English to be heard. There are no red cards for taunting.

Teams are large, sometimes eighty or more players, all male, aged twelve to thirty-five. They come and go, different groups warming up on the "sidelines" while others play.

"Where's my goal, which side am I on?" a kid yells, quickly lacing up his cleats. He throws his sandals in a pile and races to join a team, not sure what his position is, knowing it really doesn't matter. With so many on each side, ball possession is key. Once a player passes, it could be ten or more minutes before his feet touch a ball again.

"No passing—you hold onto the ball," says Zak, laughing. "I play *striker* down there! And I'm a *defender*! I score goals there!"

Nothing is out of bounds. There are times when players jump

on the small concert stage at the end of the field and play off the front boards. Everything's a showcase, players outdoing one another's moves in good-natured fashion, dazzling with footwork, speed, and intensity.

Despite qualms about getting hurt, many Blue Devils are in the mix, their blue long-sleeved shirts standing out in the fray. Here they learn how to dribble in tight quarters, leave fear behind, take a beating, and keep running. It is obvious where the team gets its remarkable ball-handling skills, its fierce attacking style, and the ability to handle heavy defensive traffic. No one here waits for the ball—it's all about attack and counter attack, and it can get rough. Players use their bodies to ward off whatever defender might be in their path. It's a master class in how to perfect a first touch, the moment a player first makes contact with the ball. From every angle, and at every pace, players take control, deadening the ball's speed and its spin before it hits the ground, flicking it quickly to a teammate running through to score, or simply taking the shot. Just as one side seems to dominate, the ball flying down the field, a counter attack turns it around, clearing the ball just before it gets inside the goal markers, sending it in the other direction.

It is here that they also hone their communication skills. Yelling at each other in Somali or Arabic, the Blue Devils unconsciously develop strategies that will keep their opposition in the dark when they hit the pitch at the high school. It goes beyond telling one another who to mark or where to pass. It strengthens their connection to one another on the field, developing a cohesive team spirit.

Some nights, Coach McGraw discreetly parks his car behind the pizza house and sits on an old railroad tie so he can watch the action. He knows they bring a lot of Somali Stadium with them when they don their Blue Devils uniforms. His players often stay on the field long after the sun goes down and he can barely see them.

In the winter, the game continues. Sometimes the kids shovel the basketball courts at Kennedy Park to play, but it's easier to throw on parkas and head to the Colisée, usually the first place plowed.

"It's really cold," Abdi H. admits, "but you run around, you're set, you're good."

Built in 1958, the Androscoggin Colisée sits high on the hill next to Drouin Field, home to the L/A Fighting Spirit, a hockey team that plays in the North American 3 league. In the 1970s, it was home ice for the Maine Nordiques, and more recently for the Lewiston MAINEiacs. The Boston Celtics played exhibition games on the floor, and Lewiston High School's hockey teams have won many state championships on its ice.

But the Colisée's biggest claim to fame—and Lewiston's, too—came in May 25, 1965, when Muhammad Ali squared off against Sonny Liston for the heavyweight championship title. The bout, which lasted just a few minutes before Ali's famous "phantom punch" took Liston down, is one of the most famous sports moments in history.

Lewiston was an unlikely host for such a marquee sports event. The bout was supposed to happen in the fall of 1964 at the Boston Garden, a rematch for Liston to recapture his title from Ali, who had just changed his name from Cassius Clay. But Ali's emergency hernia operation just days before the fight put things on hold. The delay sent promoters into a frantic search to find a new site; Lewiston fit the bill.

"Clay-Liston Championship Match Set for Lewiston's CMYC May 25," the *Lewiston Evening Journal* declared on May 7, 1965. With just a few weeks to prepare and a seating capacity of only 5,000, the Colisée—then called the Central Maine Youth Center—would be one of the smallest arenas ever to host a heavyweight bout.

Two days before the fight, Ali, increasingly controversial because of his commitment to the Nation of Islam, rolled into town, staying at the Holiday Inn in Auburn. He greeted hundreds of fans before heading out for one of his legendary training runs, which Maine state police cut short because pedestrians aren't allowed on the turnpike. Locals photographed him hanging out on his hotel balcony, relaxed and ready.

The night of the fight, fans who couldn't afford a ticket gathered high on the hill behind the arena in Marcotte Park. Looking out across the city, the basilica in the background, people peered through binoculars hoping to catch luminaries entering the building as packs of international media assembled to cover the action.

The crowd, which was about half capacity, cheered for Liston and booed Ali, who was introduced by his new name for the first time. Actor Robert Goulet, chosen to sing the national anthem despite being Canadian as a nod to Lewiston's Franco-American community, famously mangled a few of the words.

Much has been written about Ali's "phantom punch" that night. Some claim he connected a short right to Liston's face, sending the already off-balance former champion to the mat. Others insist it never happened, crying the fight was fixed. Instead of going to his neutral corner, Ali stood over Liston, daring him to get up, a ferocious look on his face. Standing ringside, camera in hand, Neil Leifer captured the moment, the most famous of Ali's career.

Liston later said he never heard the count and that relatively inexperienced "celebrity" referee Jersey Joe Walcott should have restrained Ali. When Liston finally got up, there was confusion as to whether or not it was a knockout. As the two boxers squared off, Walcott reached in and raised Ali's arm in victory, pushing Liston back to his corner. While *Sports Illustrated*'s Tex Maule called the fight "perfectly valid," Jimmy Breslin wrote that Walcott's ineptitude was "the worst mess in the history of all sports."

The Ali-Liston fight put a national spotlight on Lewiston. But it wouldn't be the last.

In July 2006, the local paper ran a headline that many national publications would soon echo: "Pig's Head Thrown into Lewiston Mosque." At ten p.m. on a Monday night, Brent Matthews, thirty-three, rolled a frozen pig's head into the Lisbon Street mosque, where some forty men knelt in prayer.

"Desecrating a place of worship," read the charge. A misdemeanor. But for Lewiston's Somali community, it meant much more than that. While Imam Nuh Iman acknowledged that the crime was the work of one man, the incident added to the fraught quality of life in Lewiston. Insults to Somalis ranged from racial slurs in school hallways to long stares at women wearing hijabs— "Dress American!"—to vicious letters to the editor of the *Sun Journal* that regurgitated myths about the impact of "parasitic" Somali refugees.

City officials held a press conference about the mosque incident, hoping transparency and quick consequences would make the story go away. They worried when they saw that a news team from Al Jazeera, in town for a story on Somali refugees, attended the press conference. But while the then-burgeoning network included the episode in the piece that aired, it wasn't the focus.

Although the pig's head story soon disappeared from headlines, Lewiston remained on edge as a small rash of anti-Muslim, anti-Somali incidents occurred. A Somali-owned restaurant bore the wrath of vandals, while police arrested a woman for spitting on a Somali man while shouting racial slurs. What, many wondered, would be the next shoe to drop?

On April 11, 2007, less than a year after Matthews rolled the pig's head into the mosque, a middle school student put a bag of ham on a table where some Somali students were eating lunch. Allegedly, he was acting on a dare from friends who thought it was funny. The Somali kids were not amused. The student was suspended for ten days, and Superintendent of Schools Leon Levesque dubbed it a "hate incident."

The event rekindled memories of the pig's head affair, as many considered it a copycat crime. Ten days later, around eight o'clock in the morning on Saturday, April 21, a distraught Brent Matthews called 911. Within minutes of police arriving at the scene, he committed suicide with a semiautomatic handgun.

Bates College graduate Elizabeth Strout, who won the Pulitzer Prize for *Olive Kitteridge*, fictionalized the pig's head incident in *The Burgess Boys*. The story takes place in fictional Shirley Falls, a depressed Maine mill town fraught with racial and religious tensions since the arrival of thousands of Somali refugees. Through brothers Bob and Jim Burgess and their sister Susan—whose nineteen-year-old son committed the crime—Strout's nuanced perspective on the complicated relationships in Shirley Falls shows the hardships and trauma felt by all of the characters and questions who the strangers in the community really are.

Without question, the détente in Lewiston was fragile between those who considered themselves to be "real" Lewiston and the newcomers. But the city was hardly in a position to turn away people interested in living there. Not only did its economic instability help solidify longstanding patterns of white intergenerational poverty, it had a detrimental impact on population numbers, sending capable young people looking for opportunity elsewhere.

It wasn't just Lewiston's problem. Maine's entire population was growing older by the second, outpacing even Florida's. It wasn't that Maine had too many old people; it just didn't have enough young people, making it difficult to attract new business—

especially the kind Lewiston needed. For the state to sustain its workforce, according to one prediction, it needed to attract three thousand new residents a year for the next two decades.

While City Hall planned economic recovery in many ways, such as the commercial repurposing of the mill buildings, Somali refugees were a much-needed shot of energy. The school population, for example, grew more than 10 percent in ten years. The Somalis arrived at a time when Maine, one of the nation's whitest, most homogenous states, reigned supreme, according to assistant city administrator Phil Nadeau, "in all the metrics you don't want to lead in. Our population doesn't go up without the presence of foreign-born." For Lewiston's economic plan to work, potential employers needed to believe that there were enough people living, working, and buying there.

But the arrival of the Somalis, and the speed and numbers with which they came, shocked the economically fraught blue-collar city, which began to experience Islamophobic behavior. Taxi drivers refused to pick up Somali passengers, Somali women complained of white men exposing themselves on the street when they passed, and calls of "Go back!" from trucks adorned with Confederate flag decals became commonplace. "WE FEED SOMALIANS AND LET U.S. TROOPS DIE," read one lawn sign. Regardless of the actual data, rumors continued to swirl that freeloading Somalis were draining state and city resources. Lewiston was going bankrupt, fumed many, because City Hall was buying the newcomers cars and giving them large sums of cash. How else, they reasoned, could "those people" afford anything? Our grandfathers came to Lewiston to work, they seethed. These people are getting handouts.

While Somalis gave many reasons for choosing Lewiston, from available housing to schools to safety, headlines focused on the economic pull of Maine's General Assistance Program, as if it was the only viable reason. Working with state and city budgets, the program provides support for basic needs—medicine, fuel, rent, and food. While many states had weakened or eliminated General Assistance, Maine continued to provide support to individuals based solely on financial need, the majority of whom were not refugees.

"I'm just so tired of the myths," Sue Charron, Lewiston's director of social services, told the local newspaper amid the reports of free cars, air conditioners, groceries, and apartments. "Eighty-five percent of the population is still the good old American folks who come in here."

But in the early days, myths grew quickly. People claimed that schools were overcrowded because of the number of rooms devoted to Muslim prayer sessions, and the city was riddled with Somali gang warfare. Nadeau rolls his eyes when asked about this, pulling out data sheets that show otherwise. Kids—all kids—will be kids, he notes of the gang claims, regardless of where they are from. Some had made some bad choices along the way but, he emphasizes, nothing that necessitated crisis management.

"It isn't perfect," he acknowledges, always ready to squelch the next inflammatory headline. "But there's nothing to report on."

The rumors of African gangs in the streets and chickens in the kitchens went national when Patrick Reardon of the *Chicago Tribune* read about Lewiston. Reardon was in Maine to write about Richard Russo's Pulitzer Prize for *Empire Falls*, which is about an economically depressed town in Maine. Reardon's subsequent article, "A Yankee Mill Town Globalizes," published in June 2002, engendered more stories on Lewiston, including one spuriously warning of an additional 20,000 refugees on their way.

On October 1, 2002, the gossip hit an apex when then-mayor Laurier Raymond issued his now-notorious open letter to the Somali community. "Maxed-out," read the headline in the *Sun*

Journal. "Mayor appeals to Somalis to stem migration." In the letter, Raymond implored the Somali community—which had grown to more than a thousand in the last eighteen months—to tell their friends to stop coming. He prided the city for having "cheerfully accepted" and "accommodated" the new arrivals, but hoped the slight decline in their numbers in recent weeks would continue, as it was a "welcome relief, given increasing demands on city and school services."

"The Somali community must exercise some discipline and reduce the stress on our limited finances and our generosity," he wrote. "We have been overwhelmed and have responded valiantly. Now we need breathing room. Our city is maxed-out financially, physically and emotionally. I look forward to your cooperation."

Although not Raymond's intention, the three-page letter opened floodgates of racial tension, dividing the city into distinct camps. Xenophobic residents heralded Raymond's letter as a breath of fresh air, allowing them to use economic arguments to mask racist sentiments. He was right, these people said. The refugees had a detrimental impact on the city and had to be stopped.

Others called the letter blatantly racist, hurting those who'd already been told to "go back to Africa" when they walked down the street. Its language played upon age-old American racial stereotypes, evoking notions of an uncontrollable black element. The mayor's use of "we" and "our" indicated that there were two Lewistons, and that Somalis were not authentic residents.

City officials made clear that the letter, while written on city letterhead, was the mayor's opinion, not policy. Council members expressed concern he hadn't consulted them before issuing the missive. City Administrator Jim Bennett assured people that Lewiston could not and would not close its doors, but would continue to support anyone who chose to live there.

After taking a few days to determine a proper response, Somali elders delivered a letter, signed by twenty-five Somali men and women, to the mayor's office. They also held a press conference on Lisbon Street. City officials saw it as an opportunity to learn who the leaders in the Somali community were. If someone got time with the microphone, they mattered.

The elders characterized Raymond's letter as "inflammatory and disturbing," describing their "dismay, astonishment and anger" and admonishing him for failing to meet with them as they had requested. They were proud of the Lewiston they helped create, a "multi-ethnic, multi-racial city" with fewer vacant apartments and storefronts. Lewiston's downtown had come alive as they "put money in the pockets of landlords," raising property values. They emphasized their status as citizens and legal residents, with many of their children "Americans by birth." The letter, they concluded, was the work of an "ill-informed leader who is bent towards bigotry."

"Somalis Rip Mayor," shouted the *Sun Journal* over a photograph of Abdirizak Mahboub addressing the crowd. Networks like NBC and CNN covered the story, while reporters from the *Los Angeles Times* to the *New York Times* wrote about Raymond's letter. But national media wasn't the only entity paying attention.

"Who is *that*?" Phil Nadeau asked when Maggie Chisholm, director of recreation and parks, called to tell him that World Church of the Creator had contacted her. They had applied to rent space for a rally at the Multipurpose Center on Birch Street. Now known as Creativity, the group, which espouses a white supremacist worldview, announced that it planned to "unite the White people of Lewiston against the Somali invasion." These guys, Nadeau realized, weren't local. And they were looking for a fight.

News of the proposed rally propelled Lewiston into action. A coalition entitled "Many and One" brought together people from area colleges, churches, city administration, and neighborhoods to plan a counter-rally. National interest in the story swelled when Matthew Hale, leader of World Church, landed in jail for soliciting an undercover federal informant to kill a judge. City Hall moved the group to the Maine Army National Guard Armory near the turnpike. "In and out," Nadeau said of the plan. "Not downtown."

"Let there be peace," the *Sun Journal* begged the morning of January 11, 2003. "With Nazis coming, some pray for peace while police brace for trouble," read the subhead.

Lewiston got more than peace. That day, remembers Nadeau, was when everything changed, solidifying relationships that would enable the city to weather future storms. Sitting at his desk in City Hall, an enormous map of Lewiston behind him and Leifer's photo of Ali standing over Liston to his right, Nadeau marks the mayor's now-infamous letter as the moment the city figured out how to move forward. There had been a few attempts—City Hall's forums, the Franco Center's "meet your neighbors" events—to bring people together. But nothing like this.

"I think that very unintentionally, Larry's writing that letter was the watershed moment for this community, because it served as the catalyst for everything else that followed," Nadeau says. "It galvanized the community."

He notes that often it takes a tragedy of some kind to bring together this kind of response. But in Lewiston, "no one got killed, no one got stabbed," he emphasizes. "We had a letter that was written by somebody who had an opinion about something, and the reaction resulted in people coming together in a way I don't think they would've ever come together."

Lewiston had found a new identity. "PEACE PREVAILS" crowed the *Sun Journal*, noting "thousands embrace Lewiston Somalis" while calling the "racist rally" a "non-event." The "Many and One" rally filled Bates College's gymnasium, three thousand strong, while a thousand more crowded together outside in the cold, chanting and singing, cheering for speakers who came outside to greet them. Across town at the armory, several hundred rallied against the few World Church supporters who actually showed up.

"Not in our house," former Lewiston mayor John Jenkins—the first African American to win the office—repeated as he moderated speeches and testimonials from other former mayors, the governor, high school students, and community organizers who spoke to Lewiston's new self. "*Ou Est Le Mayor?*" read one sign, a nod to both the city's long history of immigration and the absence of Raymond from the event. It was something that U.S. Senator Olympia Snowe, who attended alongside colleague Susan Collins, found apt. Snowe grew up in Auburn, the daughter of a Greek immigrant.

"What is happening right now across town—that is not who we are," she said in a prepared statement handed out to reporters. "There is no place for them in Maine, no place for them in Lewiston, and no place for them in America."

Muhammad Ali also sent prepared remarks. Fighting racism, he wrote, was "a greater contest" than the one he'd fought against Liston back in 1965. Lewiston's situation is "between those ingrained in bigotry and those who have embraced freedom," he wrote. "The Many and One Coalition has my full support."

Lewiston had found a path toward a new identity, a foundation to build on. By 2010, less than 20 percent of Lewiston's General Assistance budget went to noncitizens, a number proportionate to the percentage of immigrants living in the city. The community had its flaws, Nadeau acknowledged, knowing that racism lived a robust life beneath the surface of any town, including this one. But things were improving.

CHAPTER 5

I STILL SAY SOMALIA

As Lewiston learned how to live with its new residents, schools became the front line of the many transitions taking place. The Somali influx caught school administrators off guard. They struggled to put everything from English language classes to student civil rights teams into place.

Gus LeBlanc grew up in Old Town, just north of Orono on the Penobscot River, a small mill town best known for the eponymous canoes once built there. LeBlanc is a self-described Franco; his grandparents came from Canada around the turn of the twentieth century. At dinner each night, his parents talked about the various insults thrown at them that day because they were French-speaking and Catholic. While he doesn't remember experiencing prejudice, such tales left their mark.

In Old Town, there were two Catholic churches, one French-speaking and the other English. LeBlanc's parents married in the English-speaking one because his mother was of Irish descent. His grandfather, whom he describes as "not the most enlightened guy," refused to go.

When LeBlanc left Old Town for college, he headed just a few miles down the turnpike to the University of Maine at Orono. It was important to his parents that he find something better in life. At college, he played football and pursued teaching, returning to Old Town after graduation to teach history. A long career in education had begun.

After a stint in Dexter, where he captured a few state championships coaching football, LeBlanc headed to Androscoggin County, working at Turner and Oak Hill High Schools before landing at Lewiston's Montello Elementary School in 1999. LeBlanc had experience dealing with tough situations, and with more than a thousand students, things at Montello had, he remembers, "run amok a little bit." Within a year or so of his arrival, the Somalis came.

Montello had long dealt with various levels of poverty and the problems that come with it, such as chronic absenteeism. "That had always been the issue in Lewiston," says LeBlanc. With a high student count and low property values, Lewiston is the largest recipient of school aid in Maine. Today at the high school, for example, a quarter of the population is immigrant but more than 70 percent of the students receive free or reduced-price hot lunches. Yet as the district established English Language Learner (ELL) programs, some people used the new refugee students as scapegoats for low student success rates. The refugees, they claimed, were getting much more help and were draining school resources.

"A lot of them had really never been in school—they didn't understand how to behave," LeBlanc acknowledges about Somali students. "English wasn't their first language, they had a different color skin, and many were Muslims. There was a real cultural difference."

Accommodating these students went beyond ELL classes. Many of the immigrant parents fell into the category of low-literacy adults, having come from rural areas of Somalia with little access to formal education. By federal law, Lewiston schools translated all forms and handbooks into Somali once fifty families claimed it as their first language. But LeBlanc quickly realized that, even then, many parents couldn't read the information that was going home, giving them few—if any—opportunities to voice their opinions about their children's education. His new friend, ZamZam Mohamud, whose children attended Montello, came to his aid.

In Lewiston, Mohamud is one of those people that everyone knows, from the chief of police to pretty much any teacher. "If she was white," observes one longtime Lewiston resident, "there is no doubt she would be mayor."

An elegant woman with a contagious smile, Mohamud was the first Somali to sit on the city's school committee—or hold any city office, for that matter. She has volunteered on the Lewiston Police Department's Civil Rights Team, the Downtown Neighborhood Task Force, and the library board of trustees. Her daughter, Hanan, served as co–class president at the high school in 2009 and was the first Somali student to serve on the school committee.

Everyone, it seems, knows her story. Having lost much of her family in Somalia's civil war, she arrived in Lewiston in 2001 with two children and not much else. Within a few days, her son, Jama, cut his foot. In the emergency room, a nurse noticed her command of English and asked for help with another Somali patient. Mohamud had found a job. Eventually, she graduated from Central Maine Medical Center's College of Nursing and Health Professions as a certified nursing assistant.

Mohamud, who became a U.S. citizen in 2006, was LeBlanc's first Somali friend. She has played this role for many in Lewiston. While the district floundered somewhat in formalizing its communication strategies, LeBlanc and Mohamud coordinated meetings with parents so things could be explained to them verbally, rather than read via papers sent home. Once parents began to understand what was going on, they helped educate others. When the Bantu began to arrive, LeBlanc learned about tensions they had with ethnic Somalis, some of whom were already well established in Lewiston. He met with Somali elders for help in negotiating such conflicts.

"It was a tumbleweed," remembers LeBlanc. "As we got going, between the meetings and the translations and people talking to each other about the procedures, it became smoother and smoother."

Eventually, the district hired Somalis to work as translators and parental liaisons, pushed by a mandate from the U.S. Department of Justice. Abdikadir Negeye worked as a translator at Geiger Elementary, a position with enormous impact but little recognition.

"Making phone calls, taking messages from parents to the teachers, from teachers to the parents," Negeye says of his daily tasks. "I was kind of a bridge, bridging the gap not only to translate, but also culturally, talking about a lot of things like Eid or Christmastime."

He constantly reassured teachers that they couldn't ask him a dumb question. Every now and then, he reconsidered that point.

Not for the first time, Lewiston schools established policies and created solutions for a growing population of immigrant students. Superintendent Levesque reconfigured the budgets to accommodate the exploding ELL program, with local tax dollars supplemented by the state.

"The state of Maine actually gave us a multiplier," remembers LeBlanc. "If a kid was an ELL student, we got a little bit extra, kind of like disability funding."

Many worried that the budget shifts would hurt other programs, but LeBlanc didn't believe that anything suffered because of the new priorities. Levesque, says Leblanc, tried to support the Somalis as he would any other group of students.

"His philosophy was that if we've got kids with certain needs, we're going to have to do what we have to do," says LeBlanc.

LeBlanc thinks Lewiston became a better school system with better educators. At Montello, for example, he saw vast improvements in the language arts program. Rather than instruct Somalis separately, teachers integrated each lesson, knowing how interaction with native English speakers would benefit all students.

"It made us better at dealing with the needs of our lower socioeconomic and special needs kids," asserts LeBlanc. "When we figured out what we had to do to help the Somali kids, we actually helped everyone."

Maulid Abdow recalls his early days at Montello as terrifying. Nothing made sense. One of four children that his mother had in Dadaab, when asked where he's from, he will say Somalia, even though he's never been there. But with a bit of prodding, he admits he was born in Kenya, becoming uncharacteristically quiet.

"But I still say Somalia."

His parents, Hassan Matan and Shafea Omar, came to Kenya from Jilib, the most populous city in the Middle Juba region of Somalia, and a key battleground after the fall of Mogadishu in 2006. Once a rich agricultural area on the main road between the port city of Kismayo and Mogadishu, it has good proximity to both the Jubba riverbank and the Indian Ocean. Today, ravished by drought, it sees a lot of Al-Shabaab activity.

"It was good," Omar says of life in Somalia, a country she still professes to love, "and then it collapsed."

In 2002, a few years after the United States officially recognized Bantus as a persecuted minority, the family moved to Kakuma, where they found the heat unbearable and food supplies even more limited. There was no milk or meat to eat, she remembers, just flour and beans. They were afraid to go outside, even for firewood, for fear of being attacked. Looters took most of their few possessions.

Maulid missed the peanut butter sandwiches and soda he'd had for lunch in Dadaab.

After a series of interviews with immigration officers at Kakuma, in which the family had to repeat its stories of loss again and again, they flew to Nairobi, where they lived for four-teen weeks. Verification procedures included ensuring that each of their children—Maulid, his older brother, and his two little sisters—was really theirs. It wasn't until the last interviews with the U.S. Immigration and Naturalization Service that Maulid's parents realized America was on the table. They were headed to Atlanta, officials told them. But Matan and Omar already knew about Lewiston from friends. It's a small city, people told them. Very quiet. Safe. Lots of Somalis. No one mentioned that Maine was one of the whitest states in America because in Lewiston, it felt like there were lots of black people around.

Seven-year-old Maulid had no idea where they were headed. All he remembers is falling down the stairs of one of the many buses he took between airplanes. His earliest memories—his only memories—of refugee camp life revolve around soccer. All day, every day, he ran around the dusty landscape with his father and older brother, Abdiweli. They didn't have the "fancy balls" Maulid plays with now, his father says. They improvised, wadding up paper, wrapping it in a shirt, and covering it with a plastic bag. Kicking the "ball" with bare feet sometimes hurt, but Matan says Maulid got used to it. He never tired of playing, his father remem-bers. And he was fast, says Omar. From the moment he learned how to walk, one-year-old Maulid was fast.

Like his friends, Maulid is conflicted about what he actually re-members of those days and what his parents have told him. He usually simply says that life in the refugee camps was "fine" or "nice," the go-to words for many Somali teenagers. But it isn't just that Maulid doesn't remember; he doesn't *want* to remember.

"I remember some parts, but it's nothing fun," he says, struggling for the right words. "I mean, like, it's fun but it's—whatever."

Maulid grows solemn when pressed about his journey to Lewiston. His brightly colored yellow-and-blue dashiki, which he wears with ripped jeans and sandals, belies his suddenly somber mood. He's a stylish kid; he likes clothes and wears them with flair. Dashikis are not traditional Somali dress, but many students in Lewiston wear them, some days even to soccer practice.

"Bird hunting!" he remembers, his eyes lighting up, an infectious smile breaking beneath his barely-there mustache. He seems relieved to have thought of another good memory about Africa. "Yeah, I used to *love* to go bird hunting!"

After a week or so in Georgia, Maulid's family headed north in March of 2005. Maulid remembers seeing snow on the ground and at first thinking it was salt. Cold was everywhere. It seeped through his clothes, got under his skin. He didn't understand how to counteract it, never mind go to school in it. But getting used to the cold, he soon discovered, was the least of it.

"It took a long time, but I got used to the weather—whatever," he says dismissively. "But the *people*?"

He was petrified at Montello, where he started in first grade. He spoke no English and had no idea what was going on, feeling completely alone. The hallways, the other students, the routine—all were foreign to him. He spent his days with a teacher by his side, holding his hand, walking him everywhere. He did not understand why he had to sit for such long stretches of time or what the teachers meant by "behave." The first time he needed to go to the bathroom, he panicked. He knew where it was, but he didn't know how to ask if he could go, something he saw other kids doing. He finally decided to just go, running from the classroom. Once safely inside the bathroom, he stayed there, worried about the consequences of what he'd just done.

"It was *mad* scary," he says of his early days at Montello, reliving the anxiety that came with not understanding the progression of his own days. "Abdiweli went to school with me, he was like in fourth grade, and like every time I saw him, I would cry."

Because Abdiweli was in a higher grade, he had a different schedule, something Maulid didn't understand. *Why can't we be together?* he wondered. *Why does he keep leaving me?* When Abdiweli went to lunch, Maulid went to recess. When Maulid went to recess, Abdiweli went back to class. It made no sense to the brothers; they didn't understand why they were kept apart. They didn't get grade levels or recess. Why were there so many different hallways and rooms? Why did they keep moving around?

The bus ride was even worse. Maulid remembers two kids who made fun of him every day. He didn't comprehend what they were saying, but he knew it wasn't good. He didn't want to fight; he worried he'd be sent to jail. Even if he knew whom to tell about it, he couldn't. Looking back, he knows they were making fun of his skin color, his clothes, his language, and his religion.

By fourth grade, Maulid's English had gotten "okay" and things felt more comfortable. He started to listen to rap along with the African music he had grown up with, picking up pieces of a new identity in African American culture. His father tolerated his new musical interests, letting Maulid change the radio station in the car. His mother constantly worried about the pull of America on her children; the influence of a culture she did not really understand.

Things regularly took his family by surprise. Their first summer in Lewiston, local Fourth of July celebrations—firecrackers booming throughout the city—sent them into hiding in their apartment for almost a full week, just waiting for it to end.

"Boom, boom, boom," remembers his father, shaking his head at the memory.

They thought the noise was gunfire, that people were dying in the streets, something that was all too familiar. They'd been enjoying summer; the weather reminded them of Africa. But the second his mother saw a firework—"fire in the sky"—she told her children to get inside. Eventually, Maulid learned about the holiday at school and from some of his Lewiston-born neighbors in the apartment upstairs. He remembers eventually going to the park with them to watch; they'd assured him it would be safe. He went home to tell his mother it was okay.

"No," she told him. "It's guns, it's fighting."

Maulid finally got her to understand that no one was fighting, but his parents still don't like the Fourth of July.

With Christmas—another holiday the family knew nothing about—donated bags of presents and clothing arrived at their door. Sweaters, snow pants, and soccer balls—real soccer balls. When spring came, Maulid and Abdiweli went to the park with their father to take the new balls out for a spin.

"My dad used to take us to a park near the Italian Bakery," he remembers. No one had phones; kids just showed up to play. "We would just run and kick around with him."

Matan is a tailor by trade, something he did in the refugee camps to make whatever money he could. But to support his family in Lewiston—Maulid is one of eight children—Matan works as a custodian at Country Kitchen, not far from the family's second-floor, four-bedroom apartment on Walnut Street. He still makes clothes on the side; people bring him things to work on at home, and he likes making things for his family to wear.

During the summer, Matan takes the short walk from the family's apartment to Drouin Field to see Maulid play in the high school's summer league. He and his wife are also fixtures in the stands at the high school during the fall season, sitting among the few who can carve out time between jobs to watch the team play.

A small, compact man with kind eyes and dark, graying hair, Matan's face lights up when he talks about soccer, English failing him as exuberance takes over. "Woo-woo," he calls to Maulid as he watches him race down the field dribbling the ball. He paces the sideline with sandaled feet as the ball changes directions, his hands plunged into the pockets of his gray dress pants, his short-sleeved button-down shirt shifting as he follows the game. When it's cold, he dons a black leather-like jacket, something Maulid can always see out of the corner of his eye when he's on the field.

"Arsenal!" Matan says when asked about favorite teams, joy spreading over his lined face. He loves the English Premier League and goes to the Safari to watch games.

"I played soccer in Somalia," he says proudly through a translator. Having been considered a top player in district games, Matan was relieved when he discovered there was soccer in America, and he is happy the sport has grown so much in Lewiston. "I love it very, very much." He points down to his feet. He stopped playing because he injured his toes, but he still loves to watch.

"Woo-woo," he calls again, yelling advice to Maulid and his teammates in Somali. When Maulid scores, Matan's delighted grin swallows his face.

Like her husband, Omar often walks to Drouin to watch. She sits in the shade with other women who gather to talk, watch their younger children play on the sidelines, and see the game. A relaxed group, their hijabs, *masars*, and *jilbabs* create vibrant scenery. Younger women stop to say hello to Omar, the only time her eyes ever leave the game. They bend down to clasp her hand; kiss it. She returns the gesture. Boys, too, stop to greet her, lowering their eyes in respect.

The scarves she wraps around her head frame her gentle, dark eyes before combining with the long, floral, robe-like dresses she prefers to wear. Omar works maintenance at Walmart, as does Abdiweli and his wife. She also babysits, one of the many jobs worked by Somali women that unemployment data doesn't include. The long hours and her responsibilities for her extended family take their toll, making a shady spot on the grass watching soccer a luxury. She calls the players by name, knowing what they need to do.

"HIHIHIHI!" she yells, shouting directives in Somali. "Go, Maulid!" she cheers in English. "Yes, Austin! Joséph!"

She is "very proud" of her son's soccer talents, and encourages him to join teams, travel, and play. But she is conflicted, too, because she wants him to do well in school, and she worries that soccer consumes too much time. Some days she urges him to go to the field. Other days she tells him to stop playing and focus on academics. She didn't have any opportunity to go to school, which still bothers her. It's hard to learn things now. She can speak some English but has a tough time understanding when someone talks to her. Her children, she says, tell her what she needs to know.

A social kid, Maulid likes school, although he struggles with the work and doesn't like reading. He does better during soccer season, when he needs to keep his grades up to stay eligible to play. Soccer helps him manage his time, keeps him on a schedule. Soccer helps school make more sense, he says. It keeps him focused and reduces the stress.

Maulid joined his first soccer team, the Young Strikers, in elementary school. His coach got him a uniform and let him choose from a pile of used cleats. Maulid chose a pair that looked cool, green and blue, but they were way too big. He didn't like them, or the shin guards. He wanted to play barefoot or, if that wasn't allowed, with just sneakers. "What did it matter?" he asked. The kids with brand-new cleats and balls weren't half as good as he was.

But he had a lot to learn. Maulid had great skills, but he knew little about the formal aspects of a timed game with assigned positions. His coach taught him about adhering to a practice and game schedule, and taught him about winning.

"We would come together, practice every single day, and we were undefeated for years," Maulid brags. "Never lost a game until, like, eighth grade." He pauses, trailing off at the memory. "Seventh grade, maybe."

Maulid's love of soccer was typical of many Somali boys who came to Lewiston. Kicking a ball around barefoot in the camps, playing pickup games in Lewiston's parks, were common experiences that bonded them. A group of young adults—Rilwan Osman, Jama Mohamed, and Abdikadir Negeye—wanted to capitalize on that bond, using it to ensure that they didn't lose the next generation to American culture. In 2008, they formed the Somali Bantu Youth Association (SBYA), today known as Maine Immigrant and Refugee Services (MEIRS).

As is common in most immigrant tales, refugee children lived between cultures, the typical generational divide made more profound by differences in language, dress, and food. How could Somalis successfully live in Lewiston, the founders of SBYA wondered, while maintaining their cultural identity? How could kids stay focused on family and education, rather than distractions like cigarettes, schoolyard fights, and petty crime?

Kids like Maulid are part of a 1.5 generation, a term used to describe immigrants who arrive in the United States at a young age. They learn the language and customs of the new country more easily than their parents; make friends; do well in school; and join sports teams. But they also subscribe to the traditions of where they came from.

Because the Somali community arrived so quickly and in such large numbers, it could negotiate with its new environs, rather than entirely assimilate, thereby preserving critical aspects of its culture, especially religion. While living in tough neighborhoods on the outskirts of Atlanta, many Somali parents had feared the lure of baggy jeans and gangsta rap. In Lewiston, however, they felt more in control, even as they rebutted neighbors—many of whom were the children and grandchildren of French-Canadians who'd fought similar battles—who constantly asked, "Why can't you be more like us?" From language to food to religion, kids like Maulid kept a foot in two places, serving as the go-betweens for their parents as they forged a new identity. Each child had to learn American customs, while respecting and maintaining his or her Somali identity.

In 2008, the SBYA called a meeting in the basement at Hillview Apartments, a subsidized complex where some Somalis lived. Alarmed by the number of Somali students written up for disciplinary action in school, as well as the rate at which girls were dropping out to get married, the group wanted to help kids and their parents successfully navigate life in Lewiston, making good choices and breaking the cycle of poverty that existed in the city long before they arrived. Integration, acculturation, and accommodation—as opposed to wholesale assimilation—were the keys.

They started the meeting, remembers Negeye, asking kids what they needed. Homework help, they replied. Oh, and soccer.

From the beginning, the SBYA's motto for kids was to "help or get help." All were welcome, whether they needed support or could offer it. There was no money; everyone worked other jobs and went to school. Negeye, for example, worked at L.L. Bean while taking classes at Central Maine Community College. He felt bad about neglecting his family, but he wanted to make sure the Somali community had a stake in its future in Lewiston.

The Lewiston Housing Authority let the group continue to use the basement for meetings, and they stored everything from files to soccer nets in Osman's van. Their goal was to keep the kids focused and busy so they would stay off the streets, a strategy used by community organizations throughout the United States.

"We paired school with soccer," remembers Negeye. "Do the homework, work on the academics, and then go to the field and practice."

Kids had to be respectful to stay on a team. Stay out of fights. No swearing. The Lewiston Police Department praised the organization for its work.

Finding a field that the city would let them use required patience and money. Soccer practice took place at what is now Mark W. Paradis Park, wedged among Bartlett, Pierce, and Birch Streets in the heart of downtown. When Maulid and his dad first played there, it was a grassy oasis tucked behind the apartment buildings. But as more kids discovered it, the grass died from overuse, and they nicknamed it Balding Park.

Within the first year, some 150 boys—SBYA's target audience—came out to play in two divisions. They had to move games down the street to Drouin Field. Lewiston, it seemed, was becoming a soccer town.

Lewiston wasn't alone. Most of the world has a passion for soccer, with the United States long considered an outlier. When FIFA, soccer's international governing body, did a "Big Count" of its 207 member associations in 2006, it found that 265 million people worldwide played the game, while another 5 million coached or officiated. Youth players comprised more than half of those involved.

Baseball persists in its hold as America's unofficially official pastime, and (American) football, despite problems ranging from concussions to a decrease in youth participation, still produces the largest single U.S. sporting event of the year with the Super Bowl.

But the U.S. Soccer Federation is second only to China in the number of players fielded each year. So while baseball, football, basketball, and hockey rule America's professional sports landscape, participation numbers indicate something very different.

Setting aside the record-breaking television ratings set by both the Men's World Cup in 2014 and the Women's World Cup in 2015, soccer's popularity in the States is best reflected by the number of kids who play it, whether on school teams or in the recreational leagues that govern families' weekend schedules. In 1974, when U.S. Youth Soccer first tabulated numbers, there were 103,432 children registered to play the game in the country. Flash forward to the twenty-first century: more than three million play, a mere 10,867 of whom live in Maine.

Barriers to soccer's commercial success in the United States range from the slow growth of a high-profile commercial league to difficulties in creating a profitable television broadcast of a game that almost never stops. (If there aren't any time-outs, there are no commercials.) Critics dismiss the game as tedious and low-scoring, although football fans might consider what an NFL box score would look like if touchdowns were worth just one point instead of six. And for some, soccer simply seems un-American, an immigrant game. In a way, this "patriotic" disdain has worked in the sport's favor, allowing it to thrive at the community level with a diverse roster arguably more reflective of who actually lives in the United States than all of the other "major" sports combined.

As Lewiston's SBYA soccer program grew, so did the organization. In 2013, it opened offices at the B Street Community Center, a Housing Authority site in the heart of downtown on Birch Street. The group contracted with MaineCare (formerly Medicaid) and both Osman and Negeye, who worked in the public school system as interpreters and parent liaisons, became paid staffers.

The group widened its reach, responding to requests for adult literacy, high school equivalency tests, parenting, and money management classes. Staff held open hours to help with job applications and government paperwork, while juvenile justice seminars built better bridges between immigrant youth and the police. Kids learned about the consequences of fighting and drugs, while officers learned that a Somali's refusal to make eye contact is a sign of respect, submission. Weekend citizenship classes helped people start the naturalization process, something SBYA encouraged so that they could visit family in Africa as well as vote and serve on juries. The latter was a critical part of integration, one that combatted myths that Somalis didn't really want to be in the United States.

"It was a great feeling, great day, that moment," Negeye says of his own naturalization ceremony in 2011, after which his colleagues and students at Geiger Elementary School greeted him waving American flags. "Holding my certificate, now I feel like I belong to the country."

Creating a sense of belonging was something Gus LeBlanc focused on when he became principal of Lewiston High School. The school, he says, had fallen into a "malaise," but its problems were much the same as what he'd dealt with at Montello Elementary for eight years—only bigger, as several hundred Somali students tried to navigate one of Maine's largest, most impoverished high schools.

Because "kids are the products of their parents," LeBlanc saw how some of the city's racial tensions spilled into the school's hallways and cafeteria. Accusations of "terrorist" even burst out at times when students squared off against each other. But overt clashes were rare, allowing LeBlanc to concentrate on getting help to the students who needed it most. He redoubled efforts to ensure strong support for ELL students, knowing they would be further ostracized if they didn't catch up. The high school soon had five full-time ELL teachers, three aides, and a translator. The program, says LeBlanc, just "grew and grew and grew."

But the cultural piece was harder. LeBlanc didn't want to make too many special accommodations for Somali students, worried about opening a floodgate that the school could not sustain. But he understood that the schools would have to do their own share of assimilation. Somali elders met with the superintendent to strategize about what kinds of clothing would be acceptable for Somali girls to wear in gym class. Lunchrooms labeled pork products more clearly with *doofar* (pig), and replaced hot dogs and bologna with beef versions. Female students were allowed to cover their heads; hijabs were not a violation of the "no hats, no bandanas" rule. But rumors persisted about Islamic prayer sessions and girls washing their feet in the bathrooms before lunch. LeBlanc tried to find middle ground. He didn't want to restrict anyone's personal expression, but prayer could not be made an official part of the school day. He talked to Somali students about the separation of church and state in the United States, where school and religion did not go hand in hand. An informal routine developed, with kids praying in the gym during lunch or in a quiet corner of an upstairs corridor. He made sure no one bothered them, but also that no boundaries were crossed.

"It was very doable," he says.

But LeBlanc hit a roadblock when he strengthened the attendance policy to reduce tardiness and truancy, something that had long plagued the school. He knew the religious observance of Ramadan might require some absences, as Maine law permitted absences in "observance of recognized holidays...during the regular school day." But he hadn't accounted for the number of Muslim students who wanted early dismissal on Fridays for *jum'ah*, the weekly prayer. With only 175 school days per year, he didn't see how a student could miss that many afternoons to go to the mosque. Yet he wanted to make sure the school respected the religious needs of its newer students. He met with a local imam to discuss the issue.

"Contrary to the opinion of some people, he was a perfect gentleman. He wasn't angry; he was concerned," remembers LeBlanc. "The more we talked, I said to him, 'This is no different than Catholic kids and Jewish kids. If they wanted to have all these days off to go to church or whatever, we would not allow that.'"

The imam decided that while it would be best for students to come to the mosque at noon on Fridays, they could wait until school let out. With his blessing, says LeBlanc, the issue largely went away.

The athletic department, too, was going to have to make some changes; things that Mike McGraw, for one, hadn't imagined when he first signed on as soccer coach. But the foundations put in place by the schools and community groups like SBYA, alongside McGraw's decades of coaching experience, would help set things on the right track. Perhaps even a championship track.

CHAPTER 6

GRIND MODE

Mike McGraw shuffled to his car after a meeting about a new spring youth soccer league. The modest sedan with a beat-up soccer ball between the two back headrests is his calling card, known by just about everyone in the city.

It had been another long day. Yet again, he'd missed an evening at home with Rita. So much about coaching has nothing to do with actual games. For sixty-six-year-old McGraw, it meant waking up before sunrise in the preseason to plan; working with the athletic director, guidance counselors, teachers, and administrators; serving as a player's "other" parent; engaging in crisis management; keeping the Booster Club in the loop; working with officials. A lot took place before he ever stepped on the field.

Long after they graduate, kids remember his love of the game, his love of winning, his love for them. When they return to say hello, they know he is still there, never forgetting a name or a face, and the many stories that go with each player. Oftentimes on senior night, players ask him to join the traditional family photo taken before the game.

Driving home through the rows of triple-decker apartment

houses, McGraw saw a young African boy playing with a soccer ball that made the one in his back seat look new. He pulled over.

"You do that to that ball?" he asked the kid.

The boy grabbed the ball, slowly walked over, and peered through the open passenger window.

"No," he answered defensively. He clearly thought he was in trouble. He told McGraw he only kicked the ball. Honest.

McGraw laughed and asked the kid if he had any brothers at the high school. No, the boy replied, but he had a sister there.

"I think you're gonna get a new ball," McGraw said.

The boy looked into McGraw's car, his eyes stopping with disappointment at the old ball in the back.

"Not now," McGraw told him. "You tell your sister to come find me, and I'll find a ball for you."

McGraw goes crazy keeping track of the team's balls. When a player kicks one over the fence during practice, he yells for someone, anyone, to get it, fast. He knows it's a matter of minutes before a group of kids on the other side will commandeer it for their own game. Every time he sees a kid kicking a ball in a parking lot or on one of the patches of dirt that runs between apartments houses, he wonders if it is one of his. He loves how the game saturates the city, but he has a limited budget for balls. But McGraw's heart usually wins over his head. He will make sure that kid gets a new ball.

In 1974, when math teacher Paul Nadeau (no relation to assistant city administrator Phil) decided Lewiston High School needed a soccer team, he was on trend. Soccer was having a rare heyday, the North American Soccer League taking off when the New York Cosmos brought Pelé out of retirement and signed him to a three-season contract. Even soccer haters—and in the United States, then and now, there are many—knew about O Rei, the King, as Pelé was called. The Brazilian legend broke through the international scene as a seventeen-year-old in 1958 at the World Cup, scoring a hat trick against France for a 5–2 semifinal win. In the final, he netted two more against host Sweden, ensuring Brazil's victory.

The savvy marketing strategies of the Cosmos brought tens of thousands of people to see Pelé play. His celebrity created instant soccer fans, particularly among middle- and upper-class white families. The league "Americanized" the game to cultivate fans. It replaced the offside midfield line with a thirty-five-yard line in hope of putting higher numbers on the scoreboard. To avoid ties, it added a dramatic shoot-out. American fans, it seemed, needed a game to end with a winner and, perhaps more important, a loser.

While the NASL folded in 1984 (it would reemerge in 2009), soccer continued to grow at the community level. A relatively inexpensive sport, soccer was good for kids with speed and deft feet, and for those who didn't seem to fit anywhere else—not tall enough for basketball; not beefy enough for football; couldn't skate; couldn't afford a bat, a glove, a helmet.

Paul Nadeau knew how to build a team. Born in Lewiston in 1946, he epitomized the elusive "all-rounder" athlete; good at any game he tried. In high school, he played on championship football, hockey, and baseball teams. At the University of Maine at Farmington, he played basketball, soccer, and baseball, taking the team's batting title three times.

But Nadeau, one of the school's football coaches, knew that hawking soccer in Lewiston would be no mean feat; he would need whatever support he could muster. After getting approval from the school board, he started to look for players, pillaging the football team and pulling in kids who were getting ready for hockey season.

"They liked him," McGraw says, "because his personality was so in tune for teenagers. It was like a magnet."

Nadeau also was competitive. His dark, bushy eyebrows balanced out the wry smile that made it seem like he always had a plan. Wanting to get on the map quickly, he scheduled most of the first season against teams he knew he could beat. The Blue Devils finished their inaugural season 11–0–0. Nadeau was named Maine State Coach of the Year.

It was, remembers McGraw, "an eye-opener."

"SOCCER ALIVE AND KICKING," the yearbook screamed next to a team photo of shaggy-haired teenage boys who boasted a string of familiar local names, from Boucher and Cloutier to Dumont and Gosselin. "Lewiston High's first soccer season proved to be quite successful as the new team pushed ahead to an impressive standing in the league."

Within a year, McGraw came on board as an assistant coach.

McGraw took the parochial school route to Lewiston High School, attending the now-closed St. Joseph's School. His mother's sharp eye on his grades determined whether or not he played sports on any given day. He played basketball and football, and also ran track. In the summer, the left-handed second baseman played baseball.

In tenth grade, McGraw fell in love with biology and decided he wanted to be a teacher. When he was younger, he'd wanted to be an astronaut, a popular choice in the early days of space exploration. Figuring his grades would never be good enough, he changed to becoming a pilot but soon nixed that.

"I figured I wouldn't want to be a pilot," he says of his high school self. "I wouldn't want to be a *passenger* if I was a pilot, either."

McGraw graduated from the University of Maine at Gorham, now the University of Southern Maine, in 1972. In college, he added soccer to his sports schedule. One of his roommates, Jimmy Mingo, played on the team, which needed a few extra players. McGraw at first turned down the opportunity.

"I knew nothing about the game," he remembers, "and probably was a bit put off by watching professional soccer and seeing players flopping and rolling around on the ground if they were barely touched."

McGraw preferred the "brutality, intensity, and contact" of football. But Mingo persisted, and eventually McGraw volunteered to play scrimmages. He remembers being "clueless" and "with no skill." But he was competitive and left-footed. Coach Joe Bouchard soon switched him from the scrimmage squad to the team. He learned how to clear the ball and get it to players who knew what they were doing. Bouchard put McGraw at left midfield, where he remained throughout his college career.

"I developed a bit of a touch with the ball, learned more about the game, and really enjoyed it, especially the competition," McGraw remembers. "I never developed style or finesse, because there were other players who could do that."

While McGraw never made scoring a priority, he did net two goals, both of which were accidents.

"The first was off a corner kick," he recalls. "I ducked to head the ball and missed—it hit my shoulder and went in." The second also came off a corner kick, which he fortuitously curved into the goal.

McGraw's parents came to see him play, his mother filling a scrapbook with his sports clippings, something she does today with his coaching career. She thought soccer was dangerous because there were no helmets and pads, especially after McGraw landed on his head after a bicycle kick, knocking himself out in front of the bleachers.

After graduation, McGraw returned to his usual summer job working at his father-in-law's brickyard. He'd met Rita when he was just fifteen years old at the Pal Hop, a weekly battle-of-the-bands that attracted kids from the area high schools. She stuck with him through college, something he says he still can't figure out because of his wild ways.

After getting onto Lewiston's substitute-teaching list, he took a permanent sub job at Montello teaching seventh-grade math. He was on his way.

A troubling course of events landed McGraw at the high school. Phys ed teacher Norm Parent, also former athletic director, drove off Route 202 into a brook on his way back from a hunting trip. Lewiston lost one of its sports legends. A star football player at Bates, Parent had led the team to Ohio's Glass Bowl in 1946. At Lewiston High School, his football teams, composed primarily of Franco kids whose parents worked in the mills, won state championships, driven by what one former player called a "fearsome" coaching style.

Parent's death caused some shuffling around at Lewiston High School, creating a hole in the biology schedule. McGraw was in the right place at the right time.

"I've been here ever since."

While planning his first full year as a biology teacher, McGraw had no aspirations to coach. But going into his second soccer season, Nadeau needed him.

"I know that you played soccer for Gorham," Nadeau said to McGraw. "Do you want to help?"

"I said, 'Yeah, I would,'" remembers McGraw. "And that's how I got in."

For McGraw, there is no off-season. The team is on his mind every day as he thinks through changes to make, strategies to try. He stays on top of "my kids," as he calls them, all year long, tracking their grades, sending them to conditioning classes, asking about life at home. The Somali community can be fluid, with students coming and going depending on where their family network leads them. McGraw relies on his players to keep him up-to-date on everyone's situation.

Sometimes when a player said good-bye, it didn't mean forever, such as the case of Hassan "Q" Qeyle. McGraw was crushed when he found out the amiable midfielder was moving to Syracuse after his sophomore season. Born in a Kenyan camp to Somali parents, Q landed in Lewiston via Louisville in 2010, following a similar path as Abdi H. He knew Abdi H., but they didn't have much interaction until Q arrived at Lewiston Middle School at the end of seventh grade. The next year, his soccer career began, first with the middle school team, and then at the high school. Sophomore year, he made varsity. He didn't play much, but he got a taste of pursuing a championship.

Leaving Lewiston was hard on Q, especially because he arrived in Syracuse too late to try out for soccer. But he didn't question it. His grandmother's sister lived in Syracuse, and his grandmother wanted to give it a try. He stayed in touch with his Blue Devil teammates, who texted him after each game with the score and tidbits about the other team.

When McGraw heard that Syracuse wasn't working for Q's family, he didn't dare hope the midfielder might come back. But there he was, back in Lewiston, ready for his senior year. He'd missed the heartbreak of the championship game against Cheverus, and now he was ready to get on the field and help them win.

McGraw had missed Q, and not just as a player. He was a great kid—a bit goofy, with a huge heart for his family and his friends. One coach heard Q always ate last at his house, making sure his siblings had enough to eat before he started.

He was also a good player. He had terrific ball-handling skills, able to take possession and move play forward. Q could control the middle, McGraw thought as he began to imagine next season with Q in the lineup, and feed the ball to the guys up top, like Abdi H.

But it wasn't until June that McGraw could share his ideas with his team. Just as the school year started to wind down, he was allowed to call a team meeting to discuss next season.

"Today at 2:10," said a voice over the school's PA system, "all boys interested in playing soccer should meet in room 124A."

Defender Dek Hassan was excited. It was time to stop talking about getting back to the state final; the time had come to actually get there. The hallways buzzed with motivated players. Maulid joked with backup goalie Alex Rivet, a hockey star with good hands and fast reflexes, that they should skip the meeting. Maulid and Alex are a study in contrasts, Maulid dressed in a bright dashiki he got at the Mogadishu Store on Lisbon Street, where his father used to sell clothes; Alex in a polo shirt and jeans, his dark hair taking a cue from Justin Bieber. But they share a sharp wit and an air of mischief. A serendipitous hallway encounter with McGraw nixed their plan to cut.

"We were kidding," they assured their omniscient coach. "We'll be there."

As the players filed into McGraw's classroom, they took off their hats and put their hoods down, knowing his rules. They kidded around with each other, touching base, reconnecting. Trash talk—a mixture of English, Somali, and Arabic—blended with the anxiety of what lay ahead. Students in t-shirts and shorts sat next to those in tunics and jeans. A freshman walked in wearing a beige *kameez*, the hem just grazing the top of his sandals.

Moe Khalid had considered skipping the meeting. It was easy to brush it off, pretend it didn't matter. But he knew it did. Even though the first game of the season was months away, things already felt different. They were done being devastated. They had their spirit back. The team was tighter, the stakes were higher, and they had the experience. It was time, Moe said to the group, for "grind mode."

McGraw had lost his warm and fuzzy demeanor. Gone was

the nurturing biology teacher in a button-down shirt and tie. Now wearing his blue adidas shirt emblazoned with "COACH MCGRAW," he shut the classroom door—something he rarely did when teaching—with a bang. Anyone who didn't understand what was about to happen needed only to look at the expression on his face.

"Find a chair," he barked. "If you can't find a chair, then on the floor."

He surveyed the room.

"And you," he said to no one in particular, "leg off the table."

Order immediately ensued. At the front of the classroom, where not fifteen minutes earlier he had joked with students about their end-of-the-year biology projects, McGraw stood for a moment, his blue eyes steady, his mouth in an uncharacteristic straight line. With a full season ahead and a state championship loss behind, there was nothing to smile about yet. He picked up a pile of papers and began to hand them out.

Preseason schedule. Summer schedule. Code of Conduct. Registration.

The preseason schedule was complicated: a mix of practices, double sessions, tryouts, and games, with a round-robin in Portland and a tournament hosted by Lewiston in mid-August. The summer schedule was simpler: the squad divided into two teams, Lewiston 1, composed of juniors and seniors; and Lewiston 2, freshmen and sophomores. Anyone with a signed permission slip and $10 for a shirt could play.

The Code of Conduct shot straight. Show up fifteen minutes before practice. Be on time for meetings and game departures. Care for all teammates, not just friends. Show sportsmanship. Be ready to learn. Be positive. Be a good role model. Be a good student. Be respectful—to coaches, to teammates, to teachers, to opponents, to officials. Be humble in winning, gracious in losing.

Be an intense competitor and a leader in school. Be ready to step up—in a game, in class, in practice, or in the hallways.

"Fill them out so I can read them," McGraw said about the registration form.

He picked up a pile of pens on his desk for those who came unprepared, staring hard at each kid who took one.

"The Code of Conduct means asking yourself these questions: Are you there on time? Are you coachable?"

His stern, serious demeanor left no doubt about the factors of making the team. It was not just about skills, speed, and seniority. It was about taking responsibility. By showing up to this meeting, he told them, you already have an edge over those who didn't, even if those other players are better. Are you late? Have you ignored the rules? Those are the kinds of things that erase a kid from his roster.

"Be nice to your teachers, be good to each other."

Years ago, McGraw cut two starters. When he posted the final roster, the two came and asked if he'd made a mistake. He assured them he hadn't. One kid played hockey that winter; the hockey coach thanked McGraw for helping improve the kid's attitude. The next fall, he tried out for soccer again. He made it, taking his proper position on the team, toeing the line in accordance with the code. His parents thanked McGraw, and he had a good season.

McGraw never heard from the other kid again.

"Some of you guys are gonna make it the first three days and then get out," he told them, their heads bent over the forms, hands in motion. "It's an unfortunate circumstance."

As McGraw began to collect the forms, the din in the room grew—teasing, gossiping, swatting each other in the head.

"SETTLE DOWN!" he roared. Quiet returned instantly.

He talked to them about eligibility, stressing that the spring term determined whether or not they could play in the fall. Five passing courses for freshmen and sophomores; six for juniors and seniors. Summer school counted.

Dek listened to McGraw talk about eligibility. He hadn't played junior year because of his grades, but he wasn't going to miss his senior year. He was on track and would be ready for tryouts in August.

Dek is a charming kid, kind of quiet until he's not. Then he is funny, effusive. He's one of the least shy members of the team, he proudly claims, his voice harboring a touch of African cadence. He is taller than a lot of his teammates and holds himself with a self-possessed confidence, an air of maturity that many kids his age haven't found yet.

Born in Kenya, Dek spent two years in the Atlanta suburb of Clarkston before moving to Lewiston. In Clarkston, he played soccer for the Fugees, a team celebrated in the book *Outcasts United*, which he read in seventh grade. The book follows the Fugees in their early days, before Dek was there, outlining the difficult circumstances of the many different cultures and countries represented in Atlanta's refugee-filled suburbs.

Dek liked Georgia. He liked the buzz of Atlanta, walking around the city streets, hanging out at Stone Mountain. By comparison, Lewiston seemed tame, quiet, and cold. His family moved in October, when Georgia was still warm. Dek didn't like Maine's weather, especially once the snow came. But his mother, who was determined to find a better life for her family, heard it would be easier to become citizens in Lewiston. Dek knew people in Lewiston that he'd met in the refugee camp, like teammates Moe Khalid and Abdirizak Ali. His mother said they might return to Atlanta once they were U.S. citizens. But they stayed. It was all right, Dek decided. Even the snow.

And now school was going well. He'd matured a lot in the last year, figured some things out. He had watched last year's state championship. He used the same word as everybody else to describe it: heartbreaking. He knew they could do better, and he wanted to be part of it.

He looked up at Coach, who was still talking about the forms. He wanted to do it for this man, with this man. They had to get him a title. *Coach McGraw never gives up*, Dek thought. *If there was another coach who'd never won anything in thirty years? That coach would quit, he would stop. But McGraw didn't stop because he loves the game as much as we do. It's just crazy*, Dek thought. *It's crazy how badly we want to win.* He just had to make sure he kept school in check.

"Go find your teachers and get help," McGraw thundered, breaking into Dek's thoughts. "It's all about school," he continued, explaining the equation of grades and credits toward graduation that every student-athlete had to adhere to. "Take care of eligibility."

McGraw made it clear that getting good grades was part of being an athlete, part of being on a team. To be fully devoted to a team, a player had to take care of everything else, from school to family, before stepping on the field.

"BE. ON. TIME."

McGraw threw another stern look at the hopefuls.

"Because if *you* can't, *that* guy will," he said, pointing.

For summer games, transportation is not an excuse, he told them. Figure it out. Conditioning is key.

"You guys who are fasting," he said, thinking about the start of Ramadan in just a few weeks, "get your workout in early."

Last year's record, 16–1–1, was in the history books. Done. This was a new team, new schedule. There was a burden coming back after losing a state championship, McGraw admitted. Everyone knew they were hungry. There was a target on their back and everyone, from Scarborough to Falmouth, Mt. Ararat to Brunswick, had gotten better.

"You know what we're up against," he told them. "You are not last year's team, but people are going to play you like you're last year's team. We need to finish when we're supposed to finish and take advantage of our opportunities, because pain is never-ending until the next time you get there."

Thinking about the Cheverus game dampened his spirit for a moment. Thirty-three years without a title. But then his face softened and his eyes got their twinkle back. He hoped they were ready. He was.

"Guys who don't come to this meeting are going to have to prove it," he said again. "You're already one up on them." He smiled, ever so slightly. "So thank you for being here."

McGraw was done. Dek stood up, thinking about what he'd said about school. Dek had done the work. He was determined that academic eligibility was not going to keep him out.

Eligibility rules changed when Gus LeBlanc was principal. LeBlanc liked sports. The last thing he wanted to do was kill a sports program, but he was an educator first. When he won his second state football championship in 1985, nine of the eleven defensive players were in the National Honor Society.

There's a story LeBlanc likes to tell from his first year at Lewiston High School. A senior walked into his office in August. He wanted to play football but wasn't eligible. LeBlanc looked at the kid's transcript and was outraged at what he saw. Going into senior year, this student had never missed a football season, but he had only eight of the necessary twenty-four credits for graduation.

"What the hell is going on here?" LeBlanc asked.

Academic eligibility was a joke; a wink and nod. On paper the policy had teeth, but in reality, if a kid wanted to play sports, a kid played sports. Academics weren't for everyone, LeBlanc was told. For those other kids, there were sports.

"I found that mentality archaic," LeBlanc remembers. "I believe if you raise expectations, as long as they are not unrealistic, kids will meet them and, in the end, they'll benefit from them."

LeBlanc had to raise the standards, but he felt pressure from those—including the city's school board—who worried about a higher dropout rate. It was time, he knew, to talk to the athletic director.

Down the hallway and through the cafeteria from LeBlanc's office sat Jason Fuller, who became AD the year before LeBlanc arrived at Lewiston High School. He, too, knew there was a problem. But he wasn't entirely sure how to solve it.

As athletic directors go, Fuller looks like he stepped right out of central casting, sitting in a windowless office just off the gymnasium, cases of trophies lining the wall opposite his door. A burly guy with biceps that appear as though they might pop out of his polo shirt, he speaks in a booming, rapid-fire voice, rarely able to keep still, his close-cropped hair giving him an almost military appearance. He is, he admits, a tense guy and a straight shooter; someone who not only plays by the book but also wants to make sure the book is written correctly.

"Ohgodyeah," he booms, all one word, when he agrees with something. He is doggedly loyal to the school and its students or, as he, too, calls them, "my kids." There aren't enough hours in the day for Fuller to do everything he wants to do for Blue Devils teams.

Fuller did not expect to be back at his alma mater sitting at a desk. His parents came to Lewiston for teaching jobs—his mom from Ellsworth and his father from New Hampshire. Graduating from Lewiston High School in 1992, Fuller thought he'd left the city for good when he headed to Cornell University to play football. His career in the Ivy League was short-lived when he blew out his knee his first fall, something he'd done once before in high school. He returned to Maine and enrolled at the University of Maine in Orono.

Fuller describes himself as "more hardworking than smart." He hated college but managed to grab a degree in biology in just over two years, finding time to play a season of baseball before blowing out his knee yet again.

Three times was enough. No more sports.

His plan had been to be an orthopedic surgeon, but he didn't get into medical school. At twenty-one, he was mowing lawns for cash when Skip Capone, Lewiston's football coach, called him.

"Well, it doesn't look like you're going anywhere," Capone said. "Why don't you coach football for us?"

After Fuller had been on the job a week in the fall of 1995, the principal came down to the fields.

"Mr. Fuller, can I talk to you?" the principal said.

"Sure!" Fuller replied. He felt like a student all over again, the principal calling him out of practice. *This can't be good,* he thought. *What did I do to screw things up?*

"Have you ever thought about teaching?" the principal asked.

"Yeah," Fuller answered. Following in his parents' footsteps was always in the back of his head.

"Well, good, you've got an interview tomorrow at nine o'clock," the principal said, walking away. "Science."

Fuller couldn't believe it; he'd never taken a single education class. But the next day, just fifteen minutes into his first job interview, he wrote down information about new teacher orientation. He hadn't just found a job, he realized. He'd discovered a career.

Over the next several years, Fuller took classes in order to get certified to teach science. He continued to coach—football, basketball, baseball—and enjoyed the strong relationships he developed with student-athletes. When the AD position became available in 2005, he saw it as a chance to connect with even more kids.

Fuller was just settling into his new position when LeBlanc arrived. LeBlanc wanted to talk about eligibility, and Fuller was prepared to listen. He knew well the story of the senior football player with few credits to his name. He, too, asked why the kid was still playing football. Creating new standards had nothing to do with the rising immigrant population in the school. It was about creating expectations for students and building structures to help achieve them.

"Me and him had knock-down, drag-out debates about it," remembers Fuller of LeBlanc. "We fell on a system we both could support, but Gus was the driving force. And we got a better eligibility policy out of it."

The new policy required athletes to be *initially* eligible based on the marking period before a season started, as well as *continuingly* eligible based on grades at a designated point in the term. Most important, they had to be on track to graduate. LeBlanc put safety nets into place to support students. He didn't want to lose anyone, although he knew there'd be a few.

The numbers improved, from classes passed to grade point averages. The number of student-athletes rose despite stricter standards, and by the time LeBlanc took a new job as headmaster of Lee Academy in 2012, graduation rates climbed from 58 to 73 percent. While one of every four students in Lewiston took ELL classes, more than half of them graduated in four years, with most others finishing in five. Graduating became a family affair, with Somali families requesting as many as thirty tickets for the ceremony held at the Colisée. The emphasis the Somali community put on education, LeBlanc knew, helped make the tougher standards work. Lewiston High School was going in a new direction.

CHAPTER 7

I LIVE MY THANK-YOU

Lewiston High School sits off East Street, a sprawling complex set among expansive playing fields with sweeping views of the city. Walkable via a few worn paths, it feels like a different world from downtown's stacked apartment buildings and brick mills, Maine's giant sky stretching overhead as students approach the glass entrance.

McGraw starts his day standing outside his classroom before the first bell, taking in the scene, eyes gleaming as sleepy students shuffle by. He's been awake for hours, usually beating the sun. He's in his element, and students feed off his enthusiasm.

"Hey, McGraw," rings out repeatedly. He usually responds with a personal note—"You got your hair cut!" or "You getting more sleep these days?"—displaying an ease and familiarity that comes with four decades of teaching.

Inside McGraw's classroom, sports and academics come to meet. Bright blue tables with reddish-orange chairs fill the floor. The walls are covered by lively posters explaining DNA, while soccer team photos and plaques for his service to the community fill the shelves.

As McGraw preps for his first class, players routinely drop in to chat, engaging in light, respectful banter. Maslah Hassan strolls by, hall pass in hand. Wherever he is supposed to be, it is more important for him to check in with McGraw. He stands, tall and silent, occasionally pulling on his goatee, waiting for McGraw to speak first.

"Where'd you get that shirt? I like your shirt," McGraw finally says, looking at the black hoodie the senior is wearing.

"I got it from Maulid," Maslah answers, looking down at his feet to hide the smile spreading across his face, his usual swagger somewhat checked in front of his coach.

"Ha!" McGraw laughs. "Maulid has the goods, right?"

Just after nine o'clock, students come through the door, chatting, mocking, and bantering, backpacks thrown over a mix of hoodies, jeans, and traditional African dress. Some of the girls wear brightly patterned hijabs—magenta with a band of fake flowers or turquoise adorned with jeweled leaves, metallic threads catching the fluorescent lights above. A girl in a sweatshirt and jeans, tattered Converse on her feet and her long hair tipped with hot-pink dye, walks in with a can of soda in one hand and a phone in the other.

"Do you know where that goes?" McGraw asks, pointing to the can.

"Down my throat," she answers.

He points to the phone, undeterred. "And do you know where that goes?"

She nods.

"Not in my class," he pronounces.

"HAT!" he calls to a boy walking in. The kid sheepishly throws the Red Sox cap to the floor before taking a seat.

"How you guys doing?" McGraw begins. Picking up a piece of chalk with his left hand, he writes the due date for an impending lab report on homeostasis on the board, his slight Maine accent highlighting words like "cah-bon" dioxide. This is the first of three times today he will go through a diffusion-and-osmosis song-and-dance.

Standing in the middle of the tables while he lectures, he picks up two beakers of liquid. He patiently waits until everyone's eyes are on his hands.

"What's the one thing changed?" he asks. "What's the independent variable?

The class settles into lab groups. McGraw moves throughout the room, checking in with each of them, asking questions, and telling them to "staht making ob-suh-VAY-shuns."

"You've got more skills than you're letting on," he chides a group who is fooling around. "Is iodine a solid or a liquid?"

"Liquid," one whispers. McGraw waits. "Solid," she says more forcefully. He nods and moves on.

At the next group, he leans over the working students, his blue tie grazing the desk.

"I love that shirt," McGraw tells a boy wearing a Chelsea FC shirt.

"Who's Chelsea?" another student asks.

"Are you kidding me?" McGraw asks in mock horror, shaking his head. He looks back at the kid in the soccer jersey. "Love it."

McGraw continues to work the room, his reading glasses flying on and off his face as needed, patiently explaining the assignment over and over, encouraging one to come see him at the end of the day for extra help, condemning another for texting under the table.

"What are your observations?" he keeps asking. "What does iodine do to starch? What do you see?"

He stops to talk to a girl with a striking black-and-white scarf covering her head, spilling down her back.

"Yes, yes," he says, looking at her lab report, most of which he recognizes from his lecture. "But I want to hear it from you—I want to know what *you* think."

He stays with her, helping her rethink the consequence of iodine as a starch indicator, before moving to the next table, where he asks a girl about a bracelet—blue stones strung together—on her wrist. Her boyfriend made it, she tells him. McGraw looks impressed. He tells her about a boyfriend his daughter once had who made her custom CDs. She looks confused; what's a CD?

"Which is larger," he asks her, moving on, "starch or glucose?"

At the end of the day, McGraw makes sure his classroom is in order, putting everything away in the storage closet at the front of the room. "MCGRAW IS RAD" reads the sign on the closet door. Inside, microscopes and hefty textbooks with titles like *Basic Human Physiology* are neatly stored next to soccer balls. A faded handmade poster—"LET'S GO BIG BLUE"—sits above photos of McGraw's family. Framed butterfly specimens hang next to photos of soccer stars past and present. He has a story for just about every face.

"He's a doctor, he's a baseball coach, and this one," he says, pointing to Eric Wagner in an old black-and-white photo, "is head soccer coach at Swarthmore."

Wagner still returns to Lewiston every summer to work at McGraw's youth soccer camp. An easygoing guy, he has a surfer look to him, with sandy hair that crawls across his face in modern-day muttonchops. Soft-spoken, he takes long pauses when he speaks, patient with his thoughts.

Wagner is passionate about both Lewiston and McGraw. He was a senior in 1982, when McGraw became head coach, taking over for Nadeau.

"Paul was much more of a disciplinarian, a yeller—he was a scary figure to us," Wagner recalls. "He freaked us out."

Wagner thinks the team played well for Nadeau because they

were scared not to. McGraw, on the other hand, was someone Wagner *wanted* to play for: inspirational, able to pull devotion from his players and make a strong team. When the two find time each summer to head to Gipper's, a popular sports bar in Auburn, Wagner is always amazed at how McGraw makes everyone feel like the most important person in the room. It can take an hour for McGraw to get to a table, stopping to talk to everyone who'd had him as a coach or a teacher.

"And so you're sitting down at a table with him, and everybody in the place is coming up and stopping and saying hello, and you never once feel jealous that he's not paying attention to you," says Wagner. "You just know he's popular and people like him. As soon as he's done saying hi to that person, he'll be right back, engrossed in the conversation. It's incredible."

Wagner, whose father is a retired Bates psychology professor who still lives in Lewiston, knows well the changes the high school has undergone since he graduated.

"I can tell you who the two black kids in school were," he says of his high school days. "Because there were only two."

He thinks the changes are exciting, particularly in terms of soccer. Everywhere he looks when he visits, he sees kids of all ages kicking around a ball. But it's more than how many are playing the game. It's how they are playing it, and the traditions they are creating.

A few Somali students found their way to McGraw in the earliest days of the refugee influx. Midfielders like Hamdi Naji and Mohamed "Momo" Mohamed, who was described as having the "fastest foot in town" in the 2003 yearbook, paved the way for others to follow. Within a few years, immigrants dominated the team. The Somalis no longer heard, "What're you doing here?" when they showed up for tryouts. Perhaps no one's story better represents the turning point than Shobow Saban.

Slight of build, Shobow is a potpourri of personality, demonstrating an air of worldly and philosophical wisdom one moment; a bad joke and raucous laughter the next. A graduate of Assumption College, he is a caseworker with Maine Immigrant and Refugee Services, the former SBYA, determined to give back to the community. He helps parents better communicate with their increasingly Americanized children and works with city officials and social workers to better understand Somali culture. It's his way, he says, of saying thank-you, *wad mahadsantahay*, which he would rather do through actions than words.

"I came here as an immigrant, so the taxpayers who don't even know me and I never met them, who actually spend money on me to get textbooks, to make sure the teachers get paid, to make sure that I sit in a chair, that I have a lunch—for all that, I say thank-you," he says. "I mean, I've never met them, I've never seen them. So that's the reason I say thank-you to the community. I live my thank-you."

Born in 1993, Shobow left Somalia with his family when he was less than a year old after a trespasser killed his grandfather. His memories start in Dadaab, where he learned basic math and English, and played soccer whenever he could. Life was hard, but Kenya felt safer, more peaceful, than Somalia. But when he was six, his father became ill. Disease spread rapidly in the camps, with so many people coming and going. Lacking adequate medical facilities, and with few doctors to be found, Shobow's father died. Shobow's mother, Bilow Farah, was left alone with her six sons. As the eldest, Shobow assumed much responsibility for the family.

Shobow's story is one that William "Kim" Wettlaufer, former director of the Trinity Jubilee Center, knew would get a strong reaction when he gave talks about Lewiston's Somalis. He told his audiences about this woman, a single mother, who has six sons.

"Every mother in the house would gasp," Wettlaufer remembers, smiling.

Wettlaufer met Shobow and his family at Trinity Jubilee. A graduate of Bates, where he was an All-American runner, Wettlaufer stayed in Lewiston after graduation in the days before Bates alums did such things, first writing sports for the *Sun Journal,* and then launching a chain of Subway franchises. Wettlaufer had been a longtime volunteer and board member at Trinity Jubilee when the part-time executive director left for another position. The board asked if he'd fill in. He agreed, thinking it would be a quick fix while they searched for a new director.

Part-time became full-time, and temporary became nine years.

Trinity Jubilee is housed in the basement of Trinity Church, a beautiful gray stone Gothic Revival building capped with a bright red belfry. Built in 1879, it sits on the corner of Spruce and Bates Streets just off Kennedy Park. Nearly half of the residents in the surrounding apartments live well below the poverty line.

The entrance to the center is tucked into a shady courtyard with a handful of benches usually occupied by a group of men who smoke, talk, and while away some hours. On warm days, the laughter of kids playing basketball, skateboarding, and swimming at Kennedy—where Dek Hassan works as a lifeguard—filters into the courtyard. The men will sit and listen, watching the pigeons peck away at the dirt. There is always a stash of stale bread for anyone who wants to feed the birds, but not in the courtyard. Take it across the street to the park.

In 1991, long before the first Somalis arrived, Trinity's congregation decided it wanted to work on the issues of poverty, violence, and substance abuse that saturated the broken-down apartment buildings outside its door. Now a nonprofit organization distinct from the church, Trinity Jubilee offers a number of services, including a soup kitchen that serves a hundred meals a day, six days a week, supported by both Hannaford Supermarkets and Bates College. In the summer, there is breakfast and lunch for kids who usually eat at school.

Trinity Jubilee isn't glamorous, but it hums along with a noisy, chaotic efficiency, the door from the courtyard opening and closing all day long but especially on Thursdays, when the food pantry is open. The basement hosts a small office, a large industrial kitchen lined with rows of shiny steel refrigerators, a food storage area, and a lounge for those who sleep at the local shelter and need a place to hang out during the day. A list of rules ensures shirts and shoes are worn; people ask before they take; no one swears or smokes; and weapons, alcohol, and drugs never walk through the door.

In recent years, Trinity has added a host of services for refugees and political asylum seekers, helping them navigate their new lives in Lewiston—landlords, taxes, health care, work permits, and job applications. Walmart is a popular employer, and the Trinity staff says it is one of the few companies that not only hires immigrants, but also sticks up for them. The center's small office has a fax machine and a printer and a place to receive mail.

There's also a ball pump. All day long, kids bring in soccer balls for air. No matter what is going on—phones ringing, the food pantry line out the door with women chatting, a television show blaring, people sifting through bags of donated clothes—there is always a kid with a ball that needs air.

These days, Somalis are the minority at Trinity, having built up a foundation strong enough to take care of their own. But back when Wettlaufer first became director, the initial waves of Bantu began arriving, with far fewer resources than the ethnic Somalis who'd come before. The food pantry, which once had thirty regular customers, ballooned to more than three hundred families.

Others in Lewiston were helping, to be sure. Catholic Charities' office in City Hall was the epicenter for refugee support.

But for many refugees, their violent and terrifying pasts made them suspicious of such places, worried that housing inspectors or caseworkers might take their children or deport them, or they would lose their Section 8 rental subsidies or food stamps. Trinity Jubilee, on the other hand, didn't come across as a place of authority. Tall and lanky with a calm demeanor that rarely ruffles, Kim Wettlaufer began to build a strong rapport with the Somalis who came each Thursday for a stock of fresh produce and some canned goods.

"I have been taught," he answers when asked how he came to know so much about Somali culture and custom. "Everyone was pretty forgiving of any blunders. You think you get to a point where you really know them, and you don't—there's so much we can't begin to comprehend that these families have been through."

The Somalis dubbed Trinity Jubilee "Maysha Kim," or Kim's Place. The name remains even though Wettlaufer turned his position over to fellow Bates graduate and longtime Trinity worker Erin Reed in 2014.

"Yeah, well," he says when he hears it, dismissing it in his easygoing way. "It's just easier to say than Trinity—it's hard to say that word."

The food pantry was the key to building relationships. It reassured the refugees that Trinity wasn't going to try to convert them to Christianity, something many of them had worried about in Georgia. Here, volunteers handed out food, diapers—three thousand a month—and advice, but only when asked. Judging by the numbers of people who availed themselves of the services, Wettlaufer knew they were doing something right. That sense was reinforced when Gure Ali, one of the Somali interpreters at Montello Elementary, came to visit. He'd heard good things about the work Wettlaufer was doing and wanted to take a look.

"You're doing it," Ali said to Wettlaufer after he observed a while. "You're actually helping people without asking for anything in return."

He asked Wettlaufer if he wanted to see where some of the families lived, really get to know them. Wettlaufer jumped at the opportunity.

They walked over to Knox Street, just behind the church. The first apartment they entered had no real furniture, just a few mattresses on the floor. Wettlaufer stood, absorbing what he saw. There were several generations in the room, he realized. Suddenly, the oldest woman went to another room and brought back a chair.

"Fadhiiso!" she ordered Wettlaufer. He sat. It was inconceivable to disobey such a command. *The president of the United States,* he thought, *would be sitting right now.*

At the next apartment, four floors up, they knocked. Bilow Farah opened the door. "Ahhh," she said when she saw Wettlaufer, recognizing him from the food pantry. She invited them in and gave a tour of the apartment.

"And there was Shobow, an eighth-grader," remembers Wettlaufer. "Already just a brilliant kid."

In one of the rooms, Farah showed them a makeshift desk with a lamp. She looked at Wettlaufer.

"Study," she said, tapping the desk. "Study."

It was, he understood, the only word she knew in English. *It might be,* he thought, *the most important word for her to know.*

As Wettlaufer got to know Shobow, he started to pay attention to soccer, a sport he'd never really thought much about. He knew it was important in the lives of the Somalis, and soon enough he became, like SBYA, a link between the families and the school, helping kids to understand the regimens of tryouts, practice schedules, permission slips, and medical forms.

"I'll be brutally honest: we just have good people take care of it," says Lewiston Athletic Director Jason Fuller about how the Somali students learned the protocols of playing high school sports. "It's not that we changed a lot—we had Kim Wettlaufer, who made it his priority." Each summer, Fuller and Wettlaufer meet to prepare for the new season, figuring out who needs to get a physical, a parent's signature, and so on.

"I give him all the stuff," says Fuller, "and Kim goes out and takes care of it. Without Kim Wettlaufer, this doesn't happen. Period—end of story. His role and influence is monumental in our program."

Because of his background, Wettlaufer was more typically drawn to track and cross-country, which he has periodically coached at the high school and for Lewiston's recreational team. But because of their developing relationship with Shobow and his family, he and his wife, Carolyn McNamara, who works as a nurse practitioner at the B Street Community Center, got interested in soccer.

"We started watching," Wettlaufer says, "and then we couldn't look away."

When Shobow's family left Dadaab for Decatur, Georgia, in June 2006, soccer was one of the few things that gave him comfort. It was a tough adjustment. Their neighborhood held new dangers, like drugs and guns. His mother worried constantly about what the neighbors were up to and whether or not her boys were safe while she looked for work.

Shobow just wanted to make friends and kick a ball around. He was thrilled when some boys from his middle school finally asked if he wanted to play football.

"What happened was, some of my black friends," he says, trailing off and laughing. He still thinks it's funny that he wasn't considered to be one of "the black kids" at his school. "They asked me to play football with them—and I didn't know football wasn't soccer."

Shobow wanted friends badly. Everything about America had been so hard. Even though he studied English, he had trouble understanding the Southern accent. But he understood that kids finally wanted to play with him. *This is it,* he thought. *Football will help me fit in.*

"You cannot imagine my face," he recalls. "I was *so excited.*"

He ran to get ready, the entire time thinking, *LET'S GO!* He burst outside and saw the boys throwing around what he could only describe as "an egg ball."

"Hey, Shobow," one boy yelled. "Let's play football!"

Shobow didn't move. *This egg ball is not the football I know,* he thought. *How do I kick this thing? Maybe it's some kind of warm-up ritual? They're just chilling while someone gets the real ball? Why is it taking so long?*

One of the kids came over and asked why he wasn't playing. Shobow's infectious, high-pitched laugh rings out at the memory of it.

"I said to him, 'This is an EGG BALL!'"

The kid suddenly got it. He explained to Shobow that what he called football in Africa was called soccer in America. This was Georgia; none of them played soccer.

Shobow was crushed. He saw his dream of having friends go down the drain. Middle school, a tough time for any kid, felt even harder now.

"I was trying to grow up, fit in, and it didn't work for me," he remembers. "It was tough."

So in a few months, when his mother said a friend told her to bring the boys to Lewiston because there were good schools and a growing Somali community, Shobow was all-in.

They arrived in December, completely unprepared for the climate. Shobow remembers getting out of the car and thinking he must have been sick because his body shook so badly from the cold. Winter had to be explained to him. He wasn't sure if he liked it. He definitely did not like the reaction some people had to his family. "Go back to the camp!" people yelled at them. "You don't belong here!" Just thirteen years old, he remembers thinking, "To where? Is there no country for me?"

He also hated the stereotypes, the things that people assumed about him. Yes, he was black, but he was not a drug dealer. Yes, he was Muslim, but he was not a terrorist. Yes, he was Somali, but he was not a pirate.

His mother told him to focus on his future and what he wanted to accomplish. "Shobow, it's not where you come from that matters," she told him. "It's about who you are and where your destination is."

Shobow liked school. His broken English served him much better in Maine than it had in Georgia. He began with some ELL classes but found them too easy. After he passed an exam, he was mainstreamed into regular classes.

"So I got into those, and because this was already ordained by God, I guess, I met this kid, Jonny McDonough."

The story of Shobow and Jonny's friendship has been fictionalized in Maria Padian's young adult novel, *Out of Nowhere*. It is a story that has come to represent the slow integration of Somalis into Maine, with soccer at the very center. The book, which juniors read at Lewiston High School, highlights some of the difficulties Somali students faced in the early days in their new community. It's the stuff they don't like to talk about, from racist slurs hurled at them in school hallways to the sharing of cleats and shin guards on the soccer team; a JV player ripping off his gear after a game to throw to a varsity player, who plunges his feet into the sweaty socks and shoes before taking the field, often a few minutes late.

Shobow and Jonny had the same homeroom at Lewiston Middle School and shared a science class. Homeroom didn't seem like much of anything to Shobow: stand and say the Pledge of Allegiance, go to class, and return at the end of the day for announcements. But sometimes they were allowed "laptop time" before going home, during which Shobow liked to read about soccer. He'd comb the Internet for information about his favorite players, like Thierry Henry and Ronaldo, read histories of Pelé, and watch videos to learn new skills. Jonny, the captain of the middle school soccer team, noticed. He also noticed the soccer jerseys Shobow wore to school every day. It was unusual to see a kid in Lewiston wearing shirts like that. Red Sox? Of course. Patriots? Absolutely. Arsenal or Manchester United? Never.

The two started talking about soccer, their common language. Jonny told Shobow about the school team and asked if he'd be interested in playing. It wasn't like Dadaab, where soccer happened all day without any organization. Jonny told him about the papers he'd need to fill out, the procedures he'd have to follow, and the coaches' meeting he needed to attend. Finally, Shobow had a friend.

"Soccer," he says, emotion filling his voice, "became the engine for my life."

Shobow's mother understood that soccer was "his thing." As a little boy in Dadaab, he'd dreamed of playing professionally. Soccer rescued him from his bad days, helping him negotiate his anxieties. So when he asked Farah if he could sign up for the eighth-grade team, she set aside her worries about her son hanging out with a bunch of white kids who weren't Muslim and who wouldn't understand their past. Yes, Farah told him. He could join the team.

That fall, Shobow became a standout player for the team, which started winning by large margins. Through soccer, he became more connected to his peers. Each morning after a game, the principal, Maureen LaChappelle, announced the score, often noting how many goals Shobow had made.

"Shobow Saban scored three goals!" Shobow imitates in a high falsetto American accent. He laughs, his dark eyes filled with mischief. "Now I became, like, 'Who is this mysterious Shobow? Where is he from?' Every kid was asking about me."

Shobow and Jonny were friends both on and off the field. Jonny was interested in Shobow, asking him questions about where he was from. At Shobow's apartment, Jonny tried Somali food, dishes like *hilib ari*, not just *sambusa*, for the first time.

"He was not an anthropologist," says Shobow, laughing, "but he was real interested not just in soccer, but the people, the culture, and me."

The two forged a bond, talking about what had brought Shobow's family to the United States, what their prayer rituals meant, why they didn't eat pork or touch dogs, and why they fasted during Ramadan. Shobow liked the questions, because even as a teenager, he knew that questions were an important step in the building of bridges.

While Shobow had found himself a niche, he was still the only Somali kid on the middle school soccer team, something that confused him because there were so many other Somali students. When he ate lunch in the school cafeteria with his teammates, he knew he stood out. He was conscious that his Somali peers, who ate at another table, casually segregated, thought of him as white. But he didn't care; he was happy.

"Who is the whitest kid in this photo?" Shobow would ask Jonny, looking at pictures of the team. "You," Jonny always answered, continuing the joke.

But as Shobow prepared to take the next step and play high school soccer, things were changing. He was not going to be the only Somali kid on the team anymore. The locks were starting to open.

CHAPTER 8

1-2-3 PAMOJA NDUGU

Mike McGraw is having a hectic morning. With no first-period class to teach, he has to run out to Grant's Bakery to pick up some apple pies for International Day for the U.S.A. table. He stopped there earlier on his way to school, but the pies weren't ready.

"At least we know they'll be fresh," he says, and laughs.

Like everyone else in Lewiston, the baker knows McGraw, who buys his family's Thanksgiving fare at Grant's every year.

"What will the Somalis make for this event?" the baker asks.

"Sambusa!" McGraw answers. Always *sambusa*, or "samboos," as some of his players call the savory pastry.

McGraw says the food thing has been fun with the team, learning about their different cuisines. He remembers once before a game when he saw players huddled around something on the ground. He walked over and took a look; it was a platter of fish, and it smelled delicious. "What is that?" he asked.

"VICTORY FOOD!" they hooted.

McGraw brings the pies to the cafeteria, where students are setting up for the festivities. The U.S.A. table is filled with doughnuts, hot dogs, and chips. He stops to take in the commotion, especially the large group of students gathering around the tables labeled CENTRAL AFRICA, with smaller signs representing Djibouti, Eritrea, and Somalia.

"It's a crazy day," he says to no one in particular, never skipping a beat as a flurry of students comes to greet him. A girl in hijab gives him a big hug, while another asks for a pass to get out of class to help with the tables. Still another wants to schedule a make-up exam after school.

McGraw leaves the cafeteria to get back in time for his second-period sophomore biology class. Sophomores run the maturity gamut; not as gawky as freshmen, they lack the wisdom and smoothness of the older kids. As they take their seats, McGraw hands back the permission slips and $10 bills that some had turned in for a field trip to Morse Mountain. Because of a lack of interest, he says, the field trip is canceled. Students begin to complain, saying they were just about to bring their money in. McGraw shakes his head. A deadline is a deadline; no exceptions.

A girl dressed in a cheerful pink-and-red hijab, a *jilbab* grazing her toes, crumples up a piece of paper as she enters and throws it into the trashcan.

"I'm a baller!" she says with delight. Everyone laughs, and she snatches a tan Ralph Lauren baseball hat off a classmate and puts it atop her hijab.

"No hats," says McGraw, laughing, and everyone giggles as she takes it off.

McGraw launches into the day's lesson, Darwin's theory of evolution.

"I am just gonna put the information out there," he tells them. "You believe what you want to believe."

He reviews Darwin's work but leaves room for their own perspectives, religious or otherwise. His respect, awe even, for Darwin is evident. He loves this stuff, revels in it. He hands out the assignment, patiently explaining its details and his expectations. They need to choose an animal, he says, and change its environment, writing about how it adapts to new surroundings. He talks about natural selection, the survival of the fittest, and the importance of coexistence among different animals.

"With changing environments, the ones that are gonna survive are the ones that will adapt," he says. He looks at them, taking off the reading glasses he needs to see his notes. "Life finds a way."

It's no giant stretch to see how the Darwin lesson translates to Lewiston. McGraw is asking students to think about what it means to suddenly live somewhere completely different. Every student in the room understands this. They either live in a new environment themselves or their environment has rapidly changed.

McGraw's ideas about natural selection are also deeply embedded in his coaching philosophies. Players on the bench, he says, are what keep the starters sharp. Keep developing your skills, he tells starters, because if you don't, the guys on the bench will.

"You work haaard!" he constantly threatens during practice, trying to motivate a kid to run a little faster or try for the ball more aggressively. "Or someone else will instead of you!"

But it goes beyond survival of the fittest.

"For McGraw, it's always about respect for the whole team," says Eric Wagner, who acknowledges that much of his own coaching philosophy stems from his old coach's approach. "The one thing that I'll probably spend the rest of my life trying to get closer to him in is the way he treats people with complete respect at all times—I wish I had that."

McGraw's admiration for the bench has served him especially well in recent years, when there has been an increased disconnect between the parents who are able to come to support the team and the players actually on the field.

"I am lucky that nobody complains about playing time; about

the other, ugly aspects of coaching," he admits, knowing well the tales of parents demanding field time for their kids. "I'm lucky I've got the people I have."

Fuller is a bit more blunt.

"The white kids' parents are there, even if their kids aren't playing," he says matter-of-factly. "Never a problem."

For a long time, the Blue Devils' bench was not that deep. If a kid went out for soccer, he didn't have to be all that skilled to make varsity. As McGraw began to see how the demographic changes at the high school could impact the soccer team, he wondered how it was all going to work, especially considering the skepticism, the fear, the worry, and the racial tension that still churned throughout the city. Indeed, he had to rethink some of the assumptions he himself had made.

Gus LeBlanc says that McGraw was the perfect person at the right moment. He has a big heart, likes kids, and has a lot of credibility with people locally. People trusted him to be fair. If these new kids were going to become dominant on a team, there was no better person to steer the process.

McGraw remembers the first time he really got a glimpse of not only the future of the soccer team but the future of Lewiston. A few Somali kids showed up to watch a summer game one evening. The rest was history.

"Yeah, we play soccer all the time," one said to him.

"You do?" McGraw asked.

"Yeah," he answered. "We want to play."

"Good," McGraw said. "You need to fill out some forms, get a physical, and there's a fee, and then . . ."

"Okay, no problem—when do we get our uniforms?"

McGraw laughed. "You have to try out in the fall."

"Oh, no," one answered. "We're gonna be okay. We're gonna be good, we're gonna make a champion."

McGraw chuckled. "You need to try out," he told them.

A few years later, Shobow was one of the players who did just that. Dan Gish remembers well the hot August day in 2007 when Shobow showed up for tryouts. The soon-to-be high school freshman didn't look like much, wiry and diminutive, but within minutes of warming up, he rainbowed the ball over the head of another and into the goal.

The rainbow, or rainbow flick, is a rare skill in soccer, almost never seen on a high school field. A flashy offensive move intended to move the ball *over* a defender, a player has to scoot the ball up his leg before kicking it overhead with the opposite heel. The ball arcs over the defender, where the player can run to kick it into the net. It requires precise timing, skilled footwork, and speed.

Stunned, Gish took in Shobow's move before looking over at McGraw. What the heck just happened? Gish had never imagined he'd ever see anything like that in Lewiston, but it was the kind of soccer he was hoping to coach.

Born at Andrews Air Force Base, Gish moved to Limestone, Maine, when he was in first grade, after his father was transferred to Loring. Gish has been in Maine so long that he considers himself a native, although he knows well the Maine saying, "You're always from away." Growing up on the base, he had an atypical Maine experience, with friends from all over—Japan, the Philippines, Thailand, and Mexico. He remembers an article about his high school's girls' basketball team, "Eagles flew in from all around the world," noting the base made the tiny town a "mini melting pot." He was well versed in the machinations of a diverse student body; he just didn't expect Lewiston to have one.

Gish played soccer at the University of Maine at Farmington, where he studied exercise physiology and roomed with Shawn Chabot, who would eventually succeed Gus LeBlanc as principal at Lewiston High School and become Gish's boss. After working for a few years, Gish decided to become a teacher. It was a natural fit for Gish, who has an intense sense of empathy when it comes to kids. Belying his bulked-up physique, his voice is earnest, almost pleading, his wide-open eyes probing kids for what they need.

Need cleats? See Coach Gish. Need help icing a sore knee? See Coach Gish.

At Gardiner High School, his first teaching job, he was also the head coach for girls' soccer. When a position opened in Lewiston in 2000, he took it. He had no intention of coaching, but when asked, he joined McGraw.

Gish coached a different kind of soccer than McGraw, and as players like Shobow started to drift onto the team, he saw the potential to make some changes. These kids weren't using soccer to get into shape for hockey or basketball. They played soccer to win and had a menu of skills to prove it. For a long time, Lewiston was a city where soccer played bridesmaid to football every autumn and completely disappeared once the snow started to fall and all eyes turned to sticks and pucks. But these kids were different.

Gish wanted to capitalize on the speed and deft ball-handling abilities of the new players, focusing on control and possession rather than the direct game that Lewiston had played for years. It was the kind of soccer he'd played in college and the way he thought the game should be played.

Direct soccer, better known as "kick and chase," is about moving the ball forward at all costs, mostly via long, vertical passes, and then chasing it down to kick it again. Goal kicks are punted long, and throw-ins are directed down the line for distance. McGraw's teams won a lot of games with that style for a long time, using size and strength to get the ball into the net.

Conversely, possession soccer sends the ball in multiple directions, with passes going every which way among a variety of players, side to side. It is a more patient, nuanced game, using numerous angles to expand the field of play to the outside lines. Goalies often throw, rather than punt, in order to build action from the back, or use short passes just as any field player would. Sideline throw-ins focus on possession, rather than distance, sometimes going shorter distances across the field, rather than heading toward the goal at all costs. Possession soccer favors speed, sophisticated ball handling, and a vast technical knowledge of the field and the players on it. Rather than one player moving the ball toward the goal, it relies on multiple switches among a variety of players in the same possession. When done well, the possession game leaves less time and opportunity for the opposition to attack.

"I'm not a kickball coach," Gish told McGraw. He understood that there were moments in any game when a direct style could be exploited, but he felt strongly that Lewiston should play a possession game. This wasn't anyone's grandfather's team: the new guys were fast, skilled, and had good control of the ball.

But McGraw had been doing things his way for more than twenty years when Gish arrived, and while he had never won a state championship, his record was strong, including the 1991 shot at the state title. But Gish found it frustrating to use a decades-old championship game as reason to continue doing things the same way. He thought he could make an impact, but McGraw had to let him in. AD Fuller understood this and intervened, calling a meeting to figure out how the team should navigate going forward.

"I give Mike a lot of credit," Fuller says about the changes that took place after the meeting, particularly how well McGraw listened to Gish's ideas. "He's evolved as a person and as a coach. After twenty-something years, to say, 'I've got to change how I do things'—that's a credit to him as a person."

Fuller knew that, as head coach, McGraw could have taken a "my way or the highway" attitude. But he didn't.

"Mike took some comments Dan made, and myself, and really handled it well," remembers Fuller. "It was a struggle, but Mike is a learner, going to every conference he can and taking in what he can."

It wasn't always easy.

"Oh, we've had *dialogue*," says Gish with a laugh, thinking about his relationship with McGraw. His admiration is evident in every word he says about him. "But the great thing about Coach is that he'll listen to you. We might not always agree on everything, but we know how to make it work." And it wasn't just about Shobow. Ali Hersi arrived at Lewiston Middle School too late to play but, like Shobow, made varsity his freshman year alongside his older brother, Abdijabar. These players brought serious skills to the team, with the potential to bring a different future to the Blue Devils. Kick-and-run soccer was quickly becoming a thing of the past.

But playing style wasn't the only thing that had to change. Just as the schools created support systems to help immigrant students, McGraw, too, realized that there were special challenges in bringing the team together. He used what he called "the advantage of the ball."

Soccer lends itself to a particular kind of teamwork. It is a game of continuity, with more flow than ruptures. It doesn't reorganize after a whistle, like basketball, or have a to-do list like the innings of a baseball game. To score in soccer, a team has to move the ball through an enormous amount of space, making decisions about who will take it where, from the first touch until someone sends it hurtling toward the net. Just by doing what a soccer team was supposed to do, the Blue Devils could become an example to the community.

Ronda Fournier, an assistant principal at Montello, often heard McGraw talk about "the ball" as she watched him adapt to change. An unapologetic "girl from the backwoods," Fournier grew up in Sabattus, a small town just a stone's throw from Lewiston, and attended Oak Hill High School, where football reigns supreme. A three-sport athlete herself—field hockey, basketball, and softball—she studied education at the University of New England and eventually landed in the biology classroom next to McGraw.

"He's a really special man," she says, smiling, a heavy Maine accent soaking every word. "You know? We are all blessed to have him as a part of our lives."

Over the years, she got to know a lot of soccer players. If McGraw stepped out for a moment, they knocked on her door instead.

"Mrs. Fournier, you gonna let us in so we can put away our soccer gear?" they'd ask. "Yep, no problem," she'd answer. "I'll put it in for ya."

Over the course of ten years, she and the coach developed a close working relationship. Few people had a better view to see how McGraw developed his winning formula.

"I remember him telling me of how difficult it was in the beginning, but it was all about the soccer."

By prioritizing the game, she says, McGraw could make sure "the other stuff just didn't interfere." They didn't have to have conversations about where a player was from, or what religion he practiced, or what language he spoke, or what his family had been through. Instead, they could focus on what a kid could do on the pitch.

McGraw, the players still joke, doesn't care where they're from as long as they pass the ball. "I watched Mike in the classroom for years. I see him out on the coaching field, and he does the same thing," says Fournier. "He takes a kid's strength, and he helps that kid use their strengths to overcome their weaknesses. He shows how they're related, so that a kid can capitalize."

Fournier pauses. "Any kid," she says, and then waits another moment before repeating it, with emphasis. "Any. Kid."

Fournier knows well the challenges of teaching here, but she doesn't see the Somali influx as anything other than Lewiston being Lewiston. The newest immigrants have needs, just like those who came before them, and it is the schools' job to meet them.

"It started with the French-Canadians, right?" she says.

Her own grandmother came from Canada, her grandfather from Scotland. They worked full-time shifts at the Rubber Heel, a long-gone shoe manufacturing plant in Sabattus, while growing cucumbers for the Litchfield pickle plant as a side job.

"You know, Lewiston's gonna be kind of rough," she remembers people saying when she first considered the job in 2005. "Things are going to be different—you sure you want to go teach there?"

"I don't know about you, but I don't think it matters where the kids come from," she told them, shrugging off the comments. "They all need the same thing."

She knew what people were too polite to come right out and say. Lewiston kids, among the poorest in the state, were considered problematic well before the Somalis came. But now, according to rumors, things were worse. Kids praying in the hallway, speaking different languages, dressing in "weird" clothes, eating "strange" foods. But Fournier didn't care what anyone thought they knew about Lewiston High School. Teaching was teaching.

"To me, it didn't matter at all," she says. "Kids need love, they all need to know that somebody cares about them. And now they all want to play soccer."

Fournier relied on McGraw for advice to help his players in her classes. He used the same strategies in the classroom he did on the field, emphasizing teamwork, urging her to call on a struggling student's classmates to help. There was no question McGraw knew what was best for the players, academically, on the field, or just walking down the hallway.

But McGraw, too, faced challenges. Names no longer rolled off his tongue, and at times he resorted to calling players by their numbers until he became more familiar with pronunciations. The high school yearbook showed just how rapidly surnames in Lewiston were changing; the "A" section of class photos grew quickly because of Somali surnames. In the early days, aside from class photos, the soccer pages were the only place Somali students appeared. They weren't photographed at prom. There were no casual photographs of them hanging in hallways or jumping around during Spirit Week. No one paid to put their baby picture in the back pages because such photos didn't exist; if they did, there was no money for such things.

But on the soccer field, Somali students started to lay claim, quickly becoming the majority of the varsity roster. As McGraw strategized his so-called advantage of the ball to integrate the team, he also helped incorporate the new students into the culture of the high school. He didn't think twice about it—the game came first, and trust worked both ways. He knew that when those first Somali students came to talk to him about playing, some level of trust was established. But he had to make it grow.

McGraw knew that whatever happened on the field— teamwork, communication, patience, and persistence—could impact the community as a whole. But it was going to take some serious coaching, and not just in terms of scoring goals. There'd been animosity and growing pains—all of his players had stories. Hallway skirmishes. Standoffs in the cafeteria. "Go Back to Africa," among other things, scrawled on bathroom walls or in the dirt on car windows. White kids telling Somali kids that they paid for their shoes, their food, and their apartments. Fights in the parking lot. Teachers who showed *Black Hawk Down* in class or reminded students that their behavior wasn't acceptable "in this country." McGraw knew he had to do more than yell "together" from the sideline. Moving together, winning together, wasn't going to solve the world's problems. But it was a first step. What, he wondered, was the next step?

Shobow remembers it well. It happened on a hot day in the early fall of his freshman year. McGraw saw the players getting ready as he approached the practice field. He watched them pulling up their long socks, strapping on shin guards, and huddled over cleats, trying to get knots out of tangled laces. They weren't together, he realized, and there was a pattern. The Somali kids, Shobow included, sat in the shade by the garage, leaning against the cool bricks. The white kids were over in the sun, sitting around the light pole. Both groups were talking, separately. Both groups were getting ready, separately.

This, McGraw thought, *has to change. It has to change right now.* As the coach, he had to change it. He had no doubt he could succeed at making this better; this was one of his strengths. Soccer was the connector. He had to make them see that.

"I want you guys to come over here in the middle and sit," he called as he walked over. They looked up, unsure of what he meant. He started pointing, moving players around, making sure they mixed up. Ali here, Jonny there.

"You!" McGraw roared, pointing at Shobow. His voice had yet to descend into its usual midseason rasp. "Come here—sit."

Shobow hopped up almost instantly, not only because Coach just told him to, but also because he realized what McGraw was trying to do. He wanted to bring them together. He wanted to help them be together. *This,* thought Shobow, *was good.*

McGraw continued to point, calling each of them out, until he was satisfied with the reconfiguration. *Now they are speckled,* he thought. *Perfect.* It was time to take an old-school idea of team and apply it to these players who sat before him. He wasn't trying to save the world; he wanted to win. And to do that, he needed to build relationships, something he was good at. On the field, at least, he needed them to shed their identities—white, black, Muslim, Catholic, Franco, Somali, native, immigrant—and become something new: a team.

"Okay, this is how it's gonna be," McGraw started. "It has to be this way—this is how a team plays. This is how I want you to be on the field and off the field: together."

The players looked at one another and began to relax. Almost immediately, McGraw noticed a change in their demeanors, their bodies, their faces.

"To play the game, you're gonna have to play together. It's the only way to play," he continued.

He noticed some of them starting to smile. He was on to something. *Keep going,* he thought. *Take it all the way.*

"You're going to have to talk to each other, because it's the only way we're gonna win," he continued. "Sometimes our communities don't understand each other, but you can show the adults how it is supposed to be. By playing together, that'll send a message that our cultures can get along."

But he knew it was going to take more than suiting up together. Learning how to be teammates, if not friends, was a process on and off the field.

"This is how I want you to look everywhere you go," McGraw continued. "Everywhere. If you're going to the store, if you're going to class, you guys have to do it together. High fives in the hallway. You need to hang out together. You don't have to sit together in the cafeteria if you don't want to, but you need to stick up for each other and be together. It's a brotherhood."

Wow, thought Shobow, stretching out his thin legs. From his new location on the grass, the sun on his back, he liked what he was hearing. He wanted his team to be united. A new sense of team spirit came across him, a deeper sense of connection. It was encouraging to hear Coach talk about this, to see him face it head-on. Shobow knew from his friendship with Jonny how important this was.

McGraw finished his speech. It was time for practice. The players got up and started walking onto the field to warm up.

"Good job, Coach," Shobow said to McGraw in a low voice as he walked past him, keeping his eyes down out of respect. "That was good."

McGraw smiled, satisfied. For the next decade, it would be almost impossible to talk about Blue Devils soccer without referring to the day McGraw created his so-called speckled team, his constant sideline cry of "Together! Together!" taking on new meaning.

"How would you guys say it?" he asked a few Somalis on the team one day. "How would you say 'together'?"

Pamoja ndugu, a few replied. It was Swahili, one of the many languages of the refugee camps. It meant "together brothers."

It became their rallying cry. "One, two, three!" they shouted before every game, huddled together, hands in the middle, McGraw at the center. *"PAMOJA NDUGU!"*

"We were waiting to be together," Shobow says, his eyes bright at the memory.

The new team motto created a needed break from the past. Soon everyone on the team, not just the Muslim players, understood Ramadan, that it was one of the five pillars of Islam alongside Shahadah (profession of faith), Salat (prayer), Zakat (charity), and the Hajj (pilgrimage to Mecca). Muslims around the world observed Ramadan, staying up late each night to eat. It lasted thirty days, ending with celebrations on Eid al-Fitr, when many of the African players on the team would go to Old Orchard Beach to splash in the ocean or hang out on the boardwalk, a few extra dollars in their pockets from their parents.

"I remember when I was fasting, some of the players were not eating in front of us," Shobow says of Ramadan that season, noticing how his teammates discreetly unwrapped their power bars behind the bench and kept their water bottles out of sight. "They had to wait. We didn't tell them to wait. Coach McGraw didn't tell them to wait. *They* decided to wait. If they wanted to drink, if they were thirsty so bad, sometimes, yes, they did drink—*but never in front of us.*

"That is respect," he continues. "That sense of knowing another person. I felt it. We were one team at that time, from that point. It was a big difference."

Like Shobow, McGraw felt the shift.

"They needed somebody to say, 'Break the ice, let's get it going.' So by the time they were seniors," he says of Shobow's team, "they were going to movies together, going out to play video games or foosball."

He saw a difference on the field. They played better, more in tune with one another. But what really struck him was the change off the field.

"What was nice was to see them walking together," he says. "I see it more today in school, I see them hanging out more together. They meet in the hallway and they acknowledge each other."

But there were touch-and-go moments, times when McGraw feared that a racial confrontation might break out when tensions ran high. He remembers one intense practice in particular after his "speckled" talk. Jonny McDonough and Subeer Osman were running across midfield, right in front of him, competing for the ball, getting physical, throwing elbows, grabbing each other's shirts, before finally falling to the ground. When they got up, McGraw froze as the two growled at each other. But they shook it off and continued to play. After practice, McGraw spoke to the team about it.

"I was sure Subeer was going to lose his head, and Jonny was going to punch him, and there was going to be a fight," he said. But there wasn't; they laughed about it and moved on.

Subeer is now part of Blue Devils folklore, the center of a story that has lived long after he graduated in 2010. Following McGraw's directive to hang out together, Subeer and teammate John Roy—Gish's nephew—made plans to go to a movie one night.

"I'm heading out," John called to his mom on his way out of the house.

"Well, what are you going to do?" she asked.

"I'm going to get Subeer, and then we're gonna—"

"THE HECK YOU ARE!" she yelled. "You are NOT leaving this house because I'm NOT gonna allow you—there's NO BEER!"

"No, no." He laughed. "His NAME is SUBEER."

Despite these lighter moments, McGraw knew he could not let up, especially as more Somalis came out for the team. He had to continue to work hard to make the team come together. In many ways, he figured things out with the team long before Lewiston figured them out as a community, capitalizing on the players' investment in the game and the support from their families and groups like SBYA. Just as Jackie Robinson's first at-bat predated the *Brown v. Board of Education* decision by almost a decade, revealing what integration actually looked like, for many in Lewiston, soccer showed the way. Once refugees, these players—now brothers together—had a home, a team, and one goal. Winning.

CHAPTER 9

LEWISTON PURE

There is no such thing as a part-time player in Lewiston. After practice or a game, the kids go out and play again. Coaches never need to ask them to work on a skill; it's a given that they are never done.

"Our opponents?" says Abdijabar Hersi, one of McGraw's assistant coaches and the first Somali hired by Lewiston High School's athletic department. He laughs. "They're part-time soccer players. When people ask me, 'Why is Lewiston so good?' I say, 'It's a part-time soccer player against a full-time soccer player.' And there's a big difference, you know?"

Coaching kids who prioritized soccer kept McGraw and his staff on their toes.

"I had to expand my game beyond just the hockey and baseball and basketball players that would have come out, that made soccer their second," says McGraw of the shift. "I had to change, I had to up my game to stay with them. Because they knew a lot."

At just about any waking hour of any given day, there is some version of the game being played.

"It's aaaaaaalllllll day, all the time," Hersi continues. "Downtown,

I see them dribbling around the street. Same thing if you do basketball—imagine if I walk everywhere and just dribble. Imagine! Same thing with the soccer...It's important to get touches in, you know? As much as you can."

But it isn't just pickup games. When Abdi H. tried out for the high school soccer team in 2012, he had been playing organized soccer for several years. From local recreational leagues to the SBYA teams, kids began coming to McGraw ready to play at the next level. Abdi H. had no doubt he would make varsity his freshman year, just as Shobow and Ali Hersi had.

Players took many paths to McGraw's team. Even Seacoast United, the elite pay-to-play league, began recruiting Somali players for its U-14 team. Understanding the difficulties, both cultural and financial, of taking on immigrant kids, Coach Ron Graham diligently worked with Kim Wettlaufer and Jama Mohamed, one of the SBYA founders, to make it happen. He didn't just have to figure out how to pay for it; he had to make sure the families were comfortable with it. Graham visited the homes of prospective players with Mohamed, talking with parents to gain their trust before asking if their sons could play.

Carpools, donations, and the waiving of substantial registration fees cleared the way for Lewiston kids to play for Seacoast. Colleen Whitaker, whose son Nathan played U-14, served as team administrator and remembers working with Wettlaufer to get the required birth certificates, parental permission slips, and proof of insurance. She, along with her husband Matt, created an extensive rideshare network with pickup points to get everyone to practices and games. Whitaker made name tags for each player, and a roster that included each player's photograph, name, and number, so other parents could root for them. She learned about prayer rituals and Ramadan, and that the kids from Lewiston played soccer because they wanted to, not because there was a "soccer mom" carting them around, cheering them on, and signing them up for various leagues. Initially surprised when these kids showed up for daylong tournaments with nothing—no snacks, no water bottles—she began carrying around an enormous duffel bag filled with gear she'd collected, everything from mouth guards to shin guards to protein bars.

She also got in the habit of sending the family dog to her in-laws when the kids from Lewiston slept at her house before an early-morning game departure. No dogs, Ibrahim Hussein told her. They are *najis*, unclean.

While players like Abdi H. and Maulid honed their skills with Seacoast, Austin Wing climbed through the ranks of the Lewiston/Auburn Youth Soccer Association. In the summer, he took part in McGraw's camp, McG United Soccer Academy, where Eric Wagner was one of his coaches. Wagner's eyes light up at the mention of Austin, whom he describes as "old-school Lewiston—Lewiston pure."

"He's Lewiston original, he just embodies the Lewiston that is great," Wagner says of the goalie, often the only white kid on the field. "All the great things about it—the welcoming, the hard work ethic, the good humor."

At an early age, Austin knew that he wanted to play goalie. When he was four years old, he always hung around the net. Loath to run, he hated ball-handling drills. But one of the key skills he could transfer from the t-ball field to the soccer pitch was his ability to stop a ball. "Everybody else would be scared of it," he remembers. "I'd be the only one standing in front of it."

Austin loved McGraw's summer camp, where the coach wanted kids to have fun and get comfortable with the ball. Campers played games like Around the World, taking the ball from "country" to "country" to meet new people. Austin also started training with McGraw's summer goalie clinic, working on getting more aggressive and not being afraid of players coming in on crosses. He learned how to move out of the box more, stealing the other team's scoring opportunities, rather than sitting back and waiting for the ball to come to him.

As Austin approached middle school, he discovered there were soccer players in Lewiston who weren't on his L/A team and didn't go to McGraw's camp. When he mowed his grandfather's lawn on Walnut Street, he watched them play pickup games in the Colisée parking lot and SBYA games at Drouin Field. These kids looked like a mini version of the English Premiere League, he thought.

"You come to the middle school and play with these other kids who have been playing soccer all of their lives, in different countries and pickup games on the streets, and you see all these different moves that you've never seen before," he says of playing with his future high school teammates. They racked up amazing scores in middle school, winning by ten or more goals, and focused on controlling the ball more, passing it quickly. A key to their success, Austin knew, was eighth-grade coach Abdullahi Abdi.

"If Paul Nadeau is the father of Lewiston soccer," McGraw says, "Abdullahi is the second father."

McGraw first met Abdi when his son, Ali Hersi, made the varsity squad his freshman year alongside Shobow Saban.

"He could slot a ball like no one else," McGraw says of Ali. "He could find a hole anywhere."

Ali came to practice late one day, and McGraw made him run laps. Abdi came over and introduced himself. He pointed to his son.

"Do not let him get away with anything," he said in his soft voice, touches of Africa laced through each word. "You do what you need to do—I support you."

These days, McGraw keeps Abdi on speed dial.

Growing up in Somalia, Abdullahi Abdi was the consummate athlete, good at just about everything he tried. Soccer was his first love, but he also excelled at middle-distance running until a motorcycle accident injured his right Achilles tendon. He turned to coaching, eventually becoming president of Somalia's track and field program, which led to an increasingly important role on the country's National Olympic Committee.

When civil war broke out, Abdi sent his children and his wife, Nadifo Issak, to live in Mandera, a corner of Kenya tucked between Ethiopia and Somalia. He stayed behind to work, visiting them when he could.

"It just wasn't safe for us to stay," says Halima Hersi, his daughter.

In 1996, Abdi traveled to Georgia as manager of Somalia's Olympic team, composed of a small delegation of runners. In the months leading up to the Games, the Somalis hit a snag when the Barrow County Chamber of Commerce voted they could not train at the local high school track, as had been arranged. While the Chamber claimed that the reason was money, letters to the editor of the local newspaper about the images of a U.S. soldier being dragged through the streets of Mogadishu a few years earlier countered any Olympic spirit the rural county claimed to have.

Despite such troubles, the Olympics remain one of Abdi's proudest memories. Abdi Bile's sixth-place finish in the men's 1,500 meters is Somalia's best Olympic performance to this day.

After the Olympics, Abdi stayed in Atlanta. He worked hard—at a print shop, at a gas station, at coaching—so he could send money to his family and start the process of bringing them to the States. They moved to Nairobi to begin the transition. In 1998, after two years of paperwork, Abdi secured visas for his family to join him.

The family, grateful to be reunited, settled in Gwinnet County, about an hour from the large Somali community in DeKalb. But after Issak visited friends in Lewiston, she mentioned the prospect of moving. "Lewiston is safe," she told her family. "You're going to like it." The family agreed, moving to Lewiston in 2006, where Abdi eventually got a job as an interpreter at Geiger Elementary School.

"We are diverse!" says Halima with a laugh, noting that while she and her older brothers—she's the only daughter—were born in Somalia, her middle brothers were born in Georgia, and the youngest was born Lewiston, just like her own children. Her eldest daughter, Sundus Ali, speaks fluent Somali, something Halima is proud of. At just six years old, Sundus started running for the city's recreational youth track team, coached by Kim Wettlaufer, because her grandfather told her she looked like a runner. Halima remembers her father always bringing her along to play with her brothers when she was younger, encouraging her to shoot baskets and run laps. Sport was important for everyone, he believed. Not just boys.

The track is one of the places where Somali girls, many of whom have brothers on the soccer team, shine as athletes. They don't play much soccer, although during halftime at summer games, they will kick a ball around with one another. Abdikadir Negeye knows that the girls are increasingly interested in playing but recognizes that it isn't common within Somali culture. The SBYA has fielded girls' teams since 2008. Initially, the group received some criticism from local religious leaders about girls playing. But there is nothing that prevents them from playing, Negeye assures anyone who asks, noting that their biggest challenge is finding the appropriate clothing for girls to wear on the field.

During her daughter's summer track practice at Don Roux Stadium at Lewiston High School, Halima likes to sit in the sun on the bleachers and study, writing careful notes from the textbook open next to her, frequently looking up to watch Sundus. She has worked on and off as a school interpreter but wants to finish college and become a guidance counselor. She feels the pull of life in America, wanting more for herself and her family. She loves her four children, but her parents instilled in her a need to better herself, so she tries to balance family with work and education. She sees some aspects of her culture, such as modest dress, as an extension of her character, but she also wants to explore new paths.

"These girls," she says, looking at the track, "are making their own identity as Muslim women."

Sundus loves to run and jump with her teammates, who range in age from six to fourteen. Some wear tanks and shorts, others long, dark leggings or track pants under tunics and robes. Sundus runs in an oversize t-shirt, her bright hijab—sometimes strategically tied to improve aerodynamics—streaming behind her. Wettlaufer teaches the girls how to fly over hurdles and kick across the finish line, while a Bates student explains the mechanics of the triple jump to a small group on the side. Still others work on baton passes for the relay, crying, "STICK!" until a smooth transition is made.

"Who's going to be on the relay?" they ask Wettlaufer when he strolls by, clipboard in hand. They know it's competitive, an honor to be chosen. Their collective speed is extraordinary, and they have broken many long-standing state records.

Sundus is also interested in gymnastics and cheerleading, but track feels more appropriate, safer, to Halima. "Peaceful" is the word she uses to describe watching practice in the hot sun, the sequins on her dark hijab sparkling. Gymnastics feels less so, although Halima lets Sundus take a tumbling class. Cheerleading, a big deal at Lewiston High School, whose perennial championship squad is known for gravity-defying acrobatic feats, is out of the question.

"She could get hurt," Halima worries, tempering the thoughts that fester in the head of anyone who remembers Somalia. The violence left behind always remains near, complicating the daily battle to survive. Along with the quest to learn English, go to school, and find a job, keeping family safe and close is the top priority. Family is the only thing many refugees brought with them. It is what must be preserved above all else.

"Running is better," she concludes.

While she doesn't want her daughter to play soccer, Halima is her father's progeny. She knows a lot about the sport, attending games whenever she can and talking strategy with her mother, who sometimes brings a prayer rug to games in case the team needs a little extra help. She cheers her brothers and supports her father, who coaches as many teams as he can, including high school summer soccer with his son Abdijabar. He holds impromptu sessions with players on weekday afternoons at Marcotte Park, something that once caused a rash of phone calls to the police and City Hall, the park's neighbors worried about the group of immigrants gathering. When the middle school season ends, he finds tournaments for the kids to play in, including an annual tournament each spring in Ohio. Maulid still meets with him occasionally in the Colisée parking lot to run drills.

"He is," says Abdikadir Negeye, "the coach of *everyone*."

In many ways, Abdi sealed the deal on a new era of soccer in Lewiston. Just about any player who lands on McGraw's varsity roster these days has worked with him. Like Gish, Abdi doesn't like "boot and scoot" or "kick and chase" soccer. He encourages players to keep the ball down, controlled. He wants them to understand the difference between passing and kicking, the importance of the first touch, and how to trust a teammate to take the ball.

Under Abdi's tutelage, future varsity squads capitalized on the thousands of touches they accumulate before high school, forcing McGraw to rework his strategies and figure out new ways to build on the skills that Abdi honed. Unlike McGraw's rosters of the past, most Somali players don't have the size or heft to play a physical game. They compensate for their lean build by using speed, talent, and the strong communication skills, in English or otherwise, that came from years of playing together.

Abdi is an elegant, constant presence at Lewiston games, usually dressed in dark trousers and a loose button-down shirt, sandals on his feet when weather permits. Arms folded across his chest, he often paces the sideline, usually by himself, catching every nuance of each play. Other days he sits in the bleachers off to the side.

"Quick, quick, quick," he says, sometimes to himself, sometimes so the players can hear. He wants to see fast feet, quick touches, and good passes.

His access to the team is atypical. Players never ask for permission from McGraw to confer with Abdi, which they do frequently during both practice and games. From the sideline, he will pull a player aside, putting his arm around him as they pace together, his head of short-cropped graying hair leaning in as he offers a gentle correction to what he has seen. Other times, he will beckon from the bleachers.

"Joe," he calls, without seeming to raise his voice.

Joséph Kalilwa, a defender who just took a shot on goal and is now headed for the bench, looks up and immediately jogs over to Abdi. Joe, who lived in Nashville before Lewiston, is one of a handful of players from the Democratic Republic of the Congo, a powerful athlete with more bulk than most of his teammates. He lives with his father and his older sister, Adela, an outstanding athlete who played soccer and ran track in high school before heading to the University of Southern Maine. There, she has continued her illustrious track career while staying very involved in Joe's well-being.

"Passing is better," Coach Abdi starts. Joe immediately nods.

It is a speech Joe has heard many times before. A quiet, thoughtful kid off the field, Joe loves to battle on the pitch, powering through the opposition and taking the ball downfield, dribbling the whole way. He's also funny. McGraw loves to tell the story about the time a white kid from another team yelled "Go home!" at Joe on the field. "Where, to Walnut Street?" Joe yelled back and kept running.

After a brief conversation with Abdi, Joe jogs back to the bench. When McGraw puts him back in, he passes the ball almost immediately.

Sometimes after a game or practice, Abdi will ask McGraw for a moment with the team to share something he has noticed. It is a formality, as McGraw always says yes.

"Come," Abdi says, pointing to a few players. They rise and join him in front of the team. He moves them around, explaining a new formation or strategy. They are unflaggingly respectful while he holds the floor. When he is finished, McGraw thanks him, and the players clap as the two coaches hug.

In 2014, Jason Fuller hired Abdijabar Hersi as freshman coach. It seemed fitting that Abdi's son, who graduated in 2008, would be the high school's first Somali coach.

The lack of diversity in Lewiston's teaching and coaching staffs recently came to light in February 2017, when three groups—the ACLU of Maine, Disability Rights Maine, and Pine Tree Legal Assistance—sent a letter to the school district alleging discrimination against students of color and English-language learners. Among the many accusations cited, such as discipline disparities—immigrant students are suspended at a disproportionate percentage—and communication problems, was the lack of black teachers in the schools.

While current superintendent Bill Webster refuted many of the allegations, calling it a "hatchet job" and citing Lewiston's ever-improving graduation statistics, he acknowledged the lack of black staff, but said he was hopeful for change in the future.

Hersi's hire as freshman soccer coach, which was significant for the district, also ensured players a smoother transition from his father's squad at the middle school to the high school team.

"He brings them to me," Hersi says about his dad. "I get 'em ready, and then they go to Gish or McGraw... They are ready when they come up to the varsity level."

Good-natured and sociable, his smile peeking out from the floppy L.L. Bean hat he wears to protect his light tan skin from the sun, Hersi still plays a lot of soccer. He has league games up to three times a week and loves playing at Somali Stadium in what he calls the "go-go-go" game. Hersi doesn't remember Mogadishu, where he was born, but he has what he calls a "glimpse" of Somalia. He remembers Merca, a port city on the Indian Ocean some sixty or so miles southwest of the capital. Though it was a key Al-Shabaab battle point in recent years, Hersi recalls it as a beautiful city, especially the family's large house facing the water. Even stronger are his memories of his grandparents' house in Kenya and the move to Georgia when he was nine.

Hersi liked Atlanta, where he started third grade. He appreciated the help he got from his teachers. There were no ELL programs or interpreters; it was up to him to learn English, but there was another student in his class who spoke Somali, providing some security. A self-described "people person," when he wasn't reading, he practiced imitating his peers, staring at their mouths when they spoke, listening to the sounds of their English. In a year, he was comfortable with the language.

Because of his dad, soccer and running were always part of his life. He ran with his father almost every morning. On the weekends, they found races to participate in, using them to stay in shape for soccer. His freshman year of high school in Atlanta, he tried out for the soccer team.

"I found out I was really good," he says, despite the fact that he often played basketball to fit in with the other kids. "From there on, I have just been full-time soccer."

Hersi thought about coaching for a long time. Even as a player, he liked helping teammates figure out what to do. He dabbled in coaching league and club teams, including Seacoast, but it wasn't until Halima, his sister, called him that he took the next step.

"Hey, there's a freshman position open," Halima said after consulting the school district's website. "You should go apply for it."

"Ahh, I don't know," Hersi answered. He already had two jobs: as a customer service representative for L.L. Bean, and with Direct Support Professionals working with people with autism. But Halima encouraged him, so he put in his application.

"I always wanted to get into coaching," he says. He shrugs, smiling, before saying the obvious. "My dad is a coach."

Several people applied for the job, but when Hersi walked into the interview, Fuller knew he was the right person at the right time. Hersi, too, could feel it as he answered a barrage of questions from Fuller and McGraw.

"I already knew," Hersi says Fuller later told him. "As soon as I saw your name, I was happy."

McGraw was excited to add Hersi to the coaching staff, and not just because he finally had someone who could shout directives in Somali, something he knew would be a strategic advantage, keeping other teams in the dark. He had spent years wrapping his head around the changes taking place on his roster and in his classroom. He'd buried himself in books and attended coaching conferences and clinics. But most of all he listened to the people around him, knowing he needed them if he was going to win a championship with these players.

"I needed to take who their mentors were, like Abdullahi Abdi and Abdijabar, all of those leaders in the community who coached them," he says. "I embraced them and listened to them. And I listened to the players, because I wanted, I needed, to understand."

Fuller views McGraw's relationship with Coach Abdi and the hiring of Hersi as further evidence of how much McGraw changed to accommodate his evolving roster. He became a better, more inclusive, coach, and developed a deeper level of trust with his faster, experienced players.

"He was the first coach in our department to say, 'If I'm going to be good, and I'm going to relate to these kids, I've got to go into the community.'"

Hiring Hersi represented another coming-of-age for Somalis and Blue Devils soccer, which increasingly didn't have to think about how to be "speckled." As the refugee community continued to lay strong roots in Lewiston, immigrant players became the norm. When Shobow graduated in 2011, his brothers, Benji and Garane, were already on the roster, continuing to carry the torch.

But community relationships remained fragile. While public incidents were rare, in 2009, when *Newsweek* wrote that Somalis had "revived" Lewiston, citing its All-American City award, those who still saw the newcomers as leeches became infuriated. " 'Revived' my ass," read one of the many hateful comments on the article. "They have done nothing good for our city...Seriously, find twenty people in Lewiston who are glad they are here. I know I can't."

Such talk wasn't always reserved for online commentary or private conversations. Editorials in the conservative weekly *Twin City Times* continued to rant against Somalis, taking particular offense whenever they were compared to the city's French-Canadian immigrants. "As a Franco, I find the comparison insulting!" wrote Roland Morin in 2010. "The people from Quebec came here to work—not to live off welfare!" And when the *Sun Journal* wrote about the ten-year anniversary of Somalis in Lewiston, one commenter wrote that the headline should've read, "10 years of Somalis on welfare," while others tried to connect the story of *Black Hawk Down* to immigrants living in Lewiston.

When the BBC came to Lewiston to shoot a short documentary on the Somali community in 2012, Mayor Robert MacDonald, a former police detective and teacher, said he wished Somalis would "leave their culture at the door." While the days of Mayor Raymond's infamous letter and the pig's head incident were long gone, MacDonald's remarks demonstrated how racial and ethnic tensions festered in the shadows.

Many complained that his insensitive, intolerant remarks ignored much of Lewiston's history, particularly in terms of preserving ethnic culture. Today, almost a quarter of Maine identifies as Franco-American. In Lewiston, the number hovers around 70 percent. With its French library and classes, the Franco-American Heritage Center keeps vigilant watch on the legacy of Québécois mill workers. Each month it hosts *Le Recontre*, a luncheon where only French is spoken. These days, French-speaking African asylum seekers often join their Franco neighbors at the lunch, the language bringing together the city's past and its present.

MacDonald, however, was so invested in what Lewiston once was that he had trouble articulating what it had become. His predecessor, former police chief Larry Gilbert, who held the office of mayor for consecutive terms from 2007 to 2011 between Raymond and MacDonald, had heralded the city's ethnic transformation, espousing a consistently progressive vision for the future. MacDonald, not so much.

In the BBC's four-minute segment, MacDonald is featured sitting on a park bench. A heavyset man with golden hair, he's dressed casually in a yellow polo shirt, his arm thrown over the back of the bench, eyes squinting in the brightness of the beautiful Maine day.

"The immigrants that have come in here have cost us a lot of money, and we are continuing to go with, to fight with, the federal government. You know, you brought them in, you pay for them," he says in an unconcerned tone that belies the severity of what is coming out of his mouth. "Here, if you want to come in here, and you want to become a citizen, that's fine. Welcome to America. But you know what? When you come here, you come and you accept our culture. And you leave your culture at the door."

Shobow, for one, tried to make light of the comments, telling the *Sun Journal* the mayor must have meant leave *shoes* at the door, as Somalis never wear them inside.

"I don't like saying bad things about other people, and I made my point," Shobow recalls. "Becoming a citizen is not leaving your whole culture behind, it's having the right to vote so that you can impact where you live."

Others were less mild in their reaction to the mayor's remarks, reawakening memories of Raymond's letter from a decade before. City Hall protesters demanded that MacDonald recant his remarks, carrying signs that read "LEWISTON IS BETTER THAN THIS" and "WE WANT A SINCERE APOLOGY." More than a thousand people signed a petition demanding that he resign.

MacDonald refused to apologize, instead attempting to clarify his remarks. He made things much worse. "If you believe in it so much," he said of Somali culture in an interview on WGME-TV, the local CBS affiliate, "why aren't you over there shedding blood to get it? Why are you here shirking your duties?"

A week later, he spoke to an overflowing crowd in the City Council's chamber at City Hall. Dressed in a pale beige blazer and a yellow tie, he donned his reading glasses and stared at the typed remarks in his hand. Stumbling a bit, he said the BBC took his remarks out of context. He meant Somalis needed to assimilate to American culture, not abandon their own. He acknowledged that immigrants "enriched the diversity" of the city.

"As mayor," he concluded, "I value every person in the city of Lewiston."

But the BBC interview was not an isolated incident. MacDonald's controversial policy ideas, including a public website that listed names and addresses of welfare recipients and a moratorium on subsidized housing in Lewiston, sparked national attention. His often-inflammatory column for the *Twin City Times* included comments about "submissive Somali women" who "turn into obnoxious customers at the grocery store cash register," condemning the "boo-hoo white do-gooders" who support them. He wrote that there was only "one dominant central culture," American culture. He told tales about his years working at Lewiston Middle School, claiming that the Somali girls studied hard, but the boys were indifferent to schoolwork.

The BBC interview highlighted MacDonald's positions and, more importantly, those who elected him, bringing racial and religious tensions back into the headlines. Less than a year after the BBC incident, he would be reelected, his supporters further emboldened to leave hateful comments about Somalis on the websites of local newspapers. The *Sun Journal* eventually barred anonymous posts.

But Mike McGraw doesn't read the comments section, often joking that he isn't "very observant." In terms of what some people say about his players, that's a very good thing. He keeps his focus on the field, urging players to value and trust one another, which enables him to avoid the political fray. But Fuller knows all too well how changes to the soccer roster in recent years have engendered animosity in the broader community. He has no patience for those who claim kids from the "outside" are playing more than "native" kids or that the program had been "taken" by those it didn't belong to.

"How much do *you* practice?" he responds to the hypothetical question of why a kid isn't playing varsity, his voice hitting a high pitch, arms animated. "Go to any field—any random field in Lewiston—the kids are playing! They're playing! There's a *reason* they're better."

Fuller understands that when the mayor told a reporter that Somalis shouldn't insert their culture "which obviously isn't working, into ours, which does," he'd clearly never watched a high school soccer game.

Just a few months after the BBC segment aired, in December 2012, MacDonald sat down with a group of Somali elders at the Blue Nile Café on Lisbon Street, where everything from pasta to roasted goat was on the menu. Abdi Matan, who came to the United States in 2005, opened the restaurant after running one in Kenya. "A nation's culture resides in the hearts and minds of its people," read a sign on the door the mayor walked through for the meeting.

Hussein Ahmed, who runs Global Halal Market on Lisbon Street, appreciated the meeting, but wished it hadn't taken so long to make it happen. Among the many things the group discussed, the mayor cited the soccer team as a prime example of the Somalis' refusal to assimilate. He asked why the parents of the soccer players did not support the Booster Club or volunteer at the Snack Shack during games.

"Without that booth, there is no team," he said, according to a local newspaper. "That's a complaint I hear, that the Somali parents are not as involved in that as they should be."

He clearly hadn't talked to Denis and Kathy Wing.

CHAPTER 10

SAINTS, MARTYRS, AND SUMMER SOCCER

Denis Wing is usually too busy pricing Cup Noodles to care what anyone has to say about the soccer team's Booster Club. The hours that he and wife, Kathy—they are always a "we" and never an "I"—commit to raising money for the team is a labor of love, a way of supporting not just their two sons but also these kids they've known since middle school. During their fourteen years of supporting Little League, he points out, there are always just a handful of parents who chip in. Five baseball teams, twelve kids per team, sixty-some parents; it's always the same five or ten who roll up their sleeves.

If anyone wants to take a shot at the parents of Somali soccer players, says Wing, they won't get far with him. He knows they are easy targets, painted with the same broad brush no matter what they do, under constant scrutiny with critics ready to pounce. But he refuses to let anyone say that just because they aren't at the Snack Shack on game night, they're lazy or unsupportive.

"They've got one parent working, and the other with three or four more kids at home," he says, although he notes that attendance has improved in recent years. "I understand that. I mean, it doesn't make it easier at times, but if Kathy and I, and the parents that are involved, didn't like what we were doing, we wouldn't do it. We know that's the demographic of the team—it's just how it is."

McGraw, too, knows that the combination of large families, multiple jobs, and little money—very little money—contribute to the relatively low attendance at most soccer games.

"When you think about it, if a parent comes in, it's five bucks; if a kid comes in, it's three bucks," observes McGraw about tickets for soccer games. "They might have enough money for one to come."

Some people wait in the parking lot until halftime, when the ticket booth closes. Others wait for big games, like the "Battle of the Bridge" match-up against Edward Little or the annual Senior Night game. McGraw knows to expect the unexpected on Senior Night, when players tend to show off for the bigger crowd. In 2014, defender Biwe Mohamed weaved all the way down the field to score a goal. When McGraw asked him about it later, Biwe apologized but said he'd had to do it: his mom was in the stands, and she had never seen him play before.

McGraw calls the Booster Club parents his saints and martyrs, knowing it can be a full-time job. Kathy Wing starts prepping the Snack Shack, the team's largest source of revenue, months in advance of the first game. She has a working list in the back of her mind at all times, especially when she is at the grocery store. She combs the aisles for bargains, items that will turn the biggest profit, stocking up when the price is right. Whenever she sees a case of twenty-four Cup Noodles for less than $10, she snaps it up, knowing she can sell them for a buck each on game night.

In August, before Lewiston's annual tournament, she steps it up a notch. The event brings in upward of $3,000, about half the Boosters' annual revenue. Denis even takes vacation the week of the tournament to make sure everything runs smoothly.

"You don't have a Booster Club without the Wings," affirms Fuller. "The Wings *are* the Booster Club."

Denis and Kathy Wing first got their hands wet learning the ropes of the Snack Shack Austin's freshman year. By his sophomore year, Kathy was running concessions, and Denis was vice president.

"There wasn't a whole lot of election," Denis remembers. "It was kind of, 'Okay, you guys are now in charge.'"

When one walks through the gate of Don Roux field and buys a ticket, the blue-and-white Snack Shack sits to the left just off the track. Laminated white paper hangs between its two windows listing available items. At big games, smart spectators load up early, knowing the line at halftime will be long.

The Boosters' operation is no mean feat. While Kathy manages drinks and snacks, her mother—Austin and Dalton's Mémé—helping her, Denis operates several grills and a hot dog steamer. Other parents make potluck contributions, from chili to mac and cheese, corn chowder to chicken potpie. Others make sure there is a steady supply of piping hot water for the Cup Noodles and hot chocolate. Later in the season, when Maine's fall chill turns into downright cold, it is almost impossible to keep up with the demand. Whoopie pies, Maine's signature treat, are a top seller, but only turn a profit when someone donates them.

In recent years, *sambusa*, the crispy triangular pocket of dough filled with savory meat that sits upon many a Somali table, has become a Snack Shack headliner. Making *sambusa* is a time-consuming process—an all-day affair—and there rarely is enough money in any family's budget to make extra. But many of the players' mothers and sisters send trays to games for the Snack Shack to sell, the Boosters reimbursing them for supplies. It's a win-win situation for everyone involved, financially and culturally. There's no question, says Denis, that *sambusa* brings people in. He just has to remind the Somali families to tone down the spices.

The Wings also make sure to watch their sons play. Denis usually watches from the fence in front of the Snack Shack, preferring it to the bleachers, while Kathy looks up occasionally from inside. Being the parent of a goalie is nail-biting business, so the Snack Shack offers her respite, enabling her to be at a game without losing her mind. She's nervous that her son is the team's last line of defense. Burying herself in concessions relieves some of the pressure.

The Wings work hard to strike a balance between Boosters' responsibilities and their real jobs. Denis is the manager of a Rite-Aid in nearby Lisbon, while Kathy is a billing rep for the Sisters of Charity Health System. Denis makes the store's shift rotation, which he posts on the wall next to a Blue Devils' game schedule. He goes to great lengths to ensure that his employees have the schedules they need, often taking an extra shift himself to make it work. They, in turn, understand that when it's game time, he needs coverage, especially when the team is on the road.

Unlike most of the team's parents, Denis and Kathy make sure that at least one of them attends every away game, even in summer. It didn't take long for players to get used to seeing them around. The couple welcomes players to their home, knowing to keep the family dog locked inside while the team swims in their pool.

"Mr. or Mrs. Wing must be around here somewhere," players often say when they need a ride or an extra mouth guard.

The Wings consider their ability to be there for their boys a luxury and make it a priority that each player knows he is supported. Knowing the limitations of the school's budget, they raise money to make sure players get some of the extras other teams take for granted, like team shirts and hats.

"It's always been about them," Denis emphasizes. "I mean, just to see the smile on their faces when you do something for them—it's the best part of it, the appreciation, the thank-you, and that's all I've ever wanted out of it."

"It's for the kids," Kathy simply says any time someone tries to thank her. "It's all about the kids."

Despite the best fund-raising efforts, keeping the team equipped is an ongoing battle. Over the years, some good citizens—many of whom met the players via Seacoast—have donated money to buy shoes and shin guards. The Boosters keep a collection of used gear to help out, and they buy extra mouth guards in case someone forgets one. But the Wings know they cannot outfit every player. There will never be enough money for that.

In summer games, the lack of everything is magnified. Many play without shin guards, wanting to save them for the real season. They shove newspapers or the insoles of another pair of shoes into their tall socks, mimicking the look—if not the protection—of the real thing. Maulid makes his out of packing tape. As he pulls his socks—one blue, one red—up his long legs, he brags to his teammates about his spark of ingenuity. He hopes the ref agrees.

Without the structure of the school day, McGraw has to work much harder in summer to keep in touch with players.

"Where are your forms?" he barks, standing next to the open trunk of his car in the parking lot next to the high school gym entrance.

While school has been out a few days, there is still a lot of buzz on the playing fields. Young runners drill under Kim Wettlaufer's watchful eye on the track, while a group of women in traditional African dress talk nearby. On the far baseball field, a game is just getting started.

The soccer players arrive mostly on foot via the trails that connect the back of the high school to downtown, just past the football practice field. Even in summer, when things are a bit more relaxed, they are careful to be on time.

"Playing for McGraw is like playing on a professional team," Maulid says, half smiling, half serious.

Since it is hot, they try to stay in the shade of the gym's entry-way, talking, teasing, a ball always in motion while they show off fancy footwork. It's Ramadan, and almost five o'clock, which means most of them have not had anything to eat or drink for more than twelve hours. The coaches are very conscious of the dietary restrictions, but the players shrug it off. Yes, it's Ramadan. No eating, no drinking. But they can and will play soccer.

Jason Fuller says that it took time to figure out how best to deal with the changing time line of Ramadan, which takes place in the ninth month of the Islamic calendar. Kim Wettlaufer and Coach Abdi help McGraw and Fuller create practice schedules that accommodate it. Flexibility has been key to making it work.

A few years ago, Ramadan took place in the fall, meaning that soccer players started games without eating. The second the sun went down, their parents arrived with trays of *sambusa* and tea. Halftime, remembers Fuller, became a bit of a feast, players going into the stands to sit with family and have something to eat. He and McGraw fully supported this.

"Absolutely, eat it as soon as you can," McGraw says to them whenever food arrives on the sidelines, noticing that the white players rather enjoyed the midgame snack as well.

They deal with prayer in the same way. In Islam, prayer is a physical act that requires a sequence of kneeling and standing while reciting memorized verses. Fuller has no patience for any-one who has a problem with it.

"Just let it happen," Fuller says of players bringing prayer rugs to practice or games. "These are *our* athletes: accommodate them."

When he started, Fuller admits knowing nothing—"NOTHING, NOTHING, NOTHING!" he yells, laughing at his past ignorance—about Islamic prayer rituals or the needs of athletes competing without food or water. He prioritized making sure athletes felt comfortable talking to their coaches about how they're feeling. Not up to running? Then come to practice and sit.

"As long as they're there, I can function with them not practicing," he says.

Players say that McGraw and Fuller now worry more about fasting and prayer than they do. McGraw tries to rotate the roster more frequently during Ramadan, putting in subs more quickly and asking if they're tired or dizzy. They usually reassure him that they are fine. This is their every day. Yes, they promise. We will say if we need to come out.

McGraw now works Ramadan into halftime speeches, using it as motivation for the entire team.

"You guys that are fasting? You want to feel good?" he asks, reminding them there are just forty minutes standing between them and a meal. "That's tremendous—you want to *earn* it."

"Which way is east?" a player asks as he arrives for a summer game at Maranacook High School. He glances up, a rolled-up prayer rug jutting from his backpack. The late afternoon sun still seems high, not helping him figure anything out. They are on a practice field in back of the school, a long walk from the parking lot. Carrying the bag of balls for Coach was hard enough. He didn't want to lug his prayer rug much farther.

His teammates look around. It feels like the middle of nowhere. The drive from Lewiston hadn't been much more than half an hour, scenic with lakes and ritzy summer camps. But standing there, Lewiston felt like a million miles away. No one else, they are certain, has prayer rugs.

After a bit of mumbling, they decide as long as they do it together, it doesn't matter where they face. A few grab their bags and head over to the adjacent baseball field. It's hot, they haven't eaten in about fifteen hours, and they want to get this done. There's a game to play.

During the game, a Lewiston player falls to the ground with a leg cramp in front of the other team's bench. The opposing coach tries to help him massage it out. When the player chalks the cramp up to the fact that he's dehydrated, the coach is floored, getting what Gish calls a "deer in the headlights" look. The coach just realized that the majority of players crushing his team are fasting. It's a response Lewiston players are used to.

Maulid finds playing during Ramadan tough. He is tired because he stays up late, eating, playing soccer in the Colisée parking lot or basketball in Kennedy Park, and eating again. Unlike some, who get up before sunrise to eat, Maulid eats before going to bed, around three, and then sleeps in. On the field, he feels like he just can't get it going, his legs heavy, overtaken by a laziness he can't do anything about.

Others don't feel fatigued, claiming that fasting gets easier after the first week. Lots of Muslim athletes fast, they say. Hakeem Olajuwon. Mo Farah.

"You don't really pay attention," says Moe Khalid, who plays in the raucous Ramadan tournament that Coach Abdi helps organize each year, designed to kill the long hours between school or work and eating.

When Ramadan shifts back to summer, it is clear of August's grueling double sessions and fall's varsity schedule but coincides with summer games. There is nothing glamorous about summer soccer. Rosters change, players come and go, work and family travel interfere with games. After the preseason meeting in June, McGraw divides players into two teams by age. Coaches Abdi and Hersi take freshmen and sophomores, dubbed Lewiston II. McGraw and Gish take juniors and seniors, Lewiston I. But titles are deceiving. Because of the middle school talent Abdi nurtures, there are no guarantees that playing on Lewiston I in the summer means a varsity spot in the fall. McGraw counts on the father-and-son coaching duo to be his eyes and ears on the younger set. Occasionally, a talented eighth grader—Abdi H. was one—comes on board for the summer, too.

For better or worse, McGraw runs summer season out of his car. His trunk is filled with balls, permission slips, shirts, and extra shin and mouth guards. Before traipsing from Readfield to Westbrook, Freeport to Topsham, he has to make sure everything is in order.

"You got shin guards?" he asks. "Is there gas in your car?"

Players need $10 to play. In return, they get some variation of a "Lewiston United" shirt with "SUBWAY EAT FRESH" scrawled across the back, courtesy of Wettlaufer, who sponsors the team to help build the roster.

Gish pulls up in his big pickup truck. In a few days, he will head to a nearby lake with his wife and kids for their annual camping trip, missing some of the summer schedule, but for now he is all about the team.

"Coach, I don't have my cleats," a player calls to McGraw. McGraw turns a deaf ear; he's busy hunting permissions slips. Gish asks the player where his cleats are.

"My cousin's house," he answers. Gish gives a good-natured chuckle. "Cousin" is a term that means a lot of different things in the Somali community. The cleats could be anywhere.

"Get in," he says to the kid. "Coach," he calls to McGraw, laughing. "Apparently I am leaving now—we have to go get our cleats at our cousin's house!"

McGraw looks at his list and then at the kids standing in front of him.

"If you need a ride and I have your papers and your money, get in the truck with Coach!" he yells.

Away games in summer are a mad scramble for transportation. McGraw drives the athletic department's beat-up white van, cramming as many players as he safely can into the seats. Others drive a family car, if there is enough gas in the tank. Often there isn't. The Wings always take a few. But when there aren't enough seats, players are left behind, McGraw making the final call as to who goes.

It isn't about taking friends, he reminds them. It's about what the team needs.

Few parents show up at away games during summer. Most take place on practice fields, with no real bench or bleachers to sit on. The team sprawls on the grass to suit up while McGraw greets the other coach. He knows just about everyone in the state and addresses each one with a twinkle in his eyes and a slap on the back.

"Keep the nice ones close," he often says, "and the other ones closer."

Summer home games usually are at Drouin Field on Walnut Street, an easy walk for players who live downtown. Drouin, which sits next to the Colisée, looks over Longley Elementary School and the stacked apartments of Bartlett and Birch Streets. Just above, neighborhoods filled with ranch houses and grassy lawns delineate a different kind of Lewiston living, the Colisée and Drouin creating a proverbial other side of the tracks.

A nondescript field surrounded by a fence that sways from years of kids hopping over it, Drouin is another grassy respite in the middle of the city. The bells from Saints Peter and Paul fill the wide-open sky on the hour, drowning out the constant fluttering of flags flying from the Colisée's front steps. In the vast parking lot below, a car circles as a man teaches a woman in hijab how to drive. A few feet away, a mother shows her daughter how to ride a beat-up bike without training wheels, the little girl's blond curls blowing beneath her helmet as she gathers speed. Another girl circles her mother on a scooter, her *jilbab* streaming behind her. As the sun sinks lower, more families gather in the Colisée parking lot, taking advantage of its open space.

There is no admission charge in the summer. Games at Drouin can bring in a decent crowd. Kim Wettlaufer sits on the grass at the far corner of the field in the shade, his long legs stretched in front of him. Carolyn often joins him, while their two young, blond children play with the Somali kids who gather nearby. Many of the players' younger brothers and sisters come to watch. The younger set loves to rib their brothers from the sidelines.

"Stop being lazy, Muktar," one calls. "Come ONNNNNNN!"

One of the youngest members of the varsity squad, Muktar Ali arrived in Lewiston in 2006 when he was in first grade, his family taking a circuitous route: Somalia to Kenya to Indiana to Maine. An introspective kid with a bit of a penchant for trouble, he's known to crack up his older teammates.

"Hilarious," Abdi H. says about him. "That kid is hilarious."

The coaches keep extra eyes on Muktar, using soccer eligibility as a carrot to keep him motivated in school and making sure he meets with his teachers frequently. No one brings out McGraw's accent like Muktar.

"MOOK-tahhhhhh!"

When a Lewiston player gets a corner kick at Drouin, the younger kids run over to talk to him, African music coming from the phones in their pockets, their bare toes creeping close to the line. At halftime, they'll take to the field, boys at one goal, girls at another, kicking a ball around, pretending to be their favorite Blue Devil.

These children flock to Wettlaufer, who rarely misses a name. He asks about a sibling, a parent, a job, a physical, or summer school. He doles out advice with quiet, compassionate intensity. They fire questions at him about track practice and youth soccer registration.

"Hey, guys," he pleads to a group kicking a ball behind the goal. "Guys, stay off the field, please? Come on!"

His eyes turn to a group of girls tending to a baby, and he tells them they should push back from the sideline so they don't get run over by a sprinting striker. They move a few feet. He tells a boy to drop the stick he is swirling around. The kid lets the long branch fall to the grass without hesitation. Wettlaufer remains kind and even-tempered, even when a young Somali girl uses profanity to reprimand her little brother. One look from Wettlaufer, and she apologizes.

"They're family," he says simply of these relationships that began years ago in the basement of Trinity.

Some of them have a key to his house, which sits just above Drouin, to take care of his cats when he is away. Others stop by just to say hello. Sometimes neighbors say things, he admits, asking if he knows that one of "those kids" was in his garage.

"I know," he patiently answers each time.

The Wings, too, can always be found at Drouin, setting up their camp chairs in the sun on the opposite side of the field from the players' bench and from the house where Denis grew up. They sit with other Booster parents, all of whom know the team and its coach as well as anyone could. Despite being across the field, they can hear McGraw call to the players.

"Is something wrong with your right foot?" McGraw yells at a defender. The kid looks up, shaking his head. "No? Really? THEN USE IT!"

The parents cackle, especially the kid's father.

The Somali parents wander over to Drouin from across the Colisée parking lot or the apartments down Walnut. The women often sit on the grass in the shade near their children, catching up with one another while their eyes stay on the game. The fathers gather across the field on the fence near the bench, arms crossed, focused. They don't bring chairs or join the Boosters on the sunny sideline, but Denis Wing walks over to talk with them about their sons. They know he spends a lot of time with the team. They know Austin, too, cheering when he makes a good save.

Sometimes McGraw's former players from long ago show up, occasionally with their own kid on the opposing team. They want to pay homage to their old coach, reciting the "three D's" of Lewiston soccer: Drive, Determination, Discipline. McGraw never hesitates on a name, never withholds a warm embrace, and always has a story about each one. "Captain Jack!" McGraw shouts. The alum, now in his mid-forties with three kids, apparently played a lot of Billy Joel back in his day.

The atmosphere before a summer game is loose, easy. Maulid greets McGraw's constant demands from the sideline with a sarcastic but good-natured smile and a big thumbs-up. In a halftime huddle, McGraw sees that more players are giggling than listening. He starts to growl until they clue him in.

"Someone farted?" McGraw asks, grinning. It's another word that makes the most of his accent. *Fahhh-ted.*

The team bursts out laughing. He lets them have fun for a minute before getting back to business.

Before games, players talk about going to the beach and, of course, girls, none of the pressure of the regular season yet weighing on them.

"Why are they all named Caitlyn?" asks one, puzzling about the American dating scene. His teammates crack up, understanding all too well what he's asking.

Those who hang out with white girls bear the brunt of good-natured teasing, but deep down, they know they have to be careful about such relationships. If the wrong girl says the wrong thing, there will be trouble. Despite the number of interracial couples in the hallways of the high school, for some in Lewiston there still is no such thing as a consensual relationship between a white girl and an immigrant boy.

"It was all going so well," rues one, "until her dad showed up."

"Yeah," laughs another. "She was all like, 'Sorry—I forgot to tell you that my dad is racist.'"

While they banter, most have at least one earbud in. Abdi H. and Moe mimic star players like Neymar and wear Beats. After FIFA banned the popular and pricey headphones from the World Cup because the company wasn't an official sponsor, wearing them became a badge of rebellion.

After everyone is dressed, they hit the field; some do drills in small groups, others help warm up the goalies, firing shots at the net. As they move the ball among themselves in circles, focusing on control and good touches, their speed increases. They boot the ball to the opposite line and then run back—one touch and go. They move between inside and outside rolls, side-to-side push-pulls, vees, and pull instep pushes. The moves of Somali Stadium often emerge during warm-ups, players faking each other out with Cruyffs and step overs. They laugh as each player outdoes the next, sometimes falling to the ground, faking exhaustion before the game even begins.

The captains call the group together. In a circle, they stretch on the ground, joking as hands reach to cleated feet, heads bowing down to knees. Next are formation drills, players making lines across the field. Even in summer, when things aren't as regimented, the Blue Devils are a formidable group. They jog across the field together, using a different action each time. High knees, toy soldiers, left slides, right slides, squat and step, and running leaps. Finally, they finish with a left-right dance of sorts, moving back and forth as they cross the field a final time, clapping and chanting as they go, their opponents often pausing to watch, forgetting their own warm-up routine. Finally, it is time to huddle for McGraw's pregame speech. He reminds them that technique and fundamentals have to come before power, and no move is worth a foul.

"Get there first," he advises. "If the guy takes a shot, that's why you have a goalie."

"One, two, three," McGraw yells as they put their hands in the center of the tight circle.

"*Pamoja ndugu!*" they answer.

"Was that one good enough?" he asks, taking a step back to look at them. It's just a summer game, after all. Does it matter? The hands go back in and they do it again.

"ONE, TWO, THREE...*PAMOJA NDUGU!*" rings across the field, causing the other team, stretching on the grass just a few feet away, to look up.

"That's better," grunts McGraw.

The players run onto the field and go to their knees for a final huddle before taking their positions. It is time.

A whistle blows almost as soon as the game begins.

"No mouth guard!" the ref yells, pointing at a Lewiston player. "Need a sub!"

"Ya don't need a mouth guard in the summah!" McGraw yells back, his players echoing the sentiment quietly behind him.

With three-plus decades of coaching under his belt, McGraw knows and respects just about every ref in the state. While he might mutter displeasure to his assistant coaches, he is always mindful of setting an example for his players. It is rare for him to argue a call, and when he does—"I can count how many times on one hand in fifteen-plus years," says Gish—it is usually posed as a request for more information.

The ref looks at McGraw and nods. He raises his arms in apology, and blows the whistle so the game can resume.

"After you make that pass, curl and go!" McGraw yells to a player, always in teaching mode, everything a lesson. "Head up! Control the guy, be patient."

"One-two touch!" shouts Gish, wanting players to control the ball and pass. "Nice job! Good idea!"

McGraw reels off players' names, never stumbling, even if someone is new to the squad. He wants to build the confidence of anyone who might make varsity for the first time in the fall, giving them direct orders to improve their play.

"When you get that, you *take* that!" he yells when someone passes instead of taking an open shot. "You're good enough!"

He turns to the bench players, offering a quick tutorial on how to decide between shooting and passing.

"It's summer," he says. "You can risk a couple things—try it out!"

Turning back to the game, he sees the opposing goalie ready to boot the ball back into play. "Back up!" he yells. "It's gonna go over your head!"

The players keep one ear to McGraw, the other to one another. They are intense, digging hard and controlling the ball with precision, at times laughing at one another as they move the ball faster toward the attacking third of the field, where they can fire off a bullet and score.

When the final whistle blows, they are exhausted but happy. The sun is setting, offering relief from the steaming day. For most of them, it is almost time to eat for the first time in hours. The other team has no idea they just lost by ten goals to a bunch of ravenously hungry guys.

CHAPTER 11

MANY NATIONS, ONE TEAM

In summer, McGraw often asks more experienced players to take a back seat. He wants everyone to get field time, learning how to expect the unexpected, as he often says, before fall.

"Don't carry the ball so much!" he yells at a probable varsity starter.

He calls for a substitution, bringing the player out of the game.

"I know you can carry the ball," he says in a low tone, his arm around the kid's shoulders. "We got to get it to the other guys. It's one touch to a man—it's hard, but you've got to do it."

The kid is visibly frustrated. He likes to dribble and has a hard time transitioning from the attack he enjoys at Somali Stadium to the one-touch, two-touch style McGraw wants to see. But he listens, and later in the game, McGraw praises him for doing it right.

"You love the ball and the ball loves you," he says. "You gave it up, and I know that's hard for you."

McGraw tries to stay supportive, but with the fall fast approaching, it's tough. There's a lot on the line.

"Pass the ball, goddammit," he mutters when another player

dribbles downfield, only to lose the ball to the other side. "We gotta work on that."

After the game, which they won, the team sits with McGraw, listening to what they could do better.

"So we didn't play wide as much as we should, and we didn't pass as much as should," he lectures. "You outside guys should be running nine miles a game—I want to see your heels on the white line!"

The pass, he reiterates, is mightier than the dribble.

"How many chances did we have that we didn't put in?" he asks. "It's not like you're in the parking lot at the Colisée or Somali Stadium—you don't have time here."

McGraw knows the hours they spend stoking their passion is critical to the team's success, but there are elements of the street game he wishes they would leave on the street. He hates showboating, what he calls selfish play, and gets especially frustrated when he sees a team strategy they practiced endlessly not executed properly during a game.

Marking is a big one. Whenever possession turns over, key defenders know who they're expected to shadow in the opposition's attack, staying close and goal-side to deny their opponent time and space to turn and pass, dribble, or shoot. The second there is a turnover, coaches and captains alike will yell for everyone to "Mark up!"

"I told you to mark him, mark him exclusively!" McGraw shouts at a defender after a kid who scored a few minutes ago breaks through again. "So you mark him haaaaahhhrd! If he goes and sits on the bench, I want you follow him there! Don't lose your man! What are you doing walking back? Are you TIRED? Because I've got a BENCH FULL of guys who can play better than you right now."

The bench chuckles, but a quick look from Gish and the smiles are gone.

Whenever Lewiston is awarded a corner kick, McGraw barks out a series of orders, sending one player to the keeper, another to post. Almost half the goals scored in any game come from a set piece. But it takes practice to effectively convert a kick or a throw-in from an opportunity to an actual goal, exploiting the opposition's "danger zone" and getting the ball through.

Corner and goal kicks are called when the ball rolls over the line at the end of the field. If the offense kicks it out, play restarts with a goal kick, which can be taken from anywhere, and by any player on the defense, inside the six-yard box nearest the goal. The ball has to leave the penalty area before anyone else can touch it, or the kick is retaken. If the defense kicks it out, the offense restarts play with a corner, which happens from the corner nearest to where the ball went out of bounds.

Even a throw-in, a seemingly small moment in a game, can have a huge impact. It's tricky; a legal throw-in requires the ball to be thrown over a player's head, with both feet firmly on the ground. A watchful ref will blow the whistle if the ball doesn't start far enough behind the head, if the thrower isn't facing the field of play, if the ball spins from just one hand, or if the thrower touches the ball again before someone else does.

His sophomore year, Maulid started toying around with a different kind of throw-in.

The flip throw, in which a player launches the ball from a front handspring, is an uncommon weapon in soccer, especially at the high school level. When done correctly, it can place the ball directly in front of the goal with tremendous velocity and torque, just as powerful, if not more so, as a kick.

After seeing a cousin try to flip the ball and fail, Maulid told his teammates he was going to try it. Abdi H. believed him. Maulid was the perfect candidate: strong and flexible, with ball-handling skills that made his feet seem like hands, manipulating the ball in almost any direction he wanted. He was fast, too, and graceful, the soles of his feet barely skimming the ground as he chased down a ball. He loved to fool around with different dance moves, doing backflips and creating routines with his best friend and teammate, Mwesa Mulonda. Maulid had flair, flamboyance, and loved attention. For him, the flip throw was just another performance; one that could help his team.

Maulid's apartment on Walnut makes practicing at Drouin easy. The apartment is on the second floor of a light blue triple-decker, chipped white molding circling the roof. There is no number on the door; anyone who climbs the dark wooden stairs knows where to go. A pile of shoes and sneakers and sandals sits just through the doorway of the large kitchen, the air thick from the lingering spices of soups and stews that bubble on the stove, to be eaten on the floor from a communal bowl or two, as is typical. Like most apartments in Lewiston, its bones have seen better days. The intricate woodwork on the built-ins and French doors hasn't seen a fresh coat of paint for generations. The living room is usually filled with Maulid's younger brothers and sisters sprawled in an array of seating areas, a giant television in the corner.

The oldest still living at home, Maulid has his own bedroom in the back, which he shares with the family's refrigerator. Unlike the living room, which is decorated in rich colors and patterns—a maroon-and-cream rug covering the worn hardwood, walls covered with rich tapestries and framed excerpts from the Koran—his room is sparse and messy. Socks are piled on the floor among shorts and t-shirts, the *macawis* he often wears at home draped across the foot of his unmade bed. On a small table sits the soccer scrapbook that his younger sister, Mana, keeps for him, filled with press clippings about the team.

From his bedroom, Maulid can hear if kids are playing at Drouin; if so, he can be on the field in minutes. After working on the flip on his own for a few weeks, he decided to try it in a game. "Hey, Coach!" he announced to McGraw with a sly smile. "I got a flip throw."

"All right," McGraw grunted. "Just don't break your neck."

McGraw was curious. Adding a flip throw to the team's arsenal could be a game-changer; "something dangerous," as Maulid put it. No one else in the league had one. McGraw knew Maulid had the goods to flip with the ball, but did he have the precision to make it effective? Get it to arc into the attacking third so someone could put a bullet on it with a head or lob it in from the far post? *That would be something,* McGraw thought, watching Maulid. *It would also be something if he landed on his butt.*

The mechanics of a flip throw are complicated. A player backs up from the sideline, judging where his feet will land when he comes around. Stepping over the line brings a whistle, something that happens often enough with a regular throw-in. Toeing the line while coming out of a front handspring is a whole different thing.

Speed is critical. After gaining momentum for several gazelle-like steps, Maulid holds the ball up, hands firmly planted on either side, before plunging downward to bounce it on the ground, flipping his legs over his head. When his feet land on the other side, he clenches his stomach muscles, forcing his body upward as he brings the ball over his head, launching it over the field.

Maulid tried out the move a few times toward the end of his sophomore season with poor results, the ball soaring out of bounds. But he began to perfect it the following summer. As he got more confident, his aim got better, the ball landing closer to the box. Other teams reacted by sending everyone to the net in anticipation, something Maulid sometimes played with—he'd do the run, and then just throw the ball over his head, no flip. It kept everyone on their toes.

McGraw watched Maulid, likely his only junior starter in the fall, thinking about how other teams would react to a flip throw. He liked to have some elements of surprise before starting a new season. A flip throw was exactly that: unexpected.

Also unexpected was Maslah Hassan.

Dripping with athletic gifts, Maslah walks with the swagger of a rock star, exuding confidence from head to toe. When he enters a room, all eyes shift to him. Magnetic, tall and lean, with legs that appear skinnier than his arms, he towers over most of his teammates, his angled high-top adding a few extra inches. But even if he didn't, they would still look up to him. Just as adults light up when talking about what a good kid Abdi H. is, younger players speak of Maslah in awed tones.

In late spring of 2015, Fuller caught wind that Maslah, who last played soccer for Lewiston his sophomore year, might come back. Rumors sparked that McGraw was recruiting talent to ensure a championship title, and that Maslah, who'd played as a freshman and junior for Edward Little, was shopping around for the best team. Maslah was used to gossip and trash talk. No matter where he landed, people called him a turncoat, a traitor, asking why he moved so much. "Keep your mouth shut," he said whenever gossip reached him. "You don't know anything about me."

Finally, Maslah decided to tell his story, hoping to quell the chatter. He sat for an interview with Kevin Mills, writer of the *Sun Journal*'s thoughtful, award-winning series about the impact of immigrants on local soccer, "Fútbol (R)evolution." Just a few minutes into their conversation, Mills realized that while Maslah's story started like those of so many refugees, his had an added layer of tragedy.

Maslah's parents, Salima Nuh and Abdi Maalim, married in Bu'aale, a farming city in the southern Jubba River Valley. She was seventeen years old; he was nineteen. Soon after, the horrors of civil war came to their door. The young couple lost everything as their village burned, and Nuh, like so many other Bantu women, was brutally assaulted. The couple began the dangerous two-week excursion to the Kenyan border. Their journey was typical: hiding from roaming militia during the day, traveling only at night, trying to avoid bandits looking to rob and rape, including the guards policing the Kenyan borders against invaders. Finally, the couple hired a car to complete the trip.

Life in Dadaab was tough, the dangers of refugee camp life always lurking. When out getting wood with some other women, again Nuh was raped. Getting out of the camps became even more urgent.

In 2004, they landed in Bridgeport, Connecticut, but soon headed north to Lewiston. Nuh became active in the community, building on some of the training she had received in Kenya on peace education and conflict resolution. She helped launch a number of initiatives for women in particular. One program connected women who did not speak English with jobs cleaning houses. Another helped them get their driver's licenses.

Maslah attended Lewiston schools until eighth grade, playing organized soccer for the first time in middle school. But when his parents' relationship grew strained, he moved across the Androscoggin to Auburn. His freshman year at Edward Little, he was the soccer team's top scorer. His home life still unstable, in 2013 he returned to Lewiston, playing his sophomore season alongside middle school friends. While competing for the Blue Devils meant playing with a deeper talent pool, Maslah still stood out, netting ten goals.

The Blue Devils made it to the regional final that year, as they had the year before, but lost. For Maslah, dropping the game paled to what happened a few weeks later. His mother, thirty-seven years old and seven months pregnant with her eleventh child, left

At the UNHCR refugee camp in Kakuma, Kenya, children play volleyball and soccer, mainstays during their time at the camp, where many in Lewiston's Somali Bantu community lived before relocating. *(Stash Wislocki)*

Abdikadir Negeye in his office at Maine Immigrant and Refugee Services. Founded as the Somali Bantu Youth Association, which created some of the first soccer teams in Lewiston for refugee youth, today MEIRS offers extensive support programs from offices in both Lewiston and Portland. *(Amy Bass)*

Shobow Saban, who played soccer for Lewiston High School and then returned to Lewiston to work for MEIRS, runs down a ball during the annual LHS alumni game at Drouin Field. "Soccer to me is not just kicking around, playing around," he says. "It's beyond that." *(Amy Bass)*

Assistant Coach Dan Gish and Coach Mike McGraw huddle with the team before a summer game at Drouin Field. In the distance, many of the players' mothers, who make *sambusa* for the concession stand and provide emotional support for their sons, have a huddle of their own. *(Amy Bass)*

The Blue Devils listen to Coach McGraw during an early fall practice at Marcotte Park. In the background, the spires of the Basilica of Saints Peter and Paul serve as a reminder of Lewiston's French-Canadian immigrant history. *(Amy Bass)*

As Coach McGraw offers one of his legendary pregame speeches, defender Abdiaziz Shaleh listens with deference. McGraw has used the rules of the game to bring kids of all backgrounds to the team, emphasizing the need for them to work together on the field and off. *(Amy Bass)*

Abdullahi Abdi, who coaches Lewiston Middle School's eighth-grade team and works with the high school freshmen in the summer, offers Muktar Ali a bit of sideline advice at a summer game. "The coach of everyone," community leader Abdikadir Negeye says about Abdi. *(Amy Bass)*

Assistant coaches Abdijabar Hersi and Dan Gish plot defensive strategies before a game. In 2014, Hersi became the first Somali coach hired by the high school's athletic department. *(Amy Bass)*

Always one to show off his moves, Maulid Abdow practices his handspring flip throw during gym class at Lewiston High School. By his junior year, the move became a weapon for the Blue Devils, as opponents had difficulty gauging where the ball was going to land. *(Amy Bass)*

Shafea Omar, Maulid's mother, takes in a summer soccer game at Drouin Field, shouting advice to her son and his teammates as only a mother can. *(Amy Bass)*

Abdi Shariff-Hassan and Moe Khalid practice intricate footwork, their ever-present Beats headphones keeping them focused and in sync. *(Amy Bass)*

Abdi Shariff-Hassan, Karim Abdulle, and Hassan "Q" Qeyle celebrate Abdi H.'s second-half goal against twin city rival Edward Little in the playoffs. The Blue Devils won the game 5–0, outshooting their opponents 22–2. *(Russ Dillingham,* Lewiston Sun Journal*)*

Maslah Hassan celebrates his second-half goal in the playoff game against Hampden Academy with Joe Kalilwa and cousin Maulid Abdow. The Blue Devils' victory meant a trip back to the state final. *(Daryn Slover,* Lewiston Sun Journal*)*

Muktar Ali's older brother Mohamed, who once played for Lewiston and is wearing one of his brother's extra jerseys, takes to the field to embrace his former coach to celebrate the Blue Devils' first state championship in soccer. "I was comfortably numb," McGraw says of the moment. "Like that song? Now I know what that means." (*Daryn Slover,* Lewiston Sun Journal)

Austin Wing runs into goalkeeper coach Per Henrikson's open arms seconds after the Blue Devils clinch their first state championship. Wing recovered from a brutal second-half collision to finish the game as goalie and celebrate. (*Daryn Slover,* Lewiston Sun Journal)

Lewiston teacher Ronda Fournier attempts crowd control as Blue Devils fans, including many former players, celebrate at Fitzpatrick Stadium. "All the kids wanted to celebrate," remembers Athletic Director Jason Fuller. "It was really overwhelming." *(Justin Pelletier, Lewiston Sun Journal)*

Maulid Abdow, Abdi Shariff-Hassan, Zak Abdulle, Ben Doyle, and their teammates climb up the bleachers to share the state championship trophy with family and friends. "They deserved it as much as we did," Abdi H. said. *(Daryn Slover, Lewiston Sun Journal)*

for work in nearby Brunswick in her Volkswagen Passat. She never made it. Robert Robataille, a fifty-two-year-old captain and paramedic for the Brunswick Fire Department, apparently fell asleep at the wheel of his pickup truck while driving west on Route 196 in Topsham near the Lisbon town line. As his truck headed down a steep hill, it crossed the centerline and drifted into oncoming traffic, colliding with Nuh's eastbound car. The hospital treated Robataille for mild injuries and released him. Nuh died in the crash.

For Maslah, the death of his mother meant yet another move for the already itinerant family. Soccer was the one thing he didn't need to pack each time he crossed the river. No matter where he lived, he played every day. It was his outlet. When he needed to, he took a ball outside—anywhere, no matter what the weather— to dribble and kick until he felt better. It was more than a coping mechanism. Soccer gives him, he says, a little bit of hope when he needs it. Like so many of his friends, soccer is his everything.

Maslah returned to Edward Little for junior year. While he had a great soccer season as the go-to offensive guy, the Red Eddies sat, season finished, while the Blue Devils made their failed championship run against Cheverus.

As McGraw started to put together his 2015 summer schedule, plotting the team's path back to the championship game, Maslah paid Fuller a visit. He made his priorities clear: he wanted to play soccer for Lewiston. However, Fuller wouldn't leave anything to chance. "I am happy to see you," he told the lanky teenager. "But I have to make sure everything is on the up-and-up."

As Lewiston High School principal, Shawn Chabot relies on people like the athletic director to do their jobs, and do them well. The school is too big to operate any other way. Chabot had to sign Maslah's transfer, but he trusted Jason Fuller to make sure everything was aboveboard.

While Fuller looks military, Chabot *is* military, serving as first sergeant in the medical unit of the National Guard in Augusta. He took the reins of LHS in February of 2015, when Gus LeBlanc's replacement didn't work out. Before that, he was principal of the middle school for three years, and of McMahon Elementary for six.

Chabot understood LeBlanc's legacy better than most. Chabot grew up in Dexter, Maine, home of the eponymous shoe company. He is French-Canadian on his father's side; his mother hails from Harlingen, Texas, located in the heart of the Rio Grande Valley, where her family moved from Mexico.

About a ninety-minute drive northwest from Lewiston, Dexter essentially shut down when the shoe manufacturer left. Chabot, born Christmas Eve in 1970, was the last baby born in the local hospital before it closed on New Year's Day. Chabot grew up just down the street from LeBlanc in Dexter and played on one of his state championship football squads.

"I always looked up to him, feared him, like, scared to death of him," Chabot remembers. "As a football coach, he was the *real* deal."

Although a football guy, Chabot knew about Lewiston's soccer team through his college roommate, Dan Gish. Chabot knew a lot of the players, understood that soccer was their passion and that the loss to Cheverus weighed heavily on them. He knew that beyond the game, the team was a group of nice kids—"good human beings."

When rumors about Maslah's return began to circulate, Chabot had been principal for only a few months. But he already had confidence in Fuller and the coaches to do the right thing. In June, Fuller put things into motion; made some phone calls, poked around. His investigation ended with a home visit. As he pulled up to the address on Allen Court, he smiled. He knew this building; a friend owned it. Years ago, Fuller himself had lived there, occupying an apartment on the first floor. *This is legit,* he thought. *Maslah is back.*

When Fuller told McGraw that everything checked out, the coach smiled when he heard Maslah's new address. He, too, knew the place well; his grandmother had once lived there. He'd spent many a Sunday dinner, adults speaking French and kids speaking English, in Maslah's new home.

Maulid, for one, was excited about Maslah's return. The two are cousins, although neither is sure how they are related.

"Maslah is like a brother to me," Maulid says. Maslah, too, felt good about playing on a team with family.

But McGraw wanted to make sure he had his ducks in a row. He called Matt Andreasen, Edward Little's coach, to assure him he hadn't helped persuade Maslah to move back. "I wouldn't do that," he told the rival coach. "I just want what's best for the students."

There was more to hash out than Maslah's residency. Andreasen had counted on Maslah as a star player, while McGraw saw him as one component of a very deep team. Abdi H. scored twenty-five goals in 2014; Karim, fourteen. Both were returning. McGraw needed to make sure Maslah understood that. The two talked about the role shift. McGraw wanted to put Maslah at striker and move Karim back to the midfield. "Are you capable," McGraw asked Maslah, "of playing *a* role, not *the* role, on this team?"

The role of a star player versus the strength of the team is a popular debate in sports. The final of the Men's World Cup in 2014, for example, posed Lionel Messi against a deep German squad. While Argentina's captain took home the Golden Ball for best player, he couldn't overturn his team's 1–0 extra-time loss.

Maslah listened to teammates, friends, coaches, teachers, and Fuller. It was tough to leave EL, where he was doing well academically. But the pull of family, the pull of Lewiston, and the pull of McGraw, someone Maslah saw as a second father, won out. Maslah trusted almost no one, but he trusted McGraw. He knew his coach would help him, both on and off the field. "Screw it," he told friends. "I just want to play soccer. Lewiston is home. It's where everything started. Besides," he said mischievously, "if you can't beat 'em, join 'em."

The phrase accompanied his senior photo in the yearbook.

Maslah joined the Blue Devils for summer games, where his teammates started to accept him again. But McGraw was uncomfortable with the "traitor" label tattooed on Maslah's shoulders. This team didn't need any additional drama as they pulled themselves back into the hunt for a state title. Summer games were an important time to work things out as a team; to experiment, communicate, and gather. He worried that Maslah's return might threaten these efforts and considered whether he should even let the rising senior play. Eventually, he compromised, making Maslah sit out the summer game against Edward Little. Tensions during that game would be bad enough, McGraw reasoned. They didn't need to add to it by putting Maslah on the field.

McGraw tried not to get too excited about Maslah's return. Kids came and went, he knew, especially immigrant kids. They hit the pitch over summer and disappeared come fall. But then he looked at Q, ready to tear up the midfield after spending his junior year in upstate New York. Sure, they'd graduated some good players. Mike. Speedy. Ibrahim. But the idea of adding Maslah to the core of returning veterans, to see Maslah play alongside Abdi H. and Karim and—

McGraw stopped himself. Not yet. It wasn't time to think about it yet.

When summer season ended and Maslah came to tryouts, McGraw finally began to reconfigure his game plan. He realized that Maslah wasn't the same kid who'd played for him in 2013. Maslah exhibited far more maturity, physical and mental. He reassured McGraw that he knew it wasn't always about scoring or getting the assist. The team had one goal: to return to the state final and win.

Still, McGraw worried. He worried that Maslah and Abdi H. might compete against each other for goals. He worried about the impact their relationship might have on the rest of the team. He asked Coach Abdi and Kim Wettlaufer what they thought about the two stars playing together. "It will be fine," both said. He talked to Maslah and Abdi H. "Don't worry," they told him. "We're good. We've been playing together, 365 days a year, since fifth grade." For Abdi H., welcoming Maslah defined what it meant to be on a team; something he thought about a lot. Maslah's return helped him understand it better.

"Everybody tries to work together to accomplish that one goal," he says about the day he learned Maslah was definitely back. "Trying to do your own thing is not as fun."

Abdi H.'s perspective about Maslah speaks volumes about him as a person and a player. Taking the role of captain very seriously, Abdi H. was always as supportive of the weakest member of the team as he was of the best. Going into his senior year, he was on track to be the highest-scoring soccer player in the school's history. He knew his numbers, but he wasn't worried about what having Maslah up front would mean for them. He just wanted that state trophy.

In many ways, Abdi H. doesn't see in himself the leader that others do. Every time Eric Wagner visits Lewiston from Swarthmore, he is jolted by how special a player Abdi H. is, and not just from a coach's perspective.

"He could've gone one of two ways—could've been a real arrogant, obnoxious braggart who doesn't really do any good for his team or his community," Wagner says. "But this kid is one of the most humble, soft-spoken, respectful, mature, intelligent kids to come out of Lewiston ever—and not just school smarts; people smarts, emotional smarts."

Wagner takes a moment to think about the respect he has for the young player. "It's unbelievable," he says, his voice more quiet. "Interacting with him is a really unique experience."

Watching Abdi H. play is a singular experience as well, one that leaves both fans and local sportswriters scratching their heads. More incredible than his speed, which is awesome, is his creativity, his unpredictability. He sees things on the field that no one else can, does things nobody expects.

"He's got a mentality for the game that is in a fourth dimension, a dimension of virtuoso musicians, incredible artists, unbelievable writers—people like that just have it," observes Wagner of watching Abdi H. play.

Already one of the best in the state, the summer before his senior year, Abdi H. somehow managed to get better, doubling down on his already strong work ethic. Not one to cruise on natural talent and athleticism, he worked on his game, his side-to-sides and feints, his free kicks and corners. He bettered his ability to move the ball downfield, using his agility to stop and start, skip and hesitate, beating opponents at every angle. He stayed up late watching soccer online; studying the game, thinking about strategies the team could develop. He watched soccer at Bates, taking notes on team communication.

With this intense focus, his already creative approach to the sport became even more innovative. Wagner remembers one game that summer in which the rising senior did something that utterly shocked him. A ball was coming in at a very sharp angle to Abdi H.'s run. Gauging how fast he was flying across the field, Wagner figured he would take the ball in stride and turn it in the direction he was already heading.

Abdi H. had other plans.

He flicked the ball behind the defender chasing him. He then made a sharp cut back onto the ball, leaving himself alone to goal. As the ball swished into the net, Wagner sat, stunned, wishing there was an instant replay so he could dissect what he'd just seen. It wasn't only speed. It was seeing an angle, a different facet on the field, that no one else saw, and then exploiting it in the blink of an eye.

By mid-August, the team was back together, gearing up for the twenty-team tournament that Lewiston hosts annually. The captains—Maslah, Karim, Austin, and Abdi H.—had to design a tournament shirt. Austin and Abdi H. took on the task. Austin envisioned a giant soccer ball on the front of a bright blue shirt encircled by "LEWISTON SOCCER." But what about the back? They needed a phrase that captured just how important this season, and the quest for a state title, was going to be.

It hit Abdi H. one night while watching soccer, as usual. The slogan for U.S. Soccer: "One Nation, One Team." He looked up the slick World Cup campaign on YouTube. It perfectly encapsulated how he felt about the coming season. Soccer is not just a game; it's not just a sport. It's life. They just had to alter the first part and add a third phrase.

"*Many* Nations, One Love," he texted Austin. "One Team."

Austin agreed. He would tell the Booster Club to order them.

Shirts done, it was time to start double sessions: morning and afternoon practices held on the same day. After McGraw spent a week at Old Orchard Beach with his family, an annual tradition where he stayed out late on the pier to eat French fries and listen to live music, he was ready to jump in, excited and nervous. He still got the jitters right before the first practice. *I just need to get past the first day,* he thought. *Once we're in our routine, it will all shake out.*

During preseason, McGraw wakes up around four o'clock. He has a hard time sleeping, his mind plotting and planning morning practices. Freshmen and sophomores were at eight o'clock; juniors and seniors at nine-thirty. At five p.m., he mixed everyone up and started again.

Preseason days are long, finally ending around ten p.m. on the last day, when McGraw posts the roster on the glass doors of the gymnasium entrance. As word spreads about the roster, players descend upon the school. They snap photos of the white sheets through the glass, the flashes reflecting back at them. A chain of texts erupts, the roster making its way from phone to phone. There always are a few surprises. "Expect the unexpected," McGraw says. He has listened to his assistants, had long conversations with Coach Abdi. These white sheets represent the team he thinks has the best shot to bring home that elusive state championship trophy.

The 2015 Lewiston Blue Devils.

CHAPTER 12

INSHALLAH,
WE GOT THIS

It was a good thing.

That's what McGraw says when asked about the preseason loss to Scarborough before the official start of the 2015 season. Because of the way the conferences work within Maine's Class A soccer, Lewiston couldn't face Scarborough until the playoffs. Although he would scout a few games across the season, McGraw wanted an early look at the Red Storm, still believing with every bone in his body that they'd be coming for them. Lewiston would return to the state final, he insisted, and Scarborough would be waiting.

"That's the team we're gonna have to beat," he'd told his players on that terrible bus ride home almost a year ago. "And they're gonna be very ready and very motivated."

He shared his premonition with Mark Diaz, head coach of Scarborough and someone McGraw and his assistant coaches had a great deal of respect for. "There's no way in hell you're going to lose to Cheverus again," McGraw said. "We have that in common." But it scared McGraw. While he worried about everything—from Ramadan to academic eligibility—facing Scarborough was the only thing he truly was afraid of. Unlike Lewiston and its string of playoff woes, Scarborough was no stranger to winning, having taken the state title in 2012 and 2013, 2008 and 2009, 2005, and for four straight years in the 1970s.

Could Lewiston beat Scarborough?

Not in preseason. On a Thursday afternoon during the second week of tryouts, Scarborough beat Lewiston 2–1. It didn't count, but it meant something. As always, McGraw chalked it up to a learning experience. He knew he had a talented team—the stars were aligning for an unprecedented amount of talent on the varsity roster. Dek was academically eligible, ensuring a formidable backline with Moe and Zak. Maslah and Q were back. Nuri had stepped up. Muktar was not far behind. Karim's versatility was unparalleled. Austin was on track to break every goalkeeper record he could. And Abdi H. was, well, Abdi H. But McGraw needed to see what would happen when a top team pushed them.

"The one thing I was worried about: were we gonna lose composure?" McGraw says, reflecting on the loss. "And we lost composure. We lost composure to a championship-caliber team."

McGraw saw what he needed to see. It was what preseason was for. Summer games showed him some surprises; players he didn't expect to shine sometimes did. The first part of the regular season, he focused on making adjustments. Midseason, he solidified the game plan. In the last weeks of regular-season play, he mentally prepared them for playoffs.

Against Scarborough, McGraw saw Muktar get lazy or timid—he wasn't sure which—and the other players get mad at him. He saw Zak lose his temper and get a red card. He saw how Karim reacted when his brother got ejected. He saw how the team responded when its leaders got stressed. But most of all, he saw how the team behaved when put into uncomfortable positions, play after play, from their communication to their strategy to their spirit.

After the loss, McGraw sat them down on the field to talk. They weren't leaving, he told them, until every single player understood there would be no finger-pointing, no matter what happened. They had to understand this.

"You point fingers at your teammates," he said, a trace of mid-season rasp already noticeable, "you're not really a team player, because you're selfish."

Selfish. Once he spit it out, the rasp replaced by emotion and force, he let it hang in the air. There was no room for interpretation. McGraw could not be clearer: he was not going to tolerate any excuses this season. None.

"You start making excuses—'the referees this,' or 'their player that'—you're making excuses for things that are out of your control."

Like the players, Gish listened to McGraw. But he didn't hear him.

The season opener against Brewer High School on the Saturday of Labor Day weekend was, by all accounts, a rough game. Gish hated it when a game got so physical. *This isn't intent to play,* he thought. *This is intent to injure.* There was a thin line between defending well—gamesmanship—and all-out mayhem. This was leaning toward the latter. One guy took a run at Maslah from thirty yards out, slamming into him, studs up, nailing his knee. No call. When Gish raised objections to an official, he got a yellow card for his efforts. Incensed, he held his tongue for the remaining time on the clock.

After the game was over, a 4–2 win with goals from Nuri, Abdi H., Maslah, and Abdiaziz "Shaleh" Shaleh, Gish couldn't let it go. The game crossed the line in the second half as Brewer learned what it could get away with. He approached the other referee, calmly, he thought, taking deep breaths. This was just a fact-finding mission, he assured himself. "That was just a poorly officiated game," Gish said, his usually earnest-sounding voice with a bit of an edge, his round eyes stretching wide. The ref looked at him, incredulous. *Oh, no*, thought Gish. He knew: another yellow card. Two yellows make a red. Gish was out.

In soccer, referees issue cards to note particularly egregious fouls. Refs carry two kinds of cards, yellow and red, in their shirt pocket. A yellow card is a formal warning for unsporting behavior: holding an opponent; delaying the restart of play; entering or leaving the field without the referee's permission; or arguing with an official. According to the rules of the Maine Principals Association (MPA), the offender leaves the game, replaced by a sub, but can reenter after a period of time.

A red card marks a serious foul, or when a player receives a second yellow. With a red, a player immediately leaves the game, cannot be replaced, and is forbidden to play the next game on the schedule. Straight reds are serious business, often given because a player exhibits excessive force. Slide tackles from behind, over-the-top tackles where a player strikes an opponent with his cleats, and two-footed tackles are all grounds for red. Spitting, too, can bring out a red, as can holding an opponent to stop a breakaway, preventing an opportunity to score. Inappropriate or threatening language is another surefire way to be sent off the field.

Gish had just gotten thrown out of a game that was not only over—his team had won. He would miss Lewiston's next game.

"You know you pretty much just cost us any chance at any kind of sportsmanship awards this season," Jason Fuller later fumed at Gish in his office. "You are right in what you say; it's just how you say it."

"You know what? I promise I'm not going to screw this thing up," Gish replied, thinking about games ahead, the mission they were on. "Not for you, and not for the players."

For Gish, it was more than the potential season of this stacked team. It was about behaving like a coach. He admired McGraw's ability to keep his head, practice what he preached. Gish knew he had to do a better job keeping the peace, never mind holding his tongue after a victory.

Three days later, Gish, sidelined by the red card, scouted Camden Hills while the Blue Devils beat Skowhegan 13–0 in the first of a string of four shutouts. McGraw tried to keep the score down, replacing Austin with Alex and pulling starters to give everyone a chance to play. But the defense blocked everything Skowhegan had, and the offense didn't stop, no matter how deep McGraw went into the bench, totaling some thirty shots on goal. Abdi H. and Maslah had hat tricks, Karim added two, and Shaleh, Nuri, Muktar, Ben Musese, and Abdirizak Ali each scored once.

As the Blue Devils got ready to board the bus to Bangor for their third game, McGraw realized that he had a full roster for the first time in the season. Academic eligibility wasn't the only thing that could bench a player. So-called citizenship infractions could, too. McGraw's expectations were the law, regardless of circumstances. No practice? No game. Late to practice? Late into game. Mouth off to a teacher? Take a seat. Act stupid? Do some laps.

One defender sat out the first two games of the season because he'd thrown punches at a kid at the last game of the summer season. Fuller benched another for taking food from the girls' field hockey potluck in the cafeteria and then arguing with a custodian about it. "Idiots," McGraw affectionately called them, always shaking his head when he caught wind of their various infractions. He meant it the way the Red Sox did when describing the merry band that won the World Series in 2004. The Blue Devils would play only two games with a full roster for the entire 2015 season, but it didn't faze McGraw.

"It's their responsibility to be able to play," he says. "If we lose, it's still on them, not me. They have to be able to play."

Years ago, McGraw arrived at practice to find a freshman on a tractor the parks department had left on the practice field. The kid pushed the button and started it, but didn't know how to turn it off.

"We didn't play a lot of soccer that day," McGraw remembers. "We did a *lot* of running."

Today, McGraw better understands how complicated the lives of some of his players and their parents are. Post-traumatic stress, poverty, confusion, isolation, and instability follow refugees no matter where or how they land. In many ways, their very existence is a victory. Many players' parents can't worry about how their sons are getting to practice or if they have a water bottle. They are in a constant battle to recover from the unspeakable things they have suffered as they struggle to make things work in America, especially for their children.

But McGraw's role is to teach them about being on a team. When the first Somalis came on board, McGraw learned that they had a different set of responsibilities at home than he was used to hearing about. It wasn't just about understanding Ramadan or daily prayer rituals; it was about family. While his players didn't have the same kind of responsibilities at home as their sisters, who cooked, cleaned, and cared for younger siblings while their mothers worked, allegiance to family still came before team. Dressed and ready for practice, they might suddenly be asked by their parents to go to an appointment or stay home with a younger sibling.

"Sometimes they just randomly call you and say, 'I need you to come for me,'" says Abdi H. about serving as his parents' translator. "It's our parents, so we go do it for them."

McGraw didn't want soccer to create a wedge between a player and his family or his culture. He watched how kids who assimilated too rapidly into so-called American life tended to stray from the straight and narrow. "Keep your culture," he told them. "Stay close to your parents. We will figure this out."

Working full-time for Maine Refugee and Integration Services, the former SBYA, after graduating from Assumption College, Shobow appreciates McGraw's evolving approach. McGraw understood that it wasn't the tenets of Islam that made life in America complicated. It was culture, identity.

"It's the food, the language, the way we speak, the way we behave," says Shobow. "All of it." There are logistical challenges as well. Transportation is a problem when practice takes place at the field on Randall Road, more than four miles from the high school. With parents working multiple jobs, these kids don't have anyone who can cart them around. McGraw remembers one early-morning August practice at Randall when nine players stumbled out of a cab, making it with seconds to spare after pooling their money for the fare. Another player started for practice every morning before sunrise, walking to the field early enough so he could take a nap, rest, before McGraw arrived.

Over time, listening to his players, learning from them, McGraw made adjustments.

"Maybe you don't come to practice, and then you won't start, but it doesn't mean you won't play," he now tells them. "It's not your fault, I get it, but it's the reality of being on a team. You have to learn the consequences of your actions, because the guy we're playing against? He didn't skip practice."

But as with any other team, sometimes getting benched has nothing to do with family or culture. Fuller deals with most of the disciplinary actions, taking flak from all sides—parents, the front office, and the coaches of other teams. But there's no leeway when it comes to rules.

"I don't care how good you are," he repeats often. "We have standards and expectations."

In 2014, Fuller could have let the suspended players back on the team for the state final against Cheverus. There was only one day left in their suspension, and the principal left the decision up to Fuller. But he wouldn't budge. "Part of learning to win is learning how to behave," he insists. "They are good kids, but it's part of being a student-athlete. No bending, no matter what the circumstance."

It took time for Fuller's football-loving head to grasp some of soccer's idiosyncrasies. He didn't get why every goal had to be celebrated like it was the first one ever scored, with the jumping, the somersaults, and the slides. The memory of the "taunting" call at the Mt. Ararat game still haunts him, agony flooding his usually congenial face at its mention. Fans have to be held back, and players have to take it down a notch, he asserts. It's part of winning.

So before the team left for Bangor, Fuller told McGraw that he wanted to talk to the team, knowing it was the first time of the 2015 season that no one was out because of suspensions or injuries. McGraw knew Fuller's perspective was important. As AD, he had eyes and ears on the whole state.

The team was used to these conversations. Fuller and McGraw often talked to them about behavior on and off the field. With the changing demographics over the last decade or so, Lewiston's reputation was more complicated than ever, and they were responsible for taking care of it. The Brewer game showed how ugly it could get, what kind of stuff they needed to be ready for.

"We constantly have to prove," Abdi H. told his teammates, "that we are better than our reputation."

And not just during games. When the football team had a home game, for example, McGraw encouraged them to go, to support another team, but reminded them to stay together and be gentlemen. Act smart, he'd say. Not stupid.

"You're a special team," Fuller began. "From Kittery to Fort Kent, everybody's talking about you. You're a target for everybody. Anything you do is magnified. It doesn't matter what happens because you're from Lewiston and you were in the state championship last year."

They could not hide for two reasons. One, they were *that* good. Two, the majority of them were black.

"There's a microscope on us," he warned. "Whatever we do comes back."

He looked at the young men before him. Abdi H. Maslah. Karim. Joe. Shaleh. Zak. Q. Nuri. Austin. Maulid. Never in the history of Maine sports had there been such a team. He was sure of it.

"Guys, the worst enemy here is yourself," he said, emotion creeping in. "Don't blow this. Don't. Blow. This."

The team listened. They trusted Fuller, something he couldn't have claimed just a few years back. His door was open to them. They told him about the kind of stuff they encountered on the field, the guys who told them to go back to Africa or used the n-word. The elbows the refs didn't see. They shrugged it off, telling him it didn't matter, that they didn't care. But he took it seriously, as did McGraw, who always encouraged them to take the high road, no matter what.

"If you trash talk," McGraw reminded them before each game, always the same speech, "then you can expect somebody else to retaliate. If you say nothing and the only guys you talk to are your teammates, you're gonna be fine. But if you call someone a name, you damn well better expect they're gonna call you a name. And don't come complaining to me if you're the perpetrator."

Finally, they boarded the bus for Bangor, and the usual chaos ensued. Singing, clapping, dancing, cheering. Arriving almost two hours later, the varsity squad prepared to watch the junior varsity game. Thinking about Fuller's remarks, McGraw reminded them, again, to be quiet and respectful, to just watch the game, and—

"Coach."

McGraw stopped and looked at Karim, shocked. Shocked to be

interrupted, for sure, but even more shocked that it was Karim, tall and lean, rubbing the scruff on his chin, his eyes flitting up and down, belying his normally calm demeanor. Karim didn't speak much. He never has. Unlike Zak, who plays soccer with joy on his sleeve, passionately directing traffic from the backline, Karim plays with quiet confidence, his vast understanding of the game evident in every powerful move. Off the field, his soft nature, especially when contrasted with Zak's nonstop chatter, means he rarely utters a word, and certainly not in front of a group. But now he had something to say.

"Coach," Karim repeated. He looked at McGraw, solemn. "We got this."

Coming from Karim, those four words were a veritable speech. They echoed what the team had been saying for months, through the long winter when they kicked balls beside towering snowbanks, at hot summer games while they fasted, and during evenings at Somali Stadium. "Inshallah," they answered when someone asked about winning a state championship. If God wills.

Everyone knew that was what Karim was really saying. *Inshallah,* we got this.

McGraw gazed at the team. There was a look in their eyes he'd never seen before. They were about to face one of the strongest teams on the schedule. He nodded, sensing that he needed to let them get started.

"Go warm up."

If the team's warm-up process in summer is fun to watch, before a game it gets downright intimidating. In unison, clapping and chanting, stretching and jogging, they convey without a doubt they are one team.

"Open the gate!" Abdi H. called, and the team seamlessly switched from its "windows" formation.

McGraw marveled at their method, pausing to watch as they

created four lines, moving through toy soldiers and squat lunges. That look was still in their eyes, he noticed.

"I don't know if this is going to be good or bad," he said to Gish. "But I guess we will find out."

It took only fifty-seven seconds to score their first goal. By minute seven, they had grabbed a 2–0 lead. They won 5–0, taking twenty-six shots total. Bangor had thought the home-field advantage would help. Bangor was wrong.

The following Saturday, the offensive onslaught continued as the Blue Devils shut out Lawrence High School, Muktar scoring the first of their eleven goals. Posting double digits for the second time in only four games, Lewiston seemed determined to erase the perception that soccer is a low-scoring game. Lawrence's goalie, Tim Weymouth, made twenty-eight saves. Austin and Alex combined for two.

With his team leading 5–0 at the half, McGraw pulled starters, worrying they'd become the most hated team in the league. He could hear Fuller in his head: "That's enough, Coach."

Abdi H. never complains about coming out. He knows that in a tight game, he will play the whole thing. Still on track to be the highest-scoring player in school history, he didn't worry about his numbers or wonder what they would be if McGraw left him in.

Pulling starters gave McGraw a chance to experiment with the bench. He decided to put in junior Benjamin Musese. Tall and lean, Ben is described by teammates as intense and competitive. Whether vying for a shot on goal or playing video games at home, he has little patience for failure. The only school day he ever missed was when he became an American citizen.

Ben came to Lewiston from the Democratic Republic of the Congo via Tanzania. He was just four years old when he fled his village on the back of his eight-year-old brother, escaping to the woods to hide from the warring factions who invaded. Ben's twin sister never made it.

Now that he is secure in Maine, Ben's love of soccer is ferocious. He plays it, he says, no matter what country he is in, and enjoys teaching it to kids at the community center, seeing himself as a role model. Off the field, he roots for Bayern Munich, and in winter and spring, he is a top triple jumper on the track team. Without soccer, he says, he cannot be happy. Without a championship, he worries, McGraw cannot be happy.

While McGraw knew Ben was powerful and fast, he wanted him to work on his shots, which lacked precision.

"He has no inside foot," McGraw commented to Gish. "We can't beat it out of him, so let's just let him go."

The cushion against Lawrence presented the perfect opportunity to let Ben hone his skills, so McGraw sent him in. He smiled when Ben scored, looking at Gish. This was a good idea. But then Ben scored again. And again. And again. Ben scored four times inside of thirty minutes. So much for keeping the score down.

The "Battle of the Bridge" with cross-river rival Edward Little came next; another shutout win, 6–0. Lewiston scored quickly, as had become its habit, and never stopped. Abdi H. had a hat trick; Muktar, Karim, and Maslah added one each.

"Shell-shocked," Coach Andreasen said of his team, outshot 25–1.

Early-minute goals built instant momentum for the Blue Devils, giving them time to settle in while throwing their opponent off-balance. The Red Eddies appeared stunned by Lewiston's sophisticated footwork. The Blue Devils ran over balls without touching them, moving so fast that the Red Eddies didn't know they were faking until the ball was already headed in another direction.

Maslah had no problem scoring on his old teammates. His presence in a Lewiston uniform upped the ante of an already electric rivalry, making for a rougher, more frustrating game than the scoreboard indicated. Moe got a red card in the first half for head-butting a kid who said something about his mother. He thought it was worth it. *Hooyadu waa lama huran,* Somalis say. It's not necessary to live with a mother; it's hard to live without a mother. *Sid iyo sagaal bilood ayaa hoyadaa ku so wadey.* Your mother was holding and raising you for nine months in her stomach. Moe couldn't let the kid off the hook, his temper taking over as it sometimes did.

"Anger is his biggest weakness, something he's got to work on," McGraw says of Moe. "He kicks himself in the ass all the time. He's gonna be successful if he takes care of that demon."

The Blue Devils were unfazed playing a man down. If anything, Andreasen later said, they played better after Moe's ejection. McGraw agreed. "This just gives us more space to move," he told the team. "Our packed offense can't be stopped." Abdi H. concurred; he saw it all the time in premier league games. He knew EL would try to attack more, giving him more opportunities to take the ball away from them.

Thanks for the hat trick, he thought.

Beating EL was a big deal. It's how sports rivalries work. But McGraw wanted to keep the early success in perspective. The team got stronger with each game, but it was only September. They would pay the price for complacency, he reminded them.

Between games, they practiced hard at Marcotte Park, a wide-open grassy space on the other side of the Colisée from Drouin. The field sits even higher than the Colisée, the 168-foot-tall twin spires of Saints Peter and Paul providing a dramatic backdrop. Some drive to Marcotte; others walk a path from the high school. Ben rides his bike. As they get ready, stretching on the grass, kicking off slides for cleats, Alex Rivet's mother stops by with a cooler full of frozen candy bars.

"JACKALS!" McGraw yells at them as they dive into the cooler, the food vanishing in mere minutes.

McGraw starts practice with a quick overview of the next team they are going to play, his "This is what we're gonna do" talk. He mentions specific players, sometimes proposing role-playing drills so they can strategize about number six or number twelve.

"They aren't EL," he says, knowing the team is still high from defeating its rival, "but you play 110 percent anyway—and if I don't get it from you starters, remember I've got twenty other guys who will give it to me."

The players solemnly nod. They know.

"Okay," he says, his demeanor lightening a bit. He looks around. He knows they're tired, a bit banged-up. There have been some hamstring issues, some contusions, a few sprains here and there. He needs to make them work, but he also needs to take care of them.

"No hills today, and..." McGraw stops, the immediate cheering too loud for him to continue. "Go do some laps, and STAY TOGETHER!"

The team falls into two lines and takes off, circling the field several times. When they return, the captains take over, Abdi H. calling out warm-up formations, a small smile on his face. So reserved off the field, he works hard to be more vocal on it. He makes sure his teammates get to work as he readies himself, but there is also a lightness about him, joking and laughing. As his muscles loosen, so does his state of mind.

The players are a colorful sight on the field, blue-and-white t-shirts mixing with an array of jerseys from favorite teams. Maulid wears his bright yellow dashiki, challenging Joe to a handstand contest as they run. Maulid nimbly flips forward and backward; Joe uses his upper-body strength to walk on his hands while keeping up with the line.

Practice divides into three groups. Varsity and JV stay with McGraw and Gish; Hersi is with the freshmen on another field; and goalkeeper coach Per Henrikson drills Austin and Alex, relentlessly throwing a variety of balls at them—tennis, football, softball, soccer—to improve their reflexes.

Once reluctant to work with high school kids, Henrikson wasn't looking to go anywhere now, and not just because of the small salary the Booster Club paid him. A giant of a man, long hair usually pulled back into a ponytail, beard unkempt, he has coached all over the world. After stints in the Philippines, India, and Bhutan, he returned to Maine, where he once dominated the basketball courts of Georges Valley High School in Thomaston, to care for his mother. "Intense and controversial" is how McGraw describes Henrikson, who rarely hesitates to tell a ref what he thinks of him, especially if he believes there's a racist element to a call. He worries the players aren't always safe on the field because they're "black, African, Muslim—because they're different." He hopes having Abdijabar Hersi on the sidelines in a blue shirt makes a difference, taking the level of respect up a notch. But he has doubts.

The majority of the team works in groups of three, focusing on two-touch drills. Mastering touch, perfecting how to take and keep control of the ball, is a key fundamental. Good soccer needs it; great soccer demands it.

"Here, here!" Moe calls, dancing from side to side to get his legs warm, his hand in the air. When the ball comes, his return is long and elegant, clearing it without ever looking down. He smiles, a cocky tilt to his head. He knows that was pretty.

"We've got Mt. Blue tomorrow!" McGraw roars, his voice getting thinner. "I want good touches ON THE GROUND! You're better than that! Control the ball! You've got to make yourself better! Warm up your feet!"

Practice is coordinated chaos, with a lion in the middle repeating things in triplicate as he moves about the field.

"TALK, TALK, TALK," McGraw bellows to a group not having much luck with keeping their exchanges to two touches. "Weave in and out—NO WALKING!"

He stops, pointing at a player who isn't jogging to get to the ball, throwing the kid a look that could stop a train.

"IF I SEE YOU WALKING, TEN PUSH-UPS!"

The player drops to the ground and lowers his body, up and down, up and down. The moment the player stands, McGraw roars again.

"PUSH-UP POSITION! FIVE! AND WE'RE GONNA COUNT 'EM LIKE A TEAM!"

The team drops in concert, counting together, McGraw hovering above, making comments that range from a sarcastic uncle to Sergeant Foley. When they're done, he calls for a huddle. It's time to scrimmage, but not until McGraw does what he does best: motivate.

"We need unity!" he begins.

The group huddles tighter, sweat rolling down their faces, their breath coming too fast to pause for water.

"Don't be afraid to shake a guy's hand when you run by, because you're gonna need that camaraderie!"

McGraw grunts, trying to clear the gravel out of his throat.

"Did you hear what I said?" he asks a player whose eyes have drifted to a youth league game across the street, mostly white kids populating the teams.

The player nods.

"Yeah? REPEAT WHAT I SAID!"

The player mumbles something. Satisfied, McGraw gets back to his speech.

"Who wants to score tomorrow?" he asks quietly, ensuring they keep still in order to hear him.

"I do!" a few players yell.

"NOOOOOOOO!" McGraw thunders.

Gish smiles, taking a step back so no one sees. He knows they've fallen into McGraw's trap.

"WE want to score tomorrow!" McGraw grumbles. "WE!"

The players begin to jump on their toes, growling as they come in closer, excitement for tomorrow's game taking over. Getting the team to focus the day before a game is always difficult. They just want to play, their eyes straying to the piles of red, yellow, and blue pinnies on the sideline, waiting for scrimmage.

They scrimmage in small sides, making one-two touch essential because of the tiny space. The ball bounces man-to-man, no one holding possession for more than a split second. The players never look down, their eyes seeking the ball's next target.

"FIND A TEAMMATE!" McGraw yells to a group not passing quickly enough, grabbing Joe. "Use your teammates," he says, pulling Joe's head closer to his own, his arm around the defender's back. "I know, I know, you like to dribble, but you'll get the ball back—you don't need to do this by yourself."

As practice continues, an audience gathers. A group of Somali kids—mostly sophomores—watches, their beat-up bicycles thrown every which way next to them. They play soccer in the park but say they are afraid to play with McGraw's team. They talk about the team in hushed tones, as if Real Madrid is scrimmaging in front of them. When the game across the street ends, parents migrate over to Marcotte. They, too, watch with reverence, pointing out specific plays for their kids to emulate.

Satisfied they've honed their touch, McGraw announces they have twenty-three seconds to prepare for full field drills. As he counts, players frantically get in line, balls returned to the net bags. He emphasizes possession and restricts the number of touches each player can take per drill. It's not the kind of practice McGraw ran thirty years ago, when his burly Franco players practiced booting the ball, trying to gain power and distance with each kick. Possession drills take patience and a lot of coaching. McGraw assigns laps to a handful of guys who are chatting on the end, but overall he is pleased.

"You just broke the crowd's heart!" he jokes to a player who sends the ball over the crossbar.

McGraw felt good. The team was working together, and not just because he was chanting his usual "together, together, together" from the sidelines. There was a spirit in the air that went beyond the seemingly effortless games they were playing. Something just felt different.

The team felt it, too. They needed a new rallying cry, Henrikson told them, something new to chant in their manic huddle before yelling, "One, two, three—*Pamoja ndugu!*" It had to be something uniquely theirs, rather than the U.S. Men's National Team's "I Believe That We Will Win."

"Think about what you're trying to do," Henrikson encouraged them. "Create something."

A group of them found it one night at Karim and Zak's house. Nuri remembered a soccer team he used to like in Jeddah, Al-Ittihad FC, the oldest club in the Saudi Premier League and a featured team in FIFA video games.

"I got it," Nuri said to Karim in Arabic. He looked over at Moe and Zak, who were combing the Internet. "I got it," he said again, this time in Somali so Moe would understand. Because of all the places he lived, Nuri's head contained a potpourri of languages—Arabic, Somali, English, and Turkish. If anyone could find a chant for the team, it was Nuri.

He knew that the passionate intonations of Ittihad fans were legend. He found a recording of one on YouTube and played it for his friends. As he began to write it down, he made tweaks here and there to better suit their team, writing in a colloquial Saudi dialect rather than textbook Arabic.

حبه حبه ‏(يــأكلك)‏
اكل البرشومي (يــأكلك)‏
وكمان إندومي (يــأكلك)‏
هــم هــمــهم (يــأكلك)‏
هاذا ليويستون (يــأكلك)‏
ماماجاأندوجو (يــأكلك)‏

We will eat you slowly, slowly
We will eat you like a prickly pear
We will eat you like noodles
We will eat you, yum yum yum
Lewiston is going to eat you
This is Lewiston, we are family.

"We're gonna beat 'em, we're gonna eat 'em," Nuri said to his friends, grinning.

Yes, this was it. They would teach it to the starters, hoping the others would fall into place. Nuri, despite being a sophomore, would take the lead, working with his teammates in a kind of call and response. He would deliver a line; the team would respond with "YAKULAK!" (WILL EAT YOU!).

It happened at the Mt. Blue game, just two days after Edward Little. Nuri had the team practice on the hour-long bus ride. After McGraw gave his pregame speech, they pressed together, Nuri in the middle.

"Just say 'yakulak' if nothing else," he reminded them, thinking how amazing it was to be doing this, and only a sophomore. He started. They responded. They didn't all know what they were saying—*We are going to eat someone?* Maulid thought—but they did it, together, and then yelled the words they knew by heart: one, two, three! *Pamoja ndugu!*

No question, the team was fired up.

While Lewiston beat Mt. Blue 5–1, the Cougars became the first team to get on the board since Brewer. But the Blue Devils returned to the art of the shutout against Brunswick. The 5–0 victory started fast and furious, with Maslah hitting the net on an assist from Nuri just thirty-two seconds in, beating the goalie from ten yards out. Abdi H. followed a few minutes later, taking the ball from Karim and blasting it into the far corner. He moved so fast, so many steps ahead of everyone else, it felt like there was more than one of him out there. Karim scored twice, and Maslah added another for good measure. Failing to get in a shot the entire first half, the Dragons had only two attempts in the second, and their keeper made an astonishing twenty-three saves.

Seven games into the season, Lewiston stood unbeaten with five shutouts, outscoring opponents 49–3. "It's only September," McGraw continued to warn his squad. "The other teams are getting better." But it didn't feel that way. As they rolled toward the playoffs, it felt like no one could take them on. But McGraw knew who was coming.

Camden Hills.

CHAPTER 13

OUR HOUSE

Before Camden Hills came to Lewiston, the Blue Devils added two more shutouts—Mt. Ararat and Cony—to their unbeaten record. McGraw felt especially good after Mt. Ararat, a midday Saturday home game that left him the afternoon to putter around his house, thinking about what to grill for dinner before sitting on the deck with a cigar, soaking in the last vestiges of summer air.

The Cony game, a 9–0 win, was one for the ages. As Cony stretched, Lewiston circled the field in unison, Zak, Q, and Nuri joking as they ran, amazed to be in shirtsleeves midseason in Augusta. It was fun to play soccer in weather that felt more like the past summer than the winter still to come.

Lewiston's goals came swiftly, players moving so fast, Cony's defense looked like traffic cones. Maslah, who bounded into position to start the game, was particularly energized. He had a mission, inspired by Bayern Munich striker Robert Lewandowski's five goals in less than nine minutes just a few days earlier against Wolfsburg. When Lewandowski came off the bench at the half, Munich was down 1–0. Lewandowski scored a hat trick in four minutes, the fastest in Bundesliga history, starting with a toe poke at minute fifty-one. By the sixtieth, the fans went insane when he scissor-kicked a cross from Mario Gotze into the net.

Although a Liverpool fan, Maslah decided to mimic Lewandowski, using years of playing FIFA video games to spark his creative juices. He'd been frustrated when Fuller yet again made McGraw pull the starters early against Mt. Ararat. He wasn't like Abdi H., who saw it as a sign that they'd done their jobs. It could be a beautiful game with a high score, he countered. And now he had a plan.

"I'm gonna top that," he said before the game, careful to make sure McGraw didn't hear. "I'm gonna do just what Lewandowski did."

It worked. Impossibly fast, Maslah found space on the right three times to score, leaving even the ref shaking his head in astonishment. With two Cony players marking him like glue, he collected the ball in midfield and broke away to score his fourth from the left. As the ball went in, he high-fived Abdi H. and jogged back, almost as if in slow motion compared to the speed he'd just turned on. But he wasn't done. Alone again in the attacking third, one on one with the goalie, he launched a blistering shot with highlight-reel prowess.

Five goals. One game. A school record. Maslah "Lewandowski" Hassan was born.

But Camden Hills wasn't Cony. A regional high school located in Rockport, Camden Hills' students are from the most scenic coastal destinations in Maine. While *Sports Illustrated* once named the school's athletic program the best in the state, in the fall of 2015, after a number of players had been injured in a game, the principal canceled the rest of the football season for a lack of adequate players.

While youth football in the United States has lost some 25,000 kids in the last several years or so, the principal's decision was unpopular. Football coach Thad Chilton acknowledged the impact that soccer's popularity had had on his roster. The negative press about concussions didn't help, with direct connections between chronic traumatic encephalopathy, or CTE, and the sport.

Soccer, too, has concussion problems, but has reaped the benefits of football's shaky future. For both schools and parents, soccer teams are far cheaper to field than football. At the professional level, Major League Soccer, despite struggling in many of its U.S. markets, has grown its audience, increasing ticket sales and sellouts in recent years as football has declined. Without a football team to cheer, for Camden Hills soccer became a focal point of the fall sports schedule.

In 2015, Camden Hills was a new kid in Class A sports, reclassified by the MPA when its enrollment topped the Class B limit by four students. The soccer team had a lot of success in Class B, winning consecutive Eastern Maine titles from 2011 to 2013, and reaching the regional semifinals in 2014. McGraw, with Gish's scouting report in hand, knows to expect a good game. Teams that dotted the coast—Yarmouth, Falmouth, Cumberland, Camden, Brunswick—have stepped up in the last few years, playing year-round in league teams. McGraw doesn't doubt that Camden Hills is ready for the challenge of Class A.

Camden game announcer Charlie Crockett, a longtime teacher and coach, agrees.

"Welcome to Windjammah soccah," he begins his broadcast, noting the early October day boasts "Chambah of Commerce weathah."

Crockett rues how local sports pundits underestimate his team. It is time for people to sit up and take notice.

"Aftah some of these performances, I think they're going to have to staht realizin' this is an exceptional soccah team," Crockett says. "This to me is probably the best soccah team that I have seen at Camden Hills, and maybe seen anywheah, any team."

While Camden Hills warms up on Don Roux field, the Blue Devils get ready in the bowels of the school, several flights down from the gym entrance. Ben sits on a bench, pulling his socks up over his shin guards, looking for tape to wrap around the top to prevent them from falling down. Nearby, Abdi H. adjusts the black-and-white captain's band on his arm.

The locker room is a tight space divided into two sections with bright blue lockers on both sides and benches in between. The smell of bleach and dirty mop water permeates the air. Gish's office sits to one side, the walls covered by his kids' drawings, photographs of players, and shelves of soccer balls signed by teams long graduated. There is usually a Dunkin' Donuts cup—medium coffee regular—that Gish brings for McGraw when he remembers.

A few players can't find their tall socks and ask McGraw for an extra pair. He has no time for such things, pushing them off. When he leaves the room to check on the game camera, they turn to Gish, who quickly grabs extra socks from his office and discreetly hands them out.

"Hey, before Coach gets back, let me just say: don't trash-talk out there," Gish says, remembering his talk with Fuller after his red card. "Don't get into it; let the scoreboard do the talking. They might say things, but don't let them take you out of your game—don't take the bait. Brush it off."

The players continue to get ready. Muktar sits alone on the maroon-painted cement floor against the wall in the corner, quietly lacing up his cleats. Zak, on the other hand, can't sit still, clapping and singing, bouncing from one player to the next, the noise echoing off the concrete. "Try driving to Bangor with Zak," McGraw once joked. "That'll test ya!"

Mwesa and Maulid are huddled over a phone, sharing a pair of earbuds and watching a video. The two shoot short comedic sketches with their friends that are quite funny. But as soon as McGraw returns and begins to pace, the phone disappears, headphones come off, talking ceases, and the clicking of cleats on the floor stops. Gish retreats to his office with Hersi, where they quietly sketch strategies on a small whiteboard. Henrikson grabs Austin and Alex to go outside for goalie drills.

McGraw impatiently waits for all eyes to shift to him. He's a bit tense. He knows Gish and Henrikson don't like Camden. Henrikson, especially, vents about what the refs won't see because a team filled with—as he sees it—a bunch of white, privileged kids is on the field. Despite his reservations about coaching in Lewiston early on, now he loves this team. He doesn't want to see them get hurt.

"NOW," McGraw roars. "Let's talk about something."

He stops to stare at a player fiddling with the roll of white tape Gish handed him a few minutes earlier.

"Does it take *this long* to put on a piece of tape?" he asks.

Regaining focus, McGraw blasts into his usual spiel about sportsmanship and motivation before giving out positions. He refers to the Cony game for examples about what did and didn't work. Moving someone to the outside. Bringing someone to the middle. Positioning Q to distribute the ball to Abdi H. and Maslah.

"Do not shoot with power," he warns those who will be up top. "Shoot with accuracy."

He pauses, looking around the room, shifting between the two sides so no one is looking at his back for too long.

"The most important thing is that we play smart, with poise, but aggressive and with confidence. You go play your game, Lewiston High School's game, *our* game."

Our game. The words hung in the air.

"You play fast, you play hard. When you refuse to lose, when you decide that you're not gonna get beat, you will NOT get beat! The minute you question yourself? You can't question yourself. When you make a decision, you make a decision, and every guy behind you backs you up. It's not one-on-one, it's not three-on-three, it's all of us against all of them. If you're not in the game, you're still in the game. If you're on the field, you know you have ten guys on the bench backing you up."

McGraw takes a breath.

"Those of you on the bench should be ready to go in at any moment," he continues. "We've got a good, strong, deep bench, and the guys in the game, if you give anything less than 110 percent, the guys on the bench are going to be pissed at you because they're sitting there watching *you* play, and if you're there playing half a game, they can play a full game."

They nod. They know.

"Don't you disrespect them. Don't-you-dis-re-spect-them. They are our all-stars, sitting there, waiting to get into the game. For some of you, you've yet to realize how good you are. There's a little switch of maturity that's gonna flip on, and you're gonna become an unbelievable player. But why wait until next year? Why not TODAY? WHY NOT AGAINST CAMDEN HILLS out there on that field?"

McGraw pauses again, gearing up for the big finale. It's time to get these guys up and out. He claps. Each player's head snaps up. They know. This is it. Gish and Hersi recognize their cue, and come into the room.

"They don't call us Dirty Lew!" McGraw yells, his voice straining, the words coming fast and furious as the players surround him until only his white hair is visible. "They call us..."

"SWEET LEW!" the players shout, stomping and pounding.

"Ready?" McGraw asks, putting his hand out. "One, two, three..."

"*PAMOJA NDUGU!*" the team thunders, grabbing their water bottles and bags and jogging out the door, down the hallway, and outside, their eyes squinting at the burst of light.

"We can outrun anybody," McGraw says to Gish as they hoist bags of balls and head out of the fluorescent light. Gish smiles, nods. He knows McGraw is a bit apprehensive about this one.

"We can outrun anybody," Gish echoes.

The Blue Devils cross the parking lot and walk through the gate, jogging past the elaborate webs of the orb weavers who signal that despite the mild weather, winter is coming. The silky gossamer sparkles in the late-day sun, but the players see only the field and the team on it.

The stadium is busy. Inside the Snack Shack, Austin's mom and Mémé are getting things ready, slow cookers heating up, while Denis Wing staffs the grill, hot dogs perfuming the air. Fuller buzzes about in a golf cart, trying to focus nervous energy on his last-minute checklist. A few parents sit in the stands, while Coach Abdi sits apart, wanting space to study the game. Fans Dan and Jeannie Martin choose their usual spot smack in the middle of the stands. Their daughter played soccer years ago for Lewiston, but these days they never miss a boys game, home or away. They started coming, they say, "when they showed up," talking about the Somalis. The team is important, Jeannie affirms. It's not just about Lewiston—all of Maine is watching.

"They don't like playing in the cold," Dan Martin worries, thinking about the latter half of the schedule. The Martins take their fandom seriously and know each player by name, strengths, and weaknesses. "That was the trouble at the Cheverus game."

Music blares from the PA system while the cheerleaders stretch on a blue mat on the track in front of the bleachers, their blue-and-white uniforms complemented by white bows in their hair. Their silver pom-poms shimmer as the sun crawls toward the outlines of downtown to the west, their breath starting to cloud as the air grows cold.

Walking past the visitors' bench to their own, the players drop their backpacks on the ground, saying hello to the handful of freshmen Hersi selected to be ball boys. They move into a double-line formation to start their slow jog around the field. Loping gracefully together, they loosen up, smiling occasionally.

Laps done, they stretch and get into small sides, drilling and dancing, practicing short passes in a sophisticated version of keep-away. Gish, McGraw, and Hersi throw out observations and recommendations, Hersi occasionally taking the ball himself because he just can't help it.

"It's fun!" Gish reminds them, kicking a long, low ball at Alex. "It's a game!"

Now good and warm, they break into two groups to fire balls at Austin as the captains meet with the refs. "Introduce yourselves," the refs instruct them before outlining the rules of the match. "Let's get ready!" McGraw growls as the captains return to the groups, clapping his hands as he reminds the team to put the balls in the bags by the benches.

High in the blue box atop the bleachers, Fuller reels off a string of announcements, including rules about spectators and sportsmanship, before calling the starting lineups for each team. After the players take their places on the field, they turn toward the flag for "The Star-Spangled Banner." As the last notes fade, McGraw brings the players in for final instructions before Nuri takes over for their chant.

"One, two, three, *pamoja ndugu!*" the team finishes.

"Together!" McGraw calls to their backs as they take the field.

The players gather on the grass on their knees in a circle, arms tightly around one another's shoulders, for a moment with the captains.

"ALL ABOARD!" rings out through the stadium as Ozzy Osbourne's voice descends into the "aye, aye, aye" of "Crazy Train."

"Don't focus on the stands," Abdi H. says inside the team circle. "Focus on the game. It doesn't matter who we are playing; we play them like Scarborough, we play them like Cheverus."

"Blue Devils, get out there, get out there, FIGHT!" the cheerleaders begin, signaling that it's game time.

"And let's get an early goal," Moe interjects, "so there's no pressure on defense!"

Good advice. Within five minutes of the first whistle, Maslah grabs possession from a Camden Hills throw-in and rushes to the corner. He sends the ball over to Abdi H., who kicks a short chop to put Lewiston on the board.

"That was a very nice goal!" McGraw calls, appreciating the teamwork.

The bench leaps to its feet in celebration. Gish reminds them to stay calm. They cannot risk getting a yellow card for sideline behavior.

"Let's keep it together."

Wiping his brow with the hem of his shirt, his habit to reset, Abdi H. is glad they got one. He feels more settled. He is nervous playing a team he knows so little about. Before today, he couldn't even find Camden on a map. He knows they are supposed to be a top team. But their record didn't tell him the one thing he really wanted to know: did they play fast or physical? Physical teams are always a worry for the Blue Devils. Worried about playing Lewiston? Just hurt them. Then the speed doesn't matter.

Abdi H. tends to study the game as it unfolds around him until he cracks the opposition's code. Then he breaks out, takes possession, and flies. Now we'll just go at it, he thinks, taking another quick look at the board. But his is the only goal in the first half. Camden, too, settles in and takes its defense up a notch. Gish's scouting report was right; this is no cakewalk.

While McGraw toes the sideline, following the ball, Gish, Hersi, and Henrikson stand back a few feet, operating as McGraw's eyes for the rest of field, calling out numbers for players to mark, yelling "second ball" when a shot doesn't finish, and reminding them to keep the ball on the ground. From the stands, Coach Abdi yells to players in Somali, calling them over to talk when they come out for a breather. A few rows away, Maulid's mother chimes in, giving them an extra encouraging word, taking sips of Gatorade every few minutes while her younger children play nearby. Even when her son comes out, her eyes never leave the field, the game growing increasingly fast-paced and rough.

"Did you *see* Maulid standing there?" McGraw yells, frustrated over a missed pass. "He's going to give me an aneurysm," he mutters.

"Fire up, Big Blue, fire up!" the cheerleaders repeat to the crowd. "Fire up, Big Blue, fire up!"

When a call doesn't go Lewiston's way, Gish shakes his head and walks down the line.

"I've got to give myself a time-out," he yells to no one in particular, thinking about his promise to Fuller.

At the half, McGraw takes the team to the far goalpost, glancing up the hill to the group of old men clustered at the side of the school's driveway. They used to just come for the football games, getting a good view for free, McGraw remembers. Now they watch soccer, too.

As the players splay on the grass, drinking water, sweat dripping down their faces, some of their families come in for the second half, the admission gate now closed. Abdi leaves his perch and crosses to the visitors' side, which will be closer to Lewiston's attacking third in the second half. The players don't notice anything. A one-goal advantage offers little comfort.

McGraw surveys the group, the assistant coaches behind him. He gives them detailed strategies. He reminds them they have to take possession, moving the ball and themselves. Don't just find opportunities; capitalize on them.

"We got one goal," he says calmly. "Do you think we can get a few more?"

The players nod, murmuring their agreement. It's time to get loud.

"Can that team beat you in the second half? No, they can't beat you in the second half. The only thing they have, THE ONLY THING THEY HAVE, is to try to take you out of the game by playing overly physical. They can't beat you unless we retaliate—if you get physical, guess who gets the card? COMPOSURE! Do NOT let their physicality, their words, take you out of the game. FOCUS. Let them foul. Make sure you deal with the game the way it's supposed to be dealt with." It's as far as he will ever go to address the challenges of playing in a Lewiston uniform and the nasty words that now go with it.

"They're fast, they're physical, you can't mess around with them," he continues. "But you're faster—let the ball do all the work. Can you pass better than them? Can you possess better than them? Can you play the ball back? Can you switch the field better than them? Can you run better than them?"

The murmurs grow louder.

"YES. YOU. CAN!"

In the second half, Abdi H. launches an attack thwarted by Camden's keeper, Lucas Boetsch. When Boetsch hits the ground, the ball in his hands, it pops up, hitting the ground for a slow roll toward the box.

"Second ball!" Gish yells from the sideline.

Nuri is on it. In two giant steps, he gets there and sends the ball into the open net. Goal.

Camden's coach, Ryan Hurley, is furious. During the first half of the game, he claimed a Lewiston player without a mouth guard took a chunk out of one of his players' heads. Now he wants a call because Boetsch got kicked after taking possession, causing the ball to roll free. It should be a free kick, he claims. It's a dead ball! Where's the call?

Because of Hurley's complaints, the officials later asked McGraw for the game tape. McGraw went to the meeting where referees reviewed it. There was no question, they decided. The keeper lost possession. According to McGraw, every referee said, "I can't see where he's coming from."

Leading 2–0, Lewiston's offense keeps at it. Moving the ball with rapid short passes, no single player in possession for very long, makes it seem like there are more of them on the field. Keeping their eyes on one another, never looking down, they stay a few steps ahead of Camden.

When the final whistle blows, Lewiston has outshot Camden 26–8. Nuri put another one in, and Camden's Kienan Brown answered, breaking away to boot the ball high overhead, out of Austin's reach, from twenty-five yards away. With the score 3–1, Lewiston's defense kicked into higher gear, keeping the ball out of Camden's reach as time ticked toward the end. They didn't need more scoring opportunities. They just needed to hold tight. The speed of the Blue Devils' defense, Hurley later told the press, was second to none. Most teams had speed up top. Lewiston had it front to back.

It is the first time that Lewiston doesn't score four or more in a game, but McGraw will take it. The team dutifully heads back to the far goal for a debriefing. They've got Oxford Hills in four days, and McGraw wants to make sure they have learned something from this one they could take into that one. And do your homework, he concludes.

As the players scatter, McGraw walks slowly to the bench with the assistants, exchanging observations—how to strengthen one player's left side, how to develop the inside foot of another. They never stop; it's what they love to do. As McGraw lugs the bag of balls to the trunk of his car, he thinks about what a satisfying win it was, but reminds himself, again, not to get complacent.

Four days later, the Oxford Hills Vikings came to town. McGraw heard the team was down six starters, suspended by the coach for doing something—he didn't know what—stupid. *Idiots,* he thought. *We've all got them.*

Austin sat the bench with a sore hamstring and shoulder. He'd sat out Cony, too, but played through the pain against Camden Hills. He was happy to give Alex the start against the Vikings, happier still when he realized he had the best seat in the house for Lewiston's offensive show.

The game felt over almost before it began. The Blue Devils scored two goals in the first three minutes, and never stopped. They rode the high of beating Camden Hills to demolish a greatly diminished Vikings squad, 14–1.

"Baseball scores," Maulid liked to say of such games.

Thirteen different Blue Devils scored, including a few who had seen little playing time thus far. Nuri nabbed a pair of goals; Muktar a goal and three assists; Mwesa a goal and two assists. Lewiston took thirty-one shots on goal. Alex made just two saves, and missed Oxford Hills' Kelton Loper's soaring free kick that went in just beneath the crossbar.

"Games aren't like this all the time," McGraw reminded them. "When you win like this, you need to show them respect, because you just showed them how to play the game, you set an example."

"Don't gloat," he said. "It cheapens the win. Be the better man."

It was Lewiston's top-scoring game of the season. Next, they shut out Messalonskee 7–0, with Abdi H. contributing a hat trick, before gearing up to face rival Edward Little again.

The rematch brought in Lewiston's largest home crowd of the season, 350 paid admissions, with at least another 100 coming in at the half. The game felt unbalanced from the get-go, Edward Little's 3–6–4 record paling next to Lewiston's 13–0. Making sure his former teammates knew he was there, Maslah blasted the ball into the net for Lewiston's first goal. In the second half, Karim scored at the three-minute mark. Five minutes later, he and Abdi H. netted a pair within twenty-six seconds of each other. When the final whistle blew, Lewiston outshot the Red Eddies 27–4, just one ball getting through Austin's legs.

"Blue we bleed," Joe wrote on his Facebook page of the 6–1 win. "Strong we remain."

There was just one game left in the regular season. Perennial conference foe Hampden Academy, best known as the school where Stephen King once taught English, came to Don Roux field on Saturday, October 17, 2015. An undefeated season and the top seed in the playoffs hung in the balance for Lewiston.

For eleven Blue Devils, it was Senior Night. Their families were there in full force: mothers, fathers, and siblings. There was a formal photo session before the game. Karim and Zak's dad made a rare appearance, but he couldn't stay.

"I'm sorry," he told McGraw, "but after we take the picture, I gotta go."

McGraw understood. Business was business, and he had to get back to work.

As the seniors assembled for their photos, McGraw thought about their record. In the course of four years, this group lost only twice, boasting 49–2–5. But that last regular-season loss, way back on September 14, 2013, was against Hampden, a brutal 4–0 game.

This game was another story.

The thirty-ninth straight regular-season victory for the Blue Devils started seven minutes in with a rocket from Abdi H. The ball moved with such force toward the net, it felt like time stood still, despite the scramble of defenders. Hampden keeper Kyle Townsend weakly deflected it, allowing Muktar to swoop in and pocket the rebound. A few minutes later, Abdi H. fed Maslah to go up 2–0.

With a minute left in the half, Abdi H. readied a pass to Maslah but felt the wind pick up ever so slightly. Before he had time to think, his feet made the decision, launching the ball from the left high over Townsend's reaching hands and into the top right corner of the net. *That was pretty special*, he thought as he slid on his knees in celebration, teammates piling around him. *A nice goal on Senior Night. I am going to remember this a long, long time.*

Abdi H. was in his element. His transformation when he took possession of the ball was always a sight to behold, but it was even more pronounced in this game. He looked bigger, his razor-sharp focus intense as he moved the ball downfield, two or more defenders following, a feeling of calm sweeping over his teammates and the fans because they knew the ball was with the best possible person on the field.

Early in the second half, an indirect kick put the Broncos on the board, giving them some badly needed momentum. But Lewiston wasn't having any of it, responding again and again. Even McGraw, who always found something they could work on, was pretty pleased with the 5–1 win. The Blue Devils closed their regular season 14–0. The top seed, they would have the home-field advantage for the playoffs.

"This is our house," Moe said, looking around Don Roux. Everyone from Australia's national rugby team to the New Jersey Devils used the phrase, popularized by the Bon Jovi sports anthem. But with this team, in this city, at this moment, it took on a whole new meaning.

CHAPTER 14

STRAIGHT RED

The Blue Devils entered the playoffs with as much baggage as momentum. Undefeated, they'd outscored opponents 100–7. But they also carried the weight of several years' playoff anguish.

We have work to do, Abdi H. reminded his teammates. Playoffs are different.

But if the *USA Today*/NSCAA Super 25 poll, which ranked Lewiston seventeenth in the nation, was any indication, they were ready. They were the only team ranked from Maine, and one of only three from New England.

"Where are we ranked in the world?" they asked McGraw when he told them the news.

There was no doubt their celebrity was on the rise. But none of it mattered, insisted Abdi H. Not the unbeaten streak, not the goals, not the national ranking. Not even the film crew on the sideline, directed by Lewiston alum Ian Clough, a local filmmaker who once played for McGraw and now wanted to make a documentary about his beloved coach.

None of it mattered. The Blue Devils, just one year after upstart Cheverus took them down, were starting over. And they were doing it against Edward Little.

The locker room grind felt different before the first playoff game. They still had to get dressed, find tape, and ice things that hurt. Most of them were sore, especially those who played in the park. No one stretched before games at Somali Stadium; they just hit the field hard and never stopped.

McGraw launched into a tactical discussion almost immediately, taking advantage of the rare quiet saturating the room.

"Don't get cute with the ball, because they're good enough," he said, always worried that too much of their street game would show up on the field. "You make a mistake—it could cost you. Be smart, not perfect. Move quickly. Horrendous call? Nothing you can do about it—get where you need to be. If you can't go forward, go backward."

McGraw stopped, wanting to let them finish getting ready so they could focus. Who needed more tape? Who needed to add another layer for warmth? Maslah put black tights beneath his shorts, worried about the temperature after the sun went down. Once everyone settled, McGraw continued.

"Go after THIS one. There's no other game. THERE IS NO OTHER GAME. If you win this game? Then, we'll see. But you've got to play your hearts out. You have to deal with the physical part, you have to deal with the mental part, you have to deal with what you have to do in order to win the game. Pressure the ball. The minute the ball gets to them, we have to have a white shirt on 'em. Right? One white shirt, the next one in support, the third one in support of him, and we get numbers around the ball, and we get the ball, pass, bring it down, get a cross, get a shot, put it in, LET'S WIN THE GAME."

"Yeahhhh," the players droned, clustering around him, clapping, hopping, pushing to get closer, their heads buried in each other's necks.

"Huh, huh, huh, huh," they chanted, bouncing. "ONE, TWO, THREE, *PAMOJA NDUGU!*"

"LET'S GO!" Zak bellowed as he rushed into the hallway.

The team wore the look of men going to war. As they warmed up, everything felt tense, different. After the last words from McGraw—"DON'T TAKE YOURSELVES OUT OF THE GAME! BE SMAHT!"—the starters ran to midfield and fell to their knees, arms around each other, heads down.

"Win it for McGraw," someone said, thinking about the ultimate goal, believing they were the team who could make it happen. From the sideline, Gish noticed the intensity, the huddle bouncing on its knees.

"This is our house," Moe repeated as the huddle broke. He wanted this so badly. It almost hurt, this swelling inside of him, this anxiety, this spirit. If they could do this, it would be one of the great accomplishments of his life. *Everyone wants McGraw to win,* Moe thought. *The guys, the school, the city. This is our moment.*

Muktar and Maslah jogged to the center of the field.

"Have fun, all right?" McGraw yelled after Muktar. "Just have fun and do your job!"

With a quick touch, the game began.

Edward Little came out hard, defending the middle, which Lewiston expected. They knew they had to play an outside game; they just didn't know it was going to be so rough. From his roost, Austin noticed that they were targeting Maslah, hacking at his ankles. Then Maulid tripped up. And Karim. Joe kicked a cannon shot; seconds later, he went down. Even on resets, there was a lot of pushing. A shoulder here, a foot there.

We're spending a lot of time on the ground, Austin thought. Things were, McGraw would say, "gettin' physical."

Finally, Abdi H. was successful. Running down the middle into the attacking third, he took a cross from Q. Barely dodging an incoming slide tackle—"Nice move, H!" yelled McGraw—in three touches he fired the ball into the net, well out of the reach of EL's diving goalie, before falling to the ground himself. *Goal!* Maulid and Q ran to embrace him, Muktar and Joe not far behind.

"That's the one we needed," Gish said to McGraw.

It was the only goal in the first half.

At halftime, a few Lewiston fans observed an official mocking Maslah's reaction to getting manhandled. Kim Wettlaufer and Carolyn McNamara were incensed. McNamara wasn't just a rabid Lewiston soccer fan; a lot of these players were her patients, her vested interest in their health adding to her anxiety over what she was seeing. She let the referees know. As Coach Abdi paced the bleachers, coffee in hand, an official came over to speak with McNamara. "I'm going to talk to Fuller," he told her, "if you guys don't shut up."

"Go ahead!" McNamara yelled, laughing at the absurdity of Fuller throwing her, of all people, out of a soccer game. "Tell Fuller! Do you want me to get him for you?"

Maulid just shook his head at the ref. He could take whatever another player threw at him, but he hated it when the refs made a bad call. He respected the refs; he would never argue, since he couldn't change what they did. But there were times when it got to him, when he wanted to walk off the field and give up. Sometimes it felt like they had an extra opponent on the field. But he learned to play on, to use it to play better and score more. Bad calls, for whatever reason, were just part of being a Blue Devil.

Looking at Maslah, Gish had no doubt that he was injured. He wasn't the kind of player who flopped. Gish saw him get pushed when he was in the air, going down hard on his ankle. Yet inexplicably, the foul was called on *him*.

Kill it with kindness, Gish repeated in his head, his mother's mantra, as he walked over to the ref.

"Sir," he began, his voice quiet, "what did you see?"

"He—Maslah—totally created that," the ref replied. Gish thanked him and walked away, his head exploding. They were playing two games, he thought, one against EL, the other against the officials.

McGraw didn't care about officiating. He had a game to win. When he addressed the team at the half, he made sure they knew that.

"You have forty minutes," he said. "It doesn't matter *who* scores, it's *us* who scores. Work as a team. Do things as a team. Pass. Help each other. As soon as you can, put the ball on the ground."

But he wasn't blind. He saw what everyone else did.

"Listen: do not lose composure when there's a grab, an elbow, push—play your game, wear 'em down, break 'em down. It's play-offs. It's do or die . . . The next goal is a very important goal."

"ONE, TWO, THREE, *PAMOJA NDUGU!*"

In the second half, Lewiston launched an aggressive attack to the delight of the growing home crowd, some 275 paid admissions. But neither a rocket from Abdi H. nor a shot from Maslah, who beat off an entire scrum of Red Eddies, hit the net.

Finally, from the outside right corner, Maulid capitalized on a short chop from Abdi H., lobbing the ball into the goal on a gorgeous run that didn't stop until he went down on bended knee, hands high overhead. Leaping to his feet, he ran back to midfield, his arms around Dek. With thirty minutes left, Lewiston led 2–0.

"Did I call it?" McGraw shouted at the bench. "Did I call it?"

"I heard you!" Alex Rivet replied, running over to celebrate, staying warm in case Austin needed to come out.

"You know what that was?" McGraw asked Hersi, who was

calling out reset instructions in Somali. "Guys were persistent. They stayed right with it."

With eleven minutes left on the clock, Lewiston's offense picked up its pace. Abdi H. sprinted downfield, three maroon shirts marking him, and took a long pass from Karim. Stopping short, just a few yards to go, he flicked the ball with the outside of his right foot over EL's defense. Not waiting for the ball to land, Maslah threw his right leg into the air for a one-touch goal, Tae Kwon Do style.

Zlatan Ibrahimović himself could not have done it better.

Maulid ran and jumped on his cousin's back, ecstatic. *This is how it's supposed to feel,* he thought, joy surging as the scoreboard clicked to 3–0.

"Let's get another one," McGraw yelled, putting his hands into the pockets of his big blue parka, settling into its warmth. He knew they had their rhythm now. It was going to be all right.

"One more!"

He doesn't stop, thought Austin, who pounced on two balls to preserve the shutout. *Even if we're up by seven goals, he never stops.*

Less than a minute after Maslah's goal, Muktar passed a short ball to Abdi H., who was surrounded by no less than eight Red Eddies in front of the box. Out of the corner of his right eye, Abdi H. saw Karim a few yards back. He passed. Karim juggled for a moment, and then left-footed the ball through the traffic, sending EL's keeper, Owen Mower, into a fruitless dive.

Four to nothing.

They kept attacking, feeling no need to step back into a defensive shell and protect their lead. Nuri brought the ball down the left side and crossed to Maslah, who hit the crossbar with a header. As Maslah headed the rebound, Maulid ran toward it.

"SECOND BALL!" screamed McGraw and Gish.

Maulid turned left and launched himself high, his back to the net, scissor-kicking the ball up and over. Landing on the ground, he turned to see Mower punch the ball over the crossbar and out of bounds.

"Damn," Maulid yelled. "If that had gone in, it would've been niiiiiice."

With less than a minute left, Abdi H. lobbed the ball into the net on a free kick.

"What a nice shot!" McGraw croaked, his voice almost gone, as the team celebrated. "What a NICE SHOT!"

At the whistle, Lewiston had outshot EL 22–2. Alex body-slammed Austin, while Jason Fuller, buried in his blue hood to ward off the encroaching cold, thanked the officials. After Coach Abdi conferred with McGraw for a few minutes about the game, the two embraced, taking a moment to rejoice in the 5–0 quar-terfinal win. But they knew it wasn't over.

"You played your game, you did what we had to do. Awesome game," McGraw told them as they packed up. "Friday, it's Bangor, right here."

The day before Halloween, a holiday that few of the players celebrated, Austin and Alex ran onto the field to warm up before Bangor arrived. The sinking sun shone bright, the trees surround-ing the field shimmering reds and golds. They were always on the field before anyone else. Being goalie could be isolating, and not just on a team with an offense like Lewiston's. Goalie drills take a long time, and Henrikson was a stickler for getting them right. Austin appreciated the work, even the damn weighted vest that Henrikson made him wear in practice. It was brutal, but his verti-cal leap had improved enormously. Now he could jump over even the tallest players to snatch the ball.

In the past year, Henrikson had taught Austin a drop kick that had become very effective. Because of Lewiston's speed,

Austin didn't have to boot the ball halfway down the field, although he certainly could. Sometimes, he threw the ball like a slingshot instead of kicking it to get it to the outside quickly, so his teammates could attack. Other times he rolled it like a bowling ball.

As the goalies warmed up, the stands began to fill. The crowd was smaller than for the EL game, but still sizable. It was a cold night to be watching soccer, a stiff breeze sending the temperature to freezing. The sky turned orange, the sun disappearing behind the city skyline. The field lights came up as the rest of the team joined the goalies. As they warmed up, their white jerseys ruffling in the wind, McGraw's words from yesterday's practice stayed in their heads.

"Do your job tomorrow," he'd said. "Let's take care of this."

In the first half, Lewiston dazzled with footwork and speed. Q, in particular, was on fire, compensating for Maslah, whose ankle still hurt. But Bangor thwarted shot after shot. After a brief sideline chat with McGraw, who noticed a gap in the defense, Abdi H. took a chance with his left foot, knowing Bangor's defenders were focused on his right. The ball soared over the traffic in the box, hitting the crossbar with tremendous force. It bounced back in front of Muktar, who took a split second to settle it before taking the shot. The keeper guessed wrong and threw himself in the opposite direction. With twelve minutes left in the first half, Lewiston was on the board.

Maulid, Abdi H., and Moe embraced Muktar. His goal fired them up. Abdi H. couldn't get over the sophomore's first touch on that ball: so composed. Now that they'd scored, they wouldn't stop. As far as Abdi H. was concerned, until the final whistle, they would play as if it was zero–zero. "Maintain the pressure," coach always said. But despite outshooting Bangor 12–0 in the first half, the score didn't budge.

"Find the gaps," McGraw reminded them at the half. "Exploit open spaces. The next goal is just a matter of time."

The second half told a different story. As Maulid prepared to flip the ball into play, Nuri, jostling for position in the box, called to Karim in Arabic.

"Should I go in?" he asked, knowing one of them usually stayed behind while others tried to get a head on the ball.

"Yeah, yeah, go ahead and try it," Karim answered. "I'll stay back."

Nuri was excited. He had loved soccer forever, kicking a ball around in the dirt in Saudi Arabia when he was little. Usually he scored with his legs. There were defenders everywhere, but he knew, deep down, that he could get a head on this ball. Straining to keep his eyes on Maulid, he waited. As the ball arched toward him, he leaped, stretching to get as far into the air as he could, hoping a defender didn't knock him down. He wasn't as tall as Karim, but this was his chance. Turned away from the net, he felt the back of his head connect with the ball.

Goal!

That's it, thought Nuri as he jumped to greet Abdi H. and Karim. *That's my favorite goal ever.*

McGraw tried to stay calm, but excitement shot through every vein. In the playoffs, Maulid's flip had become a real weapon.

Lewiston continued to attack, Muktar, Maslah, and Abdi H. moving the ball like lightning through the attacking third with cuts and scissors. Muktar, especially, seemed unstoppable, breaking away with relentless body feints, leaning one way to drag a defender with him, and then using his outside foot to accelerate in the opposite direction, leaving the defender off-balance and behind.

With twenty-two minutes left, Maslah and Muktar got the ball to Abdi H., who dribbled around and through five defenders to lob a beautiful hopping ball into the net for 3–0. As Abdi H. jogged back into position, he held his arms out wide, a smile stretching around his blue mouth guard. This felt good.

But, as McGraw always said, expect the unexpected.

It happened as Abdi H. battled one-to-one for the ball, Maslah and Muktar waiting nearby. As Abdi H. nudged the ball toward a sprinting Q, Karim came out of nowhere, studs up, flying through the air toward the ball. When he slid into the ball, he hit the foot of the defender Abdi H. battled. As the kid went down, the ref's hands went up. A whistle sounded across the field.

It was bad. They knew it was bad. Karim walked over to the ref, Nuri and Abdi H. just behind him.

Why would he do that? Zak thought, watching his brother. They were up by three, and Bangor wasn't in scoring position.

The ref reached into his pocket and raised his hand over his head. The card was red.

Karim ripped out his mouth guard and started walking to the bench, not really remembering what he did or why he did it. Nuri doubled over, grasping his head in his hands, fear gnawing at him, subsuming him. He felt like he couldn't move. *Karim won't finish the game,* he thought. *What if Bangor comes back? If we lose, this is Karim's last game.*

Abdi H. held the ball in his hands, unsure of what to do next. This was Karim. Karim was everything.

"Are you kidding me?" he said to the ref. He couldn't help it. He saw the tackle. He knew that if it looked like a foul, it usually was a foul. But straight red? "There's no way that's a red card!"

"Abdi," the ref said sternly, looking straight at him, "walk away right now."

Abdi H. understood and walked slowly away. His outburst was out of character; the ref didn't want to give him a card, too. He had to take care of his teammates, keep them calm. Any reaction from them would be a yellow card. They could not afford anyone else getting booked.

McGraw walked onto the field, the gray hoodie beneath his blue windbreaker hiding his shocked face. He stoically listened as the ref passionately explained why it was straight red and then walked back to the sideline, hands plunged into his pockets, his face expressionless. The ref had no choice. It was a hard tackle, both feet in the air. He saw what he saw.

Don't panic, McGraw reminded himself. *It won't change anything.*

Austin was tense. They didn't move the ball as well without Karim. Without him spreading the field, Austin knew they would play closer into the middle, creating more opportunities for Bangor. Sure enough, with fifteen minutes left on the clock, Garth Berenyi broke through Lewiston's defense and fired the first of his team's two shots. Austin dove hard and grabbed the ball. *Not on my watch,* he thought as he stood up.

Lewiston knew how to play with a man down. They pressed the ball forward, unsuccessfully shooting again and again. Finally, Maslah headed an arching corner kick. When Bangor's goalie punched the ball away, Maslah took advantage of the force on the rebound and sent it into the net from the air. As he jogged back into position, he held a finger up, number one, a satisfied look on his face.

The 4–0 victory had consequences. Lewiston would defend its regional title without Karim. The numbers were in their favor; they'd outscored opponents 109–7, with ten shutouts. But McGraw hated thinking about a game without Karim. The kid deserved to play. While the likes of Maslah and Abdi H. often overshadowed him, no one could touch Karim's resourcefulness or adaptability. Striker. Midfielder. Wing. Sweeper.

"Yes, Coach," he always answered whenever McGraw moved him. "Yes, Coach."

McGraw leveraged Karim's ejection to motivate the team, while emphasizing that they'd be okay without him. Every strategy, every formation, was to get Karim one more game.

"We're not just eleven on the field," he reminded them at practice. He was going to need the bench without Karim.

On Wednesday, November 4, 2015, the team gathered in the locker room before the regional final. As the clapping players crowded around McGraw, he reminded them to avoid fouls. "When you avoid fouls," he said, "you avoid set pieces. Keep the pressure on. Pressure, pressure, pressure." He couldn't say the word enough to make it matter as much as it did. "And no matter what happens, play your game." Finally, he got to the top of the mountain.

"Karim deserves to get back there," McGraw said, letting a crescendo build slowly, getting chills from his own words. "He's your captain—he has worked his tail off all year for you—and we're gonna get him back in that game. The state game. We have to win this game so Karim can play in the state final."

The players bellowed their approval and headed out under the pink-and-orange darkening sky. The American flag fluttered overhead, a light breeze behind their backs as they jogged. The cool air felt relatively tepid for a late fall night in Maine.

Soccah weathah.

A year ago, Karim had scored the two goals that sent them into the state final. Now, senior midfielder Mohamed "Moha" Abdisalan would take his place. Good on the ball, Moha brought size to the field, as tall as Karim and Maslah, but with more bulk on his frame. At midfield, he could shut down just about anyone. Up front, he was good in the air and on his feet, and got physical when needed.

But no one, thought Abdijabar Hersi as he watched Moha warm up, *could take Karim's place.* He brought maturity to the field, usually choosing to talk with his feet, but stepping up if warranted. He could attack, defend, and shoot; play high, middle, or back.

"Versatile," Hersi says when asked to characterize Karim. "The most versatile player I have ever seen."

Hersi knew that losing Karim was a problem. But he wasn't worried. Karim might have more flair and a longer stride than Moha, but Moha could get the job done.

Fuller, however, moved through his pregame tasks with a pit in his stomach. He was nervous, scared even. He thought Karim was the best player on the team. They weren't just losing *a* guy; they were losing *the* guy. Whenever Fuller talked to McGraw about something he needed the team to do, Karim was the one.

"Don't worry," McGraw would tell him. "I'll grab Karim, and he'll take care of it."

The Blue Devils were nothing if not deep. Fuller was proud of the seniors who'd received conference and regional all-star awards for the regular season and knew that the younger players—Maulid, Nuri, Muktar—would step up. McGraw seemed cautiously optimistic, but noncommittal.

"We'll see what we see," he said to Fuller.

"Good evening, ladies and gentlemen," the announcer boomed as the players warmed up. "Lewiston High School welcomes you to the Franklin Athletic Complex Don Roux field."

It was the fourth straight year that Lewiston had played in the regional final. They faced a familiar foe, the Hampden Academy Broncos, who'd upset Camden Hills to be there. As Hampden coach Josh Stevens walked onto the field, his furrowed brow said it all. This was it; the game that determined who would go to the state championship. It was hard to think of a team who wanted it more than the one his squad was about to face. But Stevens knew the Blue Devils. Lewiston's dominant play and stunning record put them under a microscope. He knew what to expect.

Or so he thought. In their regular season match-up, four Lewiston starters had sat out for various reasons. Karim had played defense in that game because Zak was benched for missing a practice.

"They were so happy," Karim remembers about the news of his red card. "They were like, 'They're missing their best defender!'"

The return of Zak, McGraw knew, was going to throw Hampden. But would it be enough to counterbalance the loss of Karim?

"For the most part, we've come out on top, we've won, we've done that," McGraw announced in the locker room. "Today? You show them how hard you can play. You show them how well you can play. No matter what your opponent throws at you, whether it's physical or mental or verbal, you play the game. The game is the purest form of competition you can play. It tells you when to pass, it tells you when to shoot. Go after them. You go after the ball. You put enough pressure on them. If they can't look up to make a pass because they've got to deal with you and the ball, you're doing your job."

As the captains took the team through its pregame paces under the lights, fans flooded the gate. Fuller couldn't believe the size of the crowd; the biggest he'd ever seen at soccer, with six hundred paid admissions and another hundred in the parking lot waiting for the half. *What a crowd,* he thought, watching Coach Abdi and Kim Wettlaufer take their places at the fence. Black. White. Catholic. Muslim. Immigrant. Young. Old. Parents. Neighbors. Strangers. Friends.

As the announcer reminded the crowd about sportsmanship, kids cheered in English while many parents yelled encouragement in Somali. The comforting aroma of the Snack Shack's grills scented the air, while cheerleaders spelled every player's name, from OTHMAN to HASSAN to WING, the crowd roaring as each took his place on the field, high fives all around.

Q looked around, not quite believing he was back. He'd missed the Cheverus game when he was up in Syracuse with his family. Now he was one game away from a state final. It was a mind-set, he knew. He looked over at Muktar. What a game-changer that kid was. Not very big, he came off the bench and energized the team, made things happen. He was like a character in a video game, with a surge button at the ready whenever he needed to pour it on. Q hoped he'd be okay, especially because he knew that a slide tackle back in September had really freaked Muktar out.

"Oh, my god," Muktar had confessed to him back then. "I'm scared!"

Q had laughed and told him he'd be fine. That was just the game.

Abdi H. also knew that Muktar worried a lot. Getting past this game wasn't just about Karim. Guys like Muktar needed to get out there and prove themselves.

Before the regional final, Abdi H. sat with the sophomore in the locker room to talk about his increasingly important offensive role. Abdi H. wanted to make sure Muktar understood that they believed in him.

"Oh, man, you seniors are so good, man," Muktar began.

"You can do a lot for the team," Abdi H. interrupted. "You should actually be a starter."

He told Muktar not to be nervous. Just go out on the field and play the game. "We have your back," Abdi H. reassured him. "There will be great opportunities to score, just like against Bangor."

Abdi H. knew they were going to be okay without Karim. The team was full of secret weapons. Q, for example, wasn't flashy, but had mad skills. The more he played, the more confident he got, starting slow but warming up to beat two, three players on footwork alone. Nuri was another, small but physical, able to get his head on just about anything.

But with Karim on the sidelines, Abdi H. knew they had to change tactics a bit. Karim's style relied heavily on his deft coordination of speed and skills, giving him opportunities to score early and often. Moha, on the other hand, liked to drift back, be more defensive, which would put more offensive burden on Nuri and Q.

"Pressure," McGraw reminded them. "Do what you gotta do, you got it?"

Lewiston got off to a feverish start, Maslah slamming the ball into the post off a pass from Abdi H. just seconds in. They kept shooting, but to no avail. But with five minutes left in the half, McGraw noticed a weakness in Hampden.

"Nuri!" he called.

Nuri ran over, panting.

"Switch the ball to the weak side quickly. They're overplaying ball side," McGraw said. "Can you tell 'em that?"

"Yeah." Nuri nodded.

Lewiston skillfully moved the ball down. Abdi H. passed to Maslah, and then bolted across the field, where Maslah found him. Abdi H. fired off a pass to Nuri, going down as he collided with a Hampden defender. Nuri finished it, drilling it past Hampden keeper Kyle Townsend, who fell to the ground, arms outstretched, hands empty.

Momentum found.

At the half, the Broncos walked onto the track to listen to Coach Stevens. As they toyed with their mouth guards, wiping sweat from their brows, he reminded them this was what soccer was all about: two good teams who wanted a state championship. They had to think, he said—animating each point with his hands—about every practice, scrimmage, and game that got them there. Now, he stressed, was when it mattered.

At the opposite end of the field, McGraw told the team they needed to change the field because Hampden had figured out that they liked playing outside. This was the seniors' last game at home, win or lose, he reminded them. One goal was not enough.

"Play like you're losing," he said.

As the teams returned to play, the Lewiston fans got organized. They, too, felt the pressure. As they began to do the wave, the jumble of cultures, ages, hats, headscarves, and languages melded into a cheering surge.

Lewiston's offense wasn't satisfied with a 1–0 shutout. Five minutes into the second half, Abdi H. launched a free kick that an army of Hampden defenders deflected. Q unleashed on the rebound, lobbing the ball high over the six Broncos who surrounded him. Townsend made a skipping sort of leap as the ball flew toward the net, but he couldn't get it. As the scoreboard flipped to 2–0, the Broncos started arguing among themselves. Hampden midfielder Nick Gilpin later described the frustration to the *Portland Press Herald*.

"The way that they pass the ball is so much better than any team I've ever seen," he said. "If somebody was keeping track of possession, they probably had the ball 90 percent of the time. And they're all unselfish. None of 'em cares who scores...It's fun to watch, but at the same time you're like, getting mad...because they're just passing it in circles around us."

With twenty minutes left, Nuri fed the ball through Maslah's nimble legs. Maslah saw Abdi H. sprinting toward the goal, two Broncos in hot pursuit. Maslah fired the ball to him. Tripping over Townsend, who tried to slide into the ball, Abdi H. popped it into the net without ever breaking stride, powering over to his teammates to celebrate. Three minutes later, Nuri fired a pass to Maslah, who beat Townsend yet again.

Hampden failed to take a shot the entire second half; Lewiston took sixteen. Townsend weathered the onslaught, undoubtedly grateful each time the ball hit the crossbar or a post, but also making spectacular saves. As the clock neared zero, Lewiston's bench stood, arms around each other. With the final whistle, they erupted. Nuri ran to the sideline, pointing at Karim, who stood tall in his blue windbreaker and black pants. The two leaped into the air and descended in an embrace, joined by Moha, Maslah, Moe, and Dek. Maulid threw his hands up over his head as he danced his way over to the bench, while Q jumped, fist out-stretched overhead.

Abdi H. was slow to join in, thinking they still had one game to go. *No*, he reconsidered. *This* was *something to celebrate*. He broke into a run to join his teammates and get ready for the award ceremony. After the Broncos hoisted their second-place plaque, it was Lewiston's turn. The announcer congratulated the Class A North Champions as each player hugged each coach, the crowd growing louder and more passionate. Finally, the regional championship plaque securely in his left hand, Abdi H. stretched his right hand overhead, his finger pointing number one, before leading the team to the stands to share the moment with family and friends, classmates and teachers. Joy enveloped them, Nuri taking a turn with the plaque to gallop around with his teammates, running to the corner of the field and sliding to his knees.

"This was just earning the right," McGraw said in their last postgame chat of the season. "Now we've got to earn the right to be number one in the state."

Next they would face Scarborough, just as McGraw had predicted.

"We are playing the best team in the south, and the only team that scored more goals than us in one game," he continued, letting the preseason loss return for a moment. "They're totally different, they're much better, but so are we. So let's let the games begin and take them on Saturday!"

Karim beamed. He'd play another game; one that the team had waited a year to play. Undefeated and with consecutive playoff shutouts, they felt ready. But on the other side of the playoff bracket, the Scarborough Red Storm had racked up their own shutout run. They'd beaten Lewiston in August, and they were looking to do it again.

CHAPTER 15

DO NOT RETALIATE

The regional championship in Class A South was a rematch between Scarborough and Cheverus. In 2014, the Stags had needed double overtime to get past Scarborough to the state final against Lewiston. A year later, they returned on an eight-game winning streak, but knew that Scarborough wanted revenge.

To beat Scarborough, Cheverus had to prevent set pieces from converting into goals. Scarborough's Matt Caron, a senior, had a legendary throw-in. From his hands, a ball went for miles before arching perfectly before the box, where a teammate could nudge it in. The Stags knew they had to clear those throw-ins if they wanted to win.

Easier said than done.

Ten minutes in, Scarborough's Josh Morrissey bicycle-kicked a corner past Cheverus keeper Jacob Tomkinson, who had played so well against Lewiston the year before. Eight minutes later, Caron stood on the sideline, ball in hand. Under the lights, his teammates' white uniforms glowed among the deep purple-blue jerseys of Cheverus. He seemed impossibly far away from where Tomkinson stood. Caron took a few quick steps and hurled the ball over his head, dragging his right foot in perfect form. As he jogged toward the action, players scrambled with eyes upward. Tomkinson greeted the ball at the near post, hands outstretched, right over left, hoping to deflect it. The ball grazed his reach en route to the net, creating the necessary touch for the goal to count. It was the first time that had ever happened to him, Caron later said. He'd never thrown in a goal before. Scarborough held its 2–0 lead until the end, its keeper Cam Nigro making six saves. Cheverus would not return for a rematch against undefeated Lewiston. It would be Scarborough.

On paper, Scarborough and Lewiston had a lot in common. Top seeds. Regional champions. Undefeated seasons. Skillful ball handling. Strong set pieces. Exceptional defense. But there were differences. Scarborough played a physical, forward game, relying on strength and athleticism to get the ball down the field, while Lewiston patiently built plays from the back, setting the pace, anticipating next moves, digging the right spots, and using speed to make up for lack of size.

Looking at team photos side by side, more obvious differences come into sharp focus. A coastal area a few miles south of Portland, Scarborough personifies Vacationland: sandy beaches, the state's largest tidal marsh, and a year-round population of eighteen thousand, over 95 percent of which is white. At the Bait Shed, diners feast on lobster rolls served in tin cake pans while sitting on a narrow pier overlooking the water. From its perch on Prouts Neck in Saco Bay, the renowned Black Point Inn brings tourists from all over the world. While rooms run upward of $600 a night over July Fourth weekend, they offer a rare opportunity for nonresidents to access the view made famous by Winslow Homer.

For many reasons, the Red Storm, with nine state titles, was a team that people liked to beat. Consistently one of the state's top soccer programs, Scarborough boasted great facilities and huge parent participation. Much, too, was made of the team's hair, which encompassed a whole lot of color and some shocking architecture. It was a Scarborough playoff tradition to sport variations on the Mohawk, shaving or trimming all but a middle strip of hair that could be gelled to new heights. Players often added color, too, from cobalt blue to the team's signature red. In their playoff run in 2014, Garrett King carved an arrow into his vibrant blue Mohawk that pointed directly down his forehead, reminiscent of Aang, the protagonist from Nickelodeon's *Avatar: The Last Airbender.*

But those who braved a cold rain in 2014 to watch Scarborough play Deering in the semifinal round weren't there because of anyone's hair. Some were there to scout Deering senior Stephen Ochan, a standout player from Sudan. Others, mostly from neighboring Portland schools, braved the elements hoping to see Deering take Scarborough down. When these teams had last met in a regular-season game in early October, people whispered, Scarborough fans had allegedly taunted Deering players with a string of racist cheers.

While Somalis and Sudanese still dominate Portland's immigrant community, in recent years a spate of asylum-seekers from Central African countries such as Burundi, Rwanda, and Congo have arrived, further diversifying the city's population. It is a change clearly seen in the city's three public high schools. First opened in 1874, Deering boasts an impressive list of notable alumni, from actresses Linda Lavin, Andrea Martin, and Anna Kendrick to writer Annie Proulx. Unlike Lewiston, Deering's diversity is broadly based, representing more than fifty countries and twenty-seven languages.

Deering embraces its global makeup, one of a handful of schools that belongs to the International Studies Schools Network (ISSN), which focuses on global competence. But not everyone sees Deering's diversity as something to celebrate. While the majority of asylum-seekers get jobs once the required 150-day waiting period lifts, a familiar hostility often paints them as parasitic, draining public coffers.

On October 7, 2014, that hostility bubbled over during a soccer game. While Scarborough got down to the business of shutting out Deering 2–0, fans allegedly hurled racist insults at Deering. Sneering chants of "USA-USA-USA" accompanied the waving of American flags. One parent told journalists that he and his wife heard people yell "Go back to Africa!" and "We're USA, you're not!" A group of Scarborough parents sitting nearby, said one observer, clearly heard them but did nothing.

Deering's coach, Joel Costigan, had dealt with such racial affronts since he took the reins of the team in 2011. The very first week he coached, a summer game, a player threw the n-word at one of his players. He soon learned that it was part and parcel of his new job.

"Me and Joel and Rocco," McGraw says, referring to longtime Portland High School soccer coach Rocco Frenzilli, "deal with things no one else in the entire state can even imagine."

Costigan, a social studies teacher, grew up in Buxton, a small town west of Portland best known as a key setting in *The Shawshank Redemption*. Studying abroad his junior year in Buenos Aires, taking in Boca Juniors' games at La Bombonera stadium, he saw firsthand the global obsession with soccer, a sport he played.

For Costigan, building chemistry on a team with kids from twelve or more countries has unique challenges. Not only does he have trouble communicating with his players; they have trouble talking to each other.

"A lot gets lost," he says about kids who come during the summer with little English in their pocket. He remembers when a player got a yellow card for failing to listen to the referee. "He doesn't speak English!" Costigan yelled from the sideline. The ref apologized, put the card away, and play continued.

While Costigan draws players from a more disparate population than McGraw, and never had the support of a group like SBYA, he encounters similar complications. A few years ago, he, like McGraw, didn't understand why "I had to move a couch for my parents" was a legitimate excuse to miss practice. Now he gets that "I have to help my parents" is a way of life, not a choice. He encourages the team, especially the captains, to figure out rules that work for everyone. It was harder to figure out ways to deal with how opposing teams treated them.

"You can see that the words that are chosen in trash talk are specific to our population," says Costigan, who talks more directly about such things than McGraw.

While the racist affronts don't surprise him, the lack of consequences does. His second season coaching Deering, an opponent hounded a Somali player. Upset, the player asked Costigan to take him out. Costigan encouraged him to shake it off, but watched as the harassment escalated throughout the game. At one point, the other player took the Deering kid down by his genitals. Even after the kid admitted he had done it, Costigan remembers, there was no card. Not yellow. Not red. Nothing.

"I want consequences for these actions," Costigan repeats.

It is never a question of *if* such things will happen, only when. In 2013, a Sanford High School player, a captain, hurled the n-word at a Deering player. The kid wrote a letter apologizing to Deering, and Sanford removed itself from the sportsmanship award voting that year.

"There were consequences," says Costigan. "That's what I want."

For Costigan, as with McGraw, it's not just about playing soccer. It's about playing soccer with integrity.

"Are we going to hit them back, sink to their level, rise above, drone it out, come out of the game—what are your options?" he asks his players before a game.

After a few local newspapers wrote about the Scarborough-Deering game in question, the superintendents of both schools announced they'd investigate the matter. While the two denounced any racist taunts that may have taken place, Scarborough's athletic director, Michael LeGage, deflected the incident as something soccer fans just did. The students, he claimed, were mimicking what they saw at European soccer games on television.

Impersonating international soccer fans is hardly something to aspire to. One parent claims he heard Scarborough fans telling Deering players to "go eat a banana," a prevalent phrase at European soccer matches. Feyenoord fans once tossed an inflatable banana at Roma's Gervinho, who hails from Côte d'Ivoire, while a Villarreal fan threw a banana at Barcelona's Dani Alves, who's from Brazil. Alves, who'd been readying for a corner, paused when the ref standing next to him failed to react. He then took a giant step forward, grabbed the banana, peeled it, and popped it into his mouth. With a quick wipe of his hands on his shorts, he drilled the ball toward the box. His father, he said later, always advised him to eat bananas to prevent cramping. Villarreal banned the banana thrower for life from El Madrigal Stadium. Alves's teammate, the legendary Neymar, posted a photograph of himself with his son on Instagram holding bananas.

"Take That, bunch of Racists," Neymar wrote. "We are all Monkeys, So What."

LeGage's FIFA defense rang hollow for Costigan. He was all for an enthusiastic fan base—it was something he tried to cultivate at Deering. But the "USA" chants revealed something far more malevolent than school spirit or a passion for soccer.

At the conclusion of the investigation, the superintendents

released a joint statement affirming Scarborough fans focused on Deering players' "places of origin," but they absolved the players and coaching staff of any wrongdoing. They pledged that steps would be taken to ensure that such an incident would not happen again. Scarborough's principal, David Creech, followed with a letter to parents. He asserted there would be zero tolerance for any kind of bias and promised more education regarding respectful behavior so "these recent allegations" would not "tarnish the great reputation our school has."

For Costigan, it was simply an expression of "our kids wouldn't do that," which dismissed the experience his players had on the field that day. To him, there was nothing "alleged" about what happened. He had his own video of the game, which he offered to everyone involved. There were no takers. So for Costigan, the investigation didn't amount to much of anything because there were no consequences.

During the 2015 playoffs, as the Blue Devils and Red Storm made their way through the brackets toward each other, Lewiston's mayoral race heightened racial tensions in the city. Ben Chin, a Bates graduate who worked as a community organizer with the progressive Maine People's Alliance and served on the board of Trinity Jubilee, announced his candidacy. MacDonald, the incumbent, claimed that Chin's pro-immigrant plans for the city—especially a past stance that noncitizens should be allowed to vote—shut out a lot of the community. MacDonald's "leave your culture at the door" anti-immigrant stance worked well for him in the past. In 2013, he had used it to ward off a challenge by former mayor Larry Gilbert, who'd espoused a progressive view of the city's increasing diversity, beating him 61 to 39 percent.

Local landlord Joe Dunne, who the Maine People's Alliance had dubbed a "corporate slumlord," made no bones about which candidate he endorsed. On three of his downtown buildings, he posted bright red signs featuring a Soviet-style hammer and sickle, a caricature of Ho Chi Minh, and the slogan "DON'T VOTE FOR HO CHI CHIN." After a slew of protestors came out against them, Dunne took the signs down and apologized in an ad in the *Sun Journal*, but not before national media, including the *Washington Post* and the *New York Times*, took note of the polarizing mayoral campaigns. Chin won the most votes on the initial ballot of five candidates, but came up just short of taking the election outright. He would go on to lose to MacDonald in the subsequent December runoff, 4,398 to 3,826.

Throughout the fall of 2015, the mayoral campaigns yet again emboldened racist chatter in Lewiston. MacDonald's anti-immigrant, anti-welfare stances overlapped with those of Maine's governor, Paul LePage, a Lewiston native whose notorious rants about everything from the Holocaust to President Obama found favor with the rising tide of support for the presidential campaign of Donald J. Trump.

"Any native Mainers on the team?" a sports fan commented on an article about Lewiston winning the regional title.

Looking ahead at Scarborough, McGraw felt confident that his players were prepared for whatever Red Storm fans might throw at them. A focus on winning, McGraw told his players, made the other stuff matter less.

"Do not retaliate," he repeated. "Just beat 'em by scoring goals. That's all you gotta do. Don't hurt 'em. Hurt the net. Hurt the ball."

While Gish had a harder time than McGraw keeping tight reins on his emotions when he saw what the players stomached, he held his tongue during playoffs because so much was on the line. But he still hated what he heard, both on and off the field. His mother was from Canada and didn't get her citizenship for years. It gave him a perspective he wished more of his friends had, especially those from Lewiston's outskirts, in the more rural parts of Androscoggin County.

"You know, I'm from Lewiston, and I know what Lewiston pride is all about," a friend said to Gish a few days before the state championship game, "and that's not it."

Gish walked away, no good-bye, not trusting himself to respond. *These kids bleed blue,* he thought. Good soccer players. Good people. That was all that mattered.

Abdi H. didn't want to waste any energy on what Scarborough fans might do or say. The team needed to focus on what he considered to be "unfinished business": their journey that had started the year before. But he knew Scarborough was going to be tough. The Blue Devils hadn't played scared since the final minute of the Cheverus game, evidenced by the number of goals they scored across the season. And if McGraw had left his starters in longer, the goal tally would be double. Confidence wasn't going to be a problem.

But McGraw still feared complacency. The Red Storm outscored its own opponents 50–8 during the regular season, and logged eight shutouts. They were not a team to take lightly, especially with that 2–1 victory over Lewiston in the preseason. It didn't count, but it hung in the air.

McGraw did his homework, studying Scarborough's games and results. They were a good team with a strong defense, coached by men he liked and respected. His own players knew that, having played with Scarborough kids on elite club teams like Seacoast. Moe, Maulid, Q, and Abdi H. considered both Matt Caron and Josh Morrissey friends, never bothered about the stories of Scarborough's fans and their notorious cheering. It wasn't these guys, they reassured themselves. Indeed, Morrissey often made the trip to Lewiston to give them rides, and sometimes they slept at his house the night before a tournament. On the road, his family often took them to dinner.

Morrissey had learned a lot from his Lewiston friends. He knew they hated dogs and hibachi. He also knew they played soccer unlike anyone else, and he was envious of their unity. When it came time for Scarborough's traditional playoff hair session, Morrissey opted for blue. It was his prediction, much like McGraw's, that he would face his friends in the final.

"They play a good soccer," Abdi H. told McGraw about Scarborough's stars. "Very physical, good style, a hardworking team."

And, of course, they're big. Scarborough's size advantage—even Lewiston's taller players, like Karim and Maslah, were significantly skinnier—and physical style meant that Lewiston's speed would be more important than ever.

"Move the ball fast and avoid hits," Abdi H. told his teammates. But he knew there would be hits. Caron, in particular, he knew to be a very physical player.

McGraw listened to Abdi H and Maslah. He listened to all of them, encouraging his captains to take the lead, ceding some of his authority. It was one of the biggest modifications he'd made as a coach as his roster had changed over the years, asking what they knew about the next team on the schedule, finding out who they'd played with and what they knew about them.

"One of the things I've learned is do less talking," he admits. "Which is hard for me."

When McGraw overhears his players on the sideline talking about what's going on in the game, he doesn't tell them to hush. He calls them over and asks questions.

"Yeah?" he encourages. "That's what we should do? Then do it—tell them out there!"

Based on stats, local pundits gave Lewiston the advantage in the showdown between the two top-ranked and unbeaten teams. While Scarborough's Caron and King were regional all-star selections, four Blue Devils made the cut: Karim and Zak, and Maslah and Abdi H., whose deadly precision-passing game had the Red Storm on high alert. While both teams had straight shutouts in the playoffs, Lewiston outscored opponents 13–0, while Scarborough topped their side of the bracket 7–0.

But McGraw knew there was one set of numbers his guys didn't have. This game marked only the third time in history that Lewiston soccer had played for a state championship. Scarborough not only had more experience playing in a state final. It had more experience winning it. A year before, Lewiston bowed to an opponent no one had given much thought. Now they were walking into the eye of a top-seeded Red Storm.

CHAPTER 16

EVERYONE BLEEDS BLUE

None of them could sleep. All throughout Lewiston, Blue Devils tossed and turned.

Up at five, the pressure of his first state final plagued Maslah. Usually so self-assured, today he was nervous. He kept thinking about sitting in the bleachers after the Cheverus game, absolutely devastated, tears rolling down his face. Cheverus was the seventh seed coming into that game, he kept thinking. And Lewiston lost. Now they were facing the best. Already showered, Maslah decided that worrying wasn't getting him anywhere. He ate something, brushed his teeth, and headed back to bed, hoping sleep would come.

Q felt the same way. He'd finally shut his eyes well after midnight, around two or so. When he woke up, he looked at the clock: six a.m. That surprised him. He usually wasn't an early riser, especially on a Saturday. But this was no ordinary Saturday. Like Maslah, he'd never played in a state final. Last year in Syracuse, he'd waited to hear from his friends about the championship game. When the texts finally came, the news wasn't good. Now he was back with his teammates. It was exciting, something he'd imagined since the moment his mother told him they were moving back to Lewiston.

Giving up on getting any more rest, Q got out of bed and pulled himself together. The oldest of eight, he wanted to get out of the apartment before anyone else woke up. *Food,* he thought. *Doughnuts.* He didn't eat doughnuts very often. They weren't cheap. But he wanted something different, something with frosting. Somali doughnuts, *kac kac,* didn't have frosting. They were more like a biscuit, eaten with tea. An American doughnut was a treat, Q thought, a breakfast of champions, maybe, to celebrate the day.

Leaving the apartment quietly, he walked over to the Italian Bakery. The white cement-block building sits on Bartlett Street next to Mark W. Paradis Park, where Maulid used to kick a ball around with his dad and Abdikadir Negeye held soccer practice in the early days of the SBYA league. The bakery is the one bit of color on the drab, run-down street, its red-and-green stripes and bright awning resembling the Italian flag. "E'molto buono!" the sign says—it's very good. The bakery opens at six every morning but Monday, its hand-cut doughnuts often selling out on the weekend.

It's early, Q noted again, as light crept across the city on his short walk to the bakery. *Really early.*

On the other side of the city, Austin, too, was awake and wanted a doughnut. He didn't go to the Italian Bakery; that was a more downtown thing. Instead, he drove over to Dunkin' Donuts, which he often did before school. The game was at noon, but Coach wanted them at the high school by ten. Everything felt off; they never played this early.

Dek didn't want doughnuts. He wanted sleep. He had been up most of the night thinking about the preseason loss to Scarborough. Now he was panicking that he wouldn't play well with so little sleep. He thought about last year's state final, which he, like Maslah, watched from the stands. It was terrifying to think about. *Cheverus was supposed to be easy,* he thought, *and Lewiston lost. What if it goes hard on us again? We need to get a wrench on these guys,* he decided. *We can't do anything stupid.* He looked at the clock. Still two hours until he had to leave. It was going to be a frustrating morning.

Like the others, Maulid had been awake for hours; up so early he took a thirty-minute nap at eight, unable to keep his eyes open. He woke up again when Q called. He wanted to come over to show Maulid his new haircut, which he was hiding from his mother. He got it cut after the ritual spaghetti dinner at Trinity the night before, a Mohawk like Nuri's. They wanted to do something cool—"beast mode," Q said—like the team had done last year when they sprayed their heads blue and white. "You look good, you play good," Gish always told them.

Let Scarborough waste time on hair, Maulid thought, his own shaped into a "box" style. But still, Q got a Mohawk? "Come over," Maulid told him. "My mom wants to see your hair. Then we'll get ready."

While the players were waking up, Gish's daughter Lilly was busy at the school decorating the team bus. "I've got to do something," she told him after they won the regional title. But Gish didn't really pay attention to her plans until his wife, Cindy, asked him about it.

"You guys decorating the bus?" she said.

"No," Gish answered. "Just want to keep things normal."

"Um, yeah," she responded. "That's not an option."

Cindy Gish knew Lewiston. Her father had worked as city clerk for decades, and she and her four sisters all graduated from the high school. Now principal of Geiger Elementary, she'd worked her way through the ranks of the school system, teaching first grade at

McMahon before serving as assistant principal there and at Montello. But back in the day, she was a state championship–winning cheerleader. She knew that Lilly's idea was a good one.

"You really need to decorate that bus," she repeated.

Gish stood firm. "We're going to keep it as normal as possible."

"Come on, we're going to decorate the bus," she replied. "They need that bus decorated."

Cindy and Lilly weren't talking about a few posters. They got blue-and-white streamers and made signs for each player to put in the windows. For the back of the bus, Lilly made a bigger sign: "WE LOVE McGRAW."

"That's awesome," Gish said when he saw it. "Just wicked."

When the players started arriving at the high school just before ten, Gish thought back to the classic husband-and-wife conversation. *My wife*, he thought, looking at the players' faces when they saw the bus, *is obviously the more intelligent person in the family.*

Q didn't see the bus when he arrived at the back of the school near the gym entrance. No one was there. He panicked. Did he miss it?

"Hey," Abdijabar Hersi called, walking over to him from his car. "You're in the wrong place."

Hersi and Q walked around to the front of the school. *Beautiful,* Q thought when he saw the bus. He'd never seen anything like it. The first time he was going to states, and he'd be riding a bus decorated like that? Unbelievable. No one had ever done anything like this for him. No one had ever done anything like this for *any* of them.

"Who did this so early in the morning?" Maulid asked when he walked up.

He shook McGraw's hand before stepping on the bus, taking in the posters, the drawings of trophies, and the streamers cascading from the ceiling all the way down the aisle. "WE R DEVILS" read a big sign in the middle. "L-H-S" read another. Maulid started to feel some of his nerves dissipate. It felt good, looking at this bus.

But Dek couldn't shake his nerves. He loved the decorations, the support they represented, but all of it made him more anxious. *I don't want to disappoint these people,* he thought, looking at the decorations. And his dad was going to the game. He didn't want to disappoint his dad.

They took their seats next to their bedazzled names, Q and Nuri's haircuts giving everyone something to talk about. Joe, too, had shaved the sides of his head. Q settled into his seat, finally smiling. Maslah, he noticed, wasn't talking to anyone, earbuds already in place. *Good idea,* Q thought, putting on his headphones.

Abdi H. was out of sorts as he approached the bus. Everything about this "noon environment," as he called it, felt weird. The routine was off. He felt better when he saw Doe Mahamud, the team statistician, waiting next to the bus, orange smoothie in hand. Always the nattiest guy on the field, Doe went all-out for the championship game with a suit and tie, a fedora topping his head. Abdi H. grabbed him and handed his phone to Gish for a photo. *That's more like it,* he thought as he boarded the bus, shaking his head. *Leave it to Doe.*

McGraw gave the team a few encouraging words as the bus pulled out of the parking lot and headed toward the turnpike. Abdi H. wondered if anyone was even listening. Because of the decorations, they couldn't see out the windows, which gave the bus an almost cave-like atmosphere.

"Listen up, listen up," McGraw rasped.

He didn't have much to say. The offense was unstoppable, the backline a wall. Usually he talked to them about the "what-ifs" of a game, about who might lure them into an offside trap, or put a shell on them. Both Mt. Blue and Mt. Ararat had done that, forcing them to make adjustments in the second half. McGraw had a hunch Scarborough would try the same to shut down Abdi H. and Maslah.

But he didn't need to tell them that. They were a mature group of guys. Mental preparation was their biggest challenge, and he'd been talking about that since the beginning of the season. *This is going to be my way* and *their way,* he thought. *I'm not going to tell them how to do this.* So he simply told them to play their game, no matter what Scarborough threw at them.

"It is going to be a game for the ages," he said. "The people down in Portland? They do not know what a great game it's going to be. It's going to be one of the games that's going to go down in history as something they're going to remember for a very, very long time."

McGraw took a moment to feel the enormity of what he was about to say. It was about more than soccer; it had been for quite a while. His players just wanted to play, just wanted to win. McGraw wanted that, too; wanted it for so long, it was hard to remember a time when he didn't want it. But he also knew where he was from, and what it meant to be coach of this team in this town with this one goal. He looked at them hard, his blue eyes serious. *Say it simple,* he thought.

"We are gonna do it together."

His shorter-than-usual speech done, McGraw got quiet. *That's rare,* thought Austin, but like everyone else, he hunkered down with his phone and his music, thinking about what was to come. *We've got this,* Austin thought.

As the bus neared the tall pines encircling Fitzpatrick Stadium, Nuri was done with the quiet. It was time to get loud, he decided. The chants began.

"*YAKULAK!*" the team yelled back at Nuri. Maulid loved that part. *We will eat them,* he thought. *We will get them.*

As the bus sat in the parking lot behind the stadium, the Blue Devils' tidal wave grew louder. "We could hear you from the field," some of the girls playing in the Gorham versus Bangor match told Austin about the chanting. "You were louder than our fans."

By Maine standards, Fitzpatrick Stadium is huge. Seating 6,000 people, it offers a full-scale turf playing field and a bright red rubberized track. It sits next to Hadlock Field, home of the Portland Sea Dogs, the Double-A affiliate of the Boston Red Sox. When the Blue Devils got off the bus, they walked behind Hadlock to the far side of the bleachers so they could have a few minutes to gather themselves.

McGraw was prepared. He'd made sure the assistant coaches had the answer to any logistical question that might come up. He wanted the players to stay focused. They were already dressed, their blue uniforms beneath their blue-and-white jackets and black pants, but still had to deal with socks and shin guards and cleats, find their hated mouth guards, and get taped.

As they approached their bench, Abdi H. ran over to the fence to greet a familiar figure. Ali Hersi, Abdijabar's younger brother, was waiting for them, the first of McGraw's alums to show up but by no means the last. Behind him, Lewiston fans started to fill the stands. AD Jason Fuller had arranged for two rooter buses to bring students. He was shocked when both sold out.

Fuller was having a crazy week. A few days before, senior Osman Doorow, born in Kenya to Somali parents and coached by Kim Wettlaufer, won the cross-country running state title. Now Fuller had another state championship on his hands. But he smiled as the buses pulled out. *That's our community, right there,* he thought, looking at the kids through the windows, faces painted blue and white regardless of what—baseball cap, ski hat, or hijab—they had on their head.

Fuller hurried home to grab his wife and three kids to head to

Portland. His kids went to Oak Hill, but were dressed head to foot in blue and white. *My kids bleed blue*, he thought, looking at them. When they arrived in Portland, Fuller was stunned by the traffic, especially because it was still an hour before game time. He knew where to park, but had no idea there would be this many people. As he walked toward the stadium, he started to get goose bumps. *This is a football crowd*, he thought. Scarborough versus Lewiston. A perfect storm.

When Shobow Saban had heard that both rooter buses sold out, he got busy. Some of the kids he worked with at MEIRS wanted to go to the game. They knew he loved soccer, that he probably was going, but they had no money. He called his cousin, some friends, anyone who had a car.

"I had to make sure that whoever asked me could get there and witness," he said of his preparations. "That they could say, 'I was there.'"

Shobow gassed up five cars that morning. But he, too, was stunned at the number of people filling the stands. It reminded him of when he went to a New England Revolution game at Gillette Stadium with McGraw. The noise, the crowds, the chanting fans. But these were Lewiston fans, Shobow thought. He flashed back to when his family had first arrived in Lewiston, the days when people told him to leave.

His mother told him then to have a big heart, to have empathy. "When you love others," she said, "sincerely love them, you will eventually get it back." Looking at the crowd of Blue Devils fans—white, black, Muslim, Catholic, Somali, Franco—Shobow realized that his mother was right. While his community wasn't perfect, it was better. He felt the stereotypes—terrorist, drug dealer, pirate—that had plagued him just a few years ago beginning to disappear. Here, he thought looking at the field, he was a proud Lewiston soccer player.

From the field, Austin kept glancing at the stands as he drilled with Alex, rotating post to post while Henrikson tossed balls at them from the eighteen. Section after section was a sea of blue and white, with a smaller wall of red representing Scarborough to the right. Austin couldn't find his family. It wasn't like a home game where his mother was in the Snack Shack and his father was grilling.

"This feels like premier league," Maulid said to Mwesa and Joe as they started jogging around the field. As they ran by their own fan section, the crowd went nuts, clanging cowbells and beating drums while yelling "WOOOOOOOOoooOOOOOO DEVILS!" They waved to people they knew, turning every time someone called their names. Maulid saw his sisters and brothers, his mom and dad, his four cousins from Vermont, and his baby niece.

"I wonder if they made her buy a ticket," he joked. She wasn't even a year old.

Maulid's family, like so many others, had made signs for the game. Abdiweli held one high over his head—an enormous #11 accompanied by a collage of newspaper clippings and photographs of Maulid, including the now-iconic photo of him leaping onto Maslah's back in the EL game. Nearby in the student section, a friend held up a sign that read "WARNING: HE COULD FLIP AT ANY TIME—#11 MAULID!" Maulid appreciated the support, but the noise was getting to him. The crowd was so close. He pulled up his hood, trying to shut it out. "It's windy," he said when teammates asked him what he was doing.

Fuller stood in front of the bleachers on the red track, his head moving in time to the beating drums. *Stay in your seats,* he silently pleaded with the fans, thinking years back to the Mt. Ararat game and the excessive celebration call. He climbed into the bleachers to sit for a bit. He wanted to remind them about what was at stake, about making good choices. And to stay in their seats.

Laps done, the Blue Devils jogged down the center of the field, cutting off Scarborough. A small smile played on Maslah's lips as he ran by. While Scarborough sat to stretch, Lewiston launched into its warm-up sequence, chanting and clapping in four lines. Intimidating as always, they made it hard for Scarborough to focus on its own warm-up routine.

As Lewiston geared up shots on goal, the crowd took notice. "That would've been NASTY!" someone called to Maslah after he just missed the net. "That would've been SICK!"

Abdi H. went into captain mode, watching everyone like a hawk. He wanted them to focus, to shed their anxieties before the first whistle. "Forget the crowd," he said. "Forget our national ranking, forget the media attention. None of those things are going to help us play better. Focus on the task at hand for the next ninety minutes. Then, only then, we celebrate."

But they kept looking for friends and family. Nuri saw his mom, Tarig Ali, down in front next to Muktar's little brother, Warsame. Her bright turquoise hijab stood in stark contrast to her long, dark coat, her arms holding a sign wishing him luck in four languages—Arabic, Somali, Turkish, and English—with "WE LOVE YOU NURI!" and "WE BELIEVE IN YOU GUYS!" scrawled above.

Outside the stadium, Lise Wagner, Eric's sister, stopped in her tracks, dumbfounded. An assistant attorney general in Portland, she'd been surprised to wake up to a *Portland Press Herald* front-page story about the Blue Devils. "With players from around the world, Lewiston soccer team may bring home a state title," read the headline, accompanied by a gorgeous photograph of Abdi H. encircled by the team. Wagner had long believed the paper had a bias against her hometown, as if there were a wall around Lewiston preventing anyone from noticing them. It was a Lewiston thing, and she was used to it. But now there were people everywhere, here to watch Lewiston play soccer. *Was it the article?* she wondered, grabbing her son, Doug, and getting into the line for tickets.

The ticket line, which wound all the way back through the streets, surprised Abdikadir Negeye, too. Seeing it jolted him back to the refugee camps, where he'd stood in long lines every day to get rations or to see a doctor. The only time he ever waited in line in Maine was when President Obama visited. Until today.

It was emotional for him, this game. He'd coached so many of these players, like Abdi H. and Maslah, when they were younger. Now here they were, trying again to bring a championship to Lewiston. Everywhere he looked, he saw someone he knew; people who'd never been to a soccer game but were here now to support the players, the team, and the community.

"It was like a rainbow," he remembers, envious of the students' blue-and-white face paint. "And loud, with people playing drums and yelling 'GO BLUE!' as they walked by."

While Lise Wagner waited in line, Eric was home in Pennsylvania. He'd paid to watch the game through the MPA's online live feed, something he'd done once before. He set up camp in his kitchen, where the pale blue walls provided a calming backdrop. His wife was at work. His two boys opted for video games in the living room. Placing his laptop on the small, dark table, he glanced at the silver mirrored clock that hung above. Almost game time. His phone buzzed with a text from Lise.

"STANDING IN LONG LINE TO GET IN."

Eric was thrilled that his sister and nephew were there, but he so wished he could join them. He knew a lot of his former teammates were in the stands. He eased atop a barstool and looked at his screen. As the signal paused, buffering, Eric was glad he had their eyes and ears to bring him the flavor, if not the action, of the game. He settled in, staring at his computer, waiting.

In the ticket line, Lise saw an elderly man who looked familiar. That's Curtis Webber, she realized, an attorney from Lewiston. She called out to the eighty-two-year-old, who seemed to be alone. *That's pretty cool,* she thought as he walked over to greet them.

"PICKED UP CURT WEBBER TO SIT WITH US," she texted Eric.

Tickets in hand, Webber in tow, they went to find seats. For the second time that morning, she stopped. Before her sat a vast, moving, loud, blue-and-white jamboree with faces both strange and familiar. Finding seats, she recognized many around her. *These are just regular Lewiston folks,* she realized, *here to see the game.*

"You look really familiar," she kept saying as the bleachers filled. There was Peter Garcia, another attorney; she went to law school with his son, Adam. She turned around to find Rob Gardiner, the former president of WCBB television. Writer Phillip Hoose, who'd won the National Book Award for his book about Claudette Colvin, was a few rows over, talking about how excited he was for the game.

"That's what was amazing to me," she says of that moment. "It wasn't just parents and students—it was the community members that were there, that were thrilled to be there, just a big love-fest."

While Lise and Doug settled in, Ronda Fournier went to the MPA table to check in. Although dressed like any other weekend sports fan in blue jeans and a gray Blue Devils hoodie, Fournier had an official reason to be at the game, volunteering to supervise the bleachers. Even though she was transitioning to her new job at Montello, she wouldn't have missed it for the world. These were her kids, and they always would be. As a colleague had told her, "Once you get that blue in your blood, it never leaves."

Nevah.

Fuller was glad to have Fournier on board to help him prevent fans from swamping the field after the final buzzer. He didn't want Lewiston ever again penalized for such behavior. Fournier understood: keep the fans in the stands, no matter what. But as she climbed through the overwhelming mass of blue and white— "Mrs. Fournier!" students cried—she realized that this was easier said than done. Students and teachers from elementary on up were everywhere, talking about which players they knew, exchanging memories about whom they'd had in class.

"This," she said to no one in particular, "is *incredible.*"

It was like the community knew: this was Lewiston's year.

As principal, Shawn Chabot felt that was true. But the game fell on a drill weekend for Chabot, putting him up in Augusta with his National Guard unit. He told his commander about the game, that he had to go. The commander agreed.

In full military dress, Chabot wanted to fly below the radar, but as he approached the stadium's gates, he gasped at the line. While things moved at a steady clip, it was a thirty-minute wait for a ticket.

Thank God I have my MPA card, Chabot thought, plunking it down for the ticket guy to see.

Walking in, he saw Fuller, but self-conscious of his military garb, he moved to the other side of the stadium. He didn't want to attract attention, a principal dressed up like a soldier. This day wasn't about him.

Chabot took in the Lewiston fan sections. All he saw was blue. Black faces, white faces, young, old. Everyone was in blue. This wasn't a turning point for the community, he thought. This was a pinnacle, a very public demonstration of what Lewiston was becoming, had become, would become. Otherwise, these people wouldn't be here, together, to watch this team. It was a proud day for Lewiston public schools, for teachers, administrators, coaches, students, and parents. There were still problems, to be sure, but that crowd sent a message. *It doesn't matter who you are,* he thought. *We're going to take you for what you do and what you stand for.*

"Welcome to Fitzpatrick Stadium for today's boys Class A state championship soccer match!" the announcer called as the teams followed the refs onto the field. At the center, Lewiston rolled off to the left, Scarborough to the right. Standing in one long line spanning almost the length of the field magnified just how much taller, bigger, the Red Storm was.

"Today's teams," the announcer continued, "the visitors in their blue uniforms with a record of seventeen wins and no losses, the northern Maine champion Blue Devils of Lewiston High School."

Zak raised his arms over his head, making a number one sign with his hands.

"And the home team, in their white uniforms, with a record of fifteen wins, no losses, and two ties, the southern Maine champion Red Storm of Scarborough High School."

As the announcer introduced game officials, both teams fidgeted, antsy. Cam Nigro took long looks down Lewiston's lineup, his massive blond Mohawk the tallest on the field. As the announcer called Lewiston's starters, the crowd howled. Zak raised his arms up and down, asking for more. When he heard his name, he placed his fist on his heart before raising it again, turning slightly toward the Lewiston bleachers. Zak was in his element. *We're so ready,* he thought, glancing at Scarborough. *They don't know what's coming for them.*

Booing could be heard throughout Lewiston's bleacher sections during Scarborough's introductions. Moe listened, his blue mouth guard dangling from his confident smile.

"This is our house," he said again. "They can be the home team, but this is our house."

CHAPTER 17

MAKE IT A GOOD ONE

Moe couldn't keep quiet. After pregame formalities finished, the team huddled tightly together, arms around one another, twitching, squirming, their feet bouncing on the bright green turf as McGraw reminded them to pressure the ball, pass, shoot. When the coach stepped away, Moe wanted to make sure their heads were exactly where they needed to be.

"Yo, listen, listen, listen up," he began, hunched in the middle, a black turtleneck underneath his jersey giving him an air of sophistication. Maulid leaned in so far, his head almost grazed Moe's, while Muktar stood still and silent trying to settle his nerves, his shaved head making him seem smaller than usual.

"All right, we're doing this for the guy on the left and for the guy on the right," Moe continued. "All right? We're doing this for the community. We're doing this for Coach McGraw, all right, who'd give up anything to be on this field right now. Last year we were here, we lost it. This is our year. No one is going to stop us, right?"

"YEAHHHHHHHHHHHHHHH," the circle roared. "HUBBA HUBBA HUBBA!"

Nuri stepped in, his hands cupping his mouth like a megaphone. Moe thought back to that night at Karim and Zak's when they found the chant and bellowed it together. Now, Nuri's voice strained as he bounced from his left foot to his right, his teammates screaming back at him.

"*YAKULAK!*"

I will do this for Coach McGraw, Nuri thought, walking to the field with Dek. *I have worked hard for him.* Moha jogged up and put his arms around them for some last-minute encouragement before heading to the bench. The embraces felt good, necessary. Abdi H. took a few leaps to make sure his legs were loose, while Dek high-kicked his way to the backline.

"CHAMPIONSHIP FOR McGRAW!"

McGraw felt a release. All season, he'd worried they'd get complacent and suffer last year's cruel fate. Now he let those worries go. They were prepared, mentally and physically, to play this game. This was it. Everything else got thrown out. Those 113 goals, the national ranking, the undefeated record? Gone. Blank slate.

"Pass the ball, shoot the ball!" he yelled at their backs. He couldn't help himself.

Standing in the goal, his neon-green jersey bright against the gray day, Austin wasn't thinking about the 113 goals or the 150 shots they didn't finish. He was thinking about the few times he'd made a save. Sometimes he thought about sleeping during a game. What did he get, 30 shots all fall? Some goalies got 30 shots a game. But he was ready to pounce on whatever came his way. "Let them take a shot," McGraw always said to the backline. "That's why you have a goalie." Flashy goals got the headlines, but, as Karim always said to his brother, "defense wins."

As defensive coordinator, Gish never got the credit he deserved for Lewiston's record. Almost nothing got past Dek, Zak, and

Moe throughout the playoffs, and when something did, Austin was there. But nothing got past Cam Nigro, either. The kid was an absolute monster, just huge, the "00" on his shirt inexplicably making him more intimidating. From across the field, Zak couldn't stop looking at Nigro's enormous yellow Mohawk. *That hair's just shocking,* he thought. Shocking and tall.

Austin knew their defense was special. They were good on the ball, which most teams didn't expect, and their communication, almost always in Somali so the other team didn't know what they were up to, was tight. No one needed to translate anything for Austin—he knew the drill, having jumped into pickup games at Drouin. They threaded the defense like clockwork. It was so stupid when someone asked him what it felt like to be the only white kid on the field. He was a piece of a whole; together brothers.

Austin snapped to attention when he heard the whistle. Scarborough put the ball into play. It was a sloppy start, every pass blocked, every ball wildly kicked. All season, Lewiston had tried to score early, throwing the opposition off-balance. But the Red Storm came out hard, launching a counter attack to break up the Blue Devils' passing rhythm.

Before the game, Scarborough coach Mark Diaz predicted a 1–0 shutout, but he wasn't sure which team would land on top. He hoped for just one offensive opportunity so they could then run out the clock. A 4–5–1 counter attack was Scarborough's best chance, creating a stronger midfield to control the game's pace and giving them more defending options. But it left only one striker to do the brunt of the offensive work.

Lewiston knew it had to spread the field and use its wide players, so they could better whatever pace Scarborough tried to set. However, the proximity of the bleachers to the field and the large media presence on the sidelines made it harder for the Blue Devils to get into their groove. There was little room to overrun anything with such a tight perimeter.

But nothing impacted them like the noise of the crowd, which kept growing. Ignoring his own advice, Abdi H. kept looking at the blur of the thousands cheering, trying to make out faces, noticing the number of Lewiston soccer shirts, alumni—old men—squeezing into vintage stock. Zak and Karim, too, kept scanning the bleachers for a glance of their parents, their little sister, their three brothers. They weren't used to having so much family at a game.

"Need to get Coach his first trophy and all that," Zak said, refocusing his attention on the game. "It's the most important thing."

McGraw knew the crowd made them nervous. "Afterwards, we can talk about how many fans there are," he told them. But it was hard. McGraw's wife, Rita, their daughter, Katie, and his sisters were there.

About four minutes in, Maulid launched his first flip throw, slipping as he put the ball on the ground and sending it straight into the air, high over his head. As the ball bounced, Nuri ran in, tossing Matt Caron to the ground as he tried to get a head on it. McGraw laughed at the throw. It felt good to laugh, loosened him up a bit. He looked at Zak and Dek, who were chuckling. *Maybe this will help,* he thought.

The ball returned to Maulid's hands. *I gotta whip it in lower,* he thought, running forward. He sent the ball straight to the box. Nigro leaped into the air, punching it away with both fists. *It was better,* Maulid thought. *But still not good.*

Both sides continued to scramble. Lacking Lewiston's technical ability, Scarborough kicked and chased down the field, dropping behind whenever Lewiston took possession, ensuring a cluster of white-shirted traffic between the ball and Nigro. Scarborough's height prevented Lewiston from getting its head on much of anything, forcing the midfield to focus on defense as the Red Storm came close to breaking through.

While everyone else struggled, Zak tempered Caron's monster throw-ins with such speed and dexterity, it felt like he was every-where, a one-man wall. For the last several days, Gish had drilled them hard on defending set pieces. It paid off: Zak was killing it.

At midfield, Q, too, shook off his nerves, impressing the crowd with his footwork. While the Red Storm tried to shut down Lewiston's stars, man-marking Abdi H. and Maslah and doubling Karim, they neglected Q. But he'd worked hard on his touch all season, and this game looked to be his opus. He loved his "flicks and turns," as he called them, and patiently moved the ball with double scissors, step overs, and perfectly executed Cruyff turns, his head up, unafraid. He was ready to take Scarborough apart. He fed the ball to Maslah, who passed to Abdi H., who sent it back to Maslah for a shot. As Nigro fell to the ground, the ball safely in his hands, he looked like he'd been trampled, knowing just how close the ball was to going in.

Lewiston's bench groaned, feeling the save in their bones as if they were out there. Watching them, Gish heard a rumbling. Usually hyper-focused, everything tuned out, he turned around for a split second. Fans spilled into the once-empty bleachers be-hind the bench. *They've had to open more sections,* an astonished Gish realized. *How many people are here?*

"BOOM BOOM!" thundered stomping feet. "DE-VILS!"

"S-T," others countered, "O-R-M!"

Lewiston's offense fought hard to get on the board in the first half but couldn't penetrate Scarborough's hopped-up defense. Neither Maulid's flips nor Nuri's corners got them anywhere. They kept attacking Scarborough's left flank, trying to create chances, but Caron always got there to block a shot, stop a cross, or take down a player. As the game got more physical, Lewiston began to fall into Scarborough's kick-and-chase style, unable to play its own game for more than a few touches at a time.

Maulid felt a fist sink into his stomach and tried to ignore it, but it came again. No foul.

Dek knew they weren't playing their game. He was so tense. It felt like the entire city was there, and he didn't want to disappoint any of them. He could hear Coach Abdi in his head reminding them to keep the ball down and pass. But they weren't doing that. It was like they forgot everything they knew.

Including McGraw's warning to never retaliate.

As Abdi H. lined up to take a corner, he heard the whistle blow several times. He saw Nigro straighten up, clapping. *What is going on?* he thought. Then he knew. As Maslah jogged over to Lewiston's bench for his ten-minute penalty, a ref held the yellow card high over his head.

"He punched him in the stomach, and I'm only giving him a yellow," the ref told McGraw, who'd walked out to find out what happened.

"Yep, yep," McGraw replied, turning back toward the bench. "NO FOULS!"

Maslah couldn't help it. He hated Scarborough—their attitude, their stupid hair. Two players kept taunting him, yanking off his captain's band whenever there was a corner kick. They did it to Abdi H., too.

"That's very clever," Abdi H. said the first time it happened. He wasn't going to let them in his head. "I've never seen that before."

But Maslah wasn't Abdi H. He hated it when people touched him on the field. The third time it happened, he snapped.

"Don't take off my captain band!" Maslah yelled, punching the kid.

Muktar replaced Maslah, who hid behind the bench, his head in his hands as teammates Ian Hussey and Yusuf Mohamed brought him water. Abdi H. finally took his kick and sent the ball to Karim, who tried to head it in, but failed. They couldn't make progress. Q could handle Nigro's gigantic goal kicks and get the ball to Karim, but with Maslah on the bench and three or four white shirts shutting down Abdi H., there was nowhere to go. Something had to change.

McGraw pulled Nuri.

"You aren't playing your game," he told the sophomore, who knew it was true. He was playing scared, and needed to calm down.

But Muktar, as usual, played best when scared. He tore up the field, passing with Abdi H. and taking shots. They started to build plays from the back, using short volleys to break Scarborough's defense.

"GOOD EFFORT!" yelled McGraw, finally liking what he saw.

With fourteen minutes left in the first half, Q drove down the field but fell when Josh Morrissey descended upon him. Caron got a lot of headlines, but Morrissey was good. He'd scored the winning goal against Lewiston in the preseason.

Q heard the whistle from the ground as his teammates ran over to make sure he was all right. Foul. Lewiston ball. As Dek's perfect free kick arched in, Karim rose above the tight traffic before the net and headed the ball as Nigro met him in the air. The two fell to the ground as the ball went in. Lewiston's fans roared while the Red Storm waved their hands in objection until they heard the whistle.

Offside.

"STAY ONSIDE!" McGraw yelled, refusing to consider whether the call was valid. It didn't matter.

Abdi H. wanted to object, but knew better. He started running backward, trying to bring his team into position as Nigro launched the ball.

"We'll get another one!" he heard Karim yell. "We'll just get another one!"

But they didn't. As the clocked ticked down, both teams battled for possession in front of the Blue Devils' backline, whose defensive dance prevented Scarborough's set pieces from doing any harm. When Maslah returned to the field, Lewiston started to build again, engaging in rapid-fire keep-away: Moe to Zak to Dek to Karim. Joe waited patiently on the outside, shepherding the ball from Dek to Q, who faked a pass to Abdi H. and sent it back to Karim to boot downfield. Nothing came of it, but they were moving the ball like they wanted, figuring out how to turn on speed while showing Scarborough no fear. With seconds left, Maulid flipped the ball in, but they couldn't capitalize before the whistle blew. For the first time all season, Lewiston was scoreless at the half.

Up in the stands, Lise Wagner glanced at her phone.

"How are we playing?" Eric texted, still unable to get his feed working.

"Well, but Scarborough is all over them," she responded. "No score at the half."

Nearby, Abdikadir Negeye felt tense. He'd been so focused; he couldn't believe it was halftime. Scarborough looked like giants next to skinny Lewiston, he thought, but the teams were well matched. Both had such strong defense. But he knew what everyone was thinking: if Lewiston didn't find their game, launch a counter attack, it would be like Cheverus all over again. They could do this. But they needed to calm down, communicate. Do what they did so very well.

Down on the field, McGraw, too, knew things still weren't right. His offense, which usually set the tone of the game, had not. He wasn't worried, not yet. But he wanted to tweak some things.

These guys beat us once, Maslah kept saying to his teammates, recalling the preseason game. We don't want it to happen again. Let's learn from our mistakes. But they were freaked. Zak, who had played the first half with such confidence, shutting down the seemingly unstoppable Jake Kacer and disarming Caron's throw-ins, started to feel last year's game creep in. Zero–zero meant that defense couldn't let a single ball past. He knew that was Scarborough's plan: play defense and look for that one goal. He couldn't let it happen.

"*We're* gonna get that one goal, not them," Q said, confident that once they put one in, everyone would want to score. "We've just got to wait for it to come."

As the team listened to McGraw, Abdijabar Hersi felt good, not nervous. At first, the crowd had intimidated him, too. Walking around before the game, he couldn't get over how many people he recognized from his own leagues and from the ones his little brother Bilal played in. Everyone was there to see what Lewiston could do. *We're on the right track,* he thought. *We're starting to play how we need to.*

"Control," he told Abdi H. "You're a captain—take control, and they won't even have a chance to score."

But Abdi H. was having a rough game. Scarborough double-marked him, so every time he received the ball, there was someone in front and behind. Hersi had a remedy for that. A few days earlier, it occurred to him they needed to rethink who played where. Moha, for example, was too good to be sitting on the bench. He was one of their largest players, powerful, excellent on the ball. He'd played well in the regional final when Karim sat out. What if they put him up top with Maslah and moved Abdi H. to left wing, where he could have a field day with his speed and his feet, needing to beat only one defender instead of the group assigned to him? Against Cheverus last year, with Abdi H. up front, they couldn't get as physical as they needed to. But Moha could get physical. Let him get banged up and pushed around. If they lost possession, his midfielder mind-set would kick in; he'd drop while Maslah stayed. When they had possession, he'd be the bull in a china shop they needed, throwing elbows as necessary.

The next day at practice, Hersi had talked to his colleagues. Henrikson and Gish immediately liked his idea. McGraw admitted that it was an interesting tactic because Scarborough likely hadn't scouted Moha, but the idea of moving Abdi H. was tough. Eventually he agreed.

It was time to put the plan into action.

"We're doing a good job," McGraw said before sending them back out. "Don't foul, play straight up, do your job." Moe flanked him while Abdi H. stayed back, thinking about his new position in the second half and worrying about the scoreboard. He knew Scarborough had one of the best defenses in the state. How could they find their rhythm?

"Forty minutes," McGraw said. "Let's see what kind of conditioning we've got—let's take advantage of the one break we're gonna get, and we'll see what we see."

"ONE, TWO, THREE: *PAMOJA NDUGU!*"

"TOGETHER!" McGraw yelled as the team ran out.

As the team's momentum unfolded, their passes sharper and more controlled, McGraw remained calm. It was only going to be a matter of time, he thought. If it went into overtime, no problem. Penalty kicks? No problem. At that point, the game was a flip of the coin anyway. His team hadn't been shut out since 2013.

McGraw's instincts were good. Lewiston created more opportunities, patiently moving the ball from Moe to Maslah to Q to Abdi H. and back to Maslah, playing wider as McGraw always begged them to. Abdi H. took the ball more easily on the left with Dek behind him, defending. Zak released to Q; Moe relayed to Maulid. Up top, Karim saw how Moha unnerved Scarborough. It felt good to have someone else with some size, especially as the game continued to get more physical, players littering the ground with each play.

After Morrissey cleared one of Nuri's kicks, Moe tried to send the ball back, and body-checked Scarborough's Jake Kacer to the ground in the process. Whistle. As everyone waited for the call, Morrissey walked over to Moe. He heard the trash talk, knew what kind of game was unfolding, and, as a captain, he wanted to set an example of good sportsmanship. He also heard racial slurs, monkey noises, hurled at Lewiston from the other side of the fence. He didn't know who was yelling such things. But it was affecting his own game, so he couldn't imagine what it was doing to his Lewiston friends. He was angry, embarrassed.

Morrissey told Moe that he was impressed by Lewiston's chemistry. There was no doubt they were the better team. It was a bittersweet epiphany, Morrissey remembers, because at that moment, he realized that Lewiston was going to win. As Moe looked at his friend, amazed by the revelation, touched by the gesture, he saw the ref reach into his pocket. Yellow card. Enough talking. There was still a game to play, but Moe was going to have to take a seat.

Karim tried to comfort Moe while Joe ran out onto the field to sub. Energized by the call, Scarborough sent the ball hurtling toward Austin, who made the save. After one of Caron's throw-ins went over the crossbar, Austin's restart grabbed momentum back for Lewiston. Karim and Q pressured; Joe relentlessly fed Maulid and Maslah. With just over seventeen minutes left, a corner kick from Nuri landed right in front of Moha, who failed to beat Nigro in a one-on-one, missing at point-blank range.

"YEAH!" screamed Nigro, leaping up and raising his hands toward the Scarborough fans. Moha grabbed his head, anguished, while Maulid prepared for the throw-in. It was his fifth flip in the half, his twelfth of the game. Maulid had protested to McGraw that it wasn't working, especially after that first one, but McGraw was resolute.

"Maulid," McGraw said to him, his eyes gleaming, "do it again."

Maulid asked a photographer crouched down on the track to move so he could make his run. He took a deep breath. He knew this could work, just like it had in the game against Bangor, when Nuri put it into the net from the left post. His grip wasn't a problem anymore. Each time he did it, it felt less risky. *You think Caron can whip it in?* Maulid silently asked the jeering Scarborough fans. *Watch this.*

He backed all the way to the outer fence, ignoring the monkey noises behind him. He wanted to make this his longest run yet. As he surveyed the field, he felt a tap on his shoulder.

"Make it a good one," said Kim Wettlaufer, who was standing at the fence with Carolyn, their infant daughter strapped to her chest. Wettlaufer never sat at big games. He had to pace when he was tense. Today, he was tense.

Maulid got fired up. He liked Wettlaufer, who'd helped his family when they first arrived in Lewiston. Maulid remembered getting in trouble for playing tag in a community garden, stomping on the plants. Wettlaufer talked to him, stood up for him, got him out of trouble. Maulid was excited that Wettlaufer was right there, just as he'd always been.

I can do this, he thought. He ran forward, gathering speed. As he catapulted his body toward the ground, ball securely between his hands as it hit the pitch, his legs flew up over his head. He whirled upright and unleashed the ball over the traffic surrounding Nigro.

"Damn," said McGraw as he watched the ball arch toward the goal. "Will somebody please put a head on that? PUT IT IN!"

Maulid couldn't have placed the ball better if it'd had a pilot aboard. Q stood at the six while Abdi H. waited next to Caron. As soon as the ball left Maulid's hands, Abdi H. rolled to the post, Caron chasing. As he angled to take a shot, Caron blocked him. Nigro leaped into the air, trying to punch the ball away from the cluster of players so tight around him, it looked like there was nowhere to land. Karim, Moha, and Nuri crowded in, purposefully blocking Nigro's view. As Nigro crashed to the ground, the ball glanced off Caron and went into the back corner of the net.

Goal!

Caron raised his hands, bewildered, while Abdi H. stared at the ball, trying to digest what had happened. Maslah fell to his knees, but then leaped up, shock and joy on his face. He launched a blistering celebration run as Abdi H. turned, arms raised, and sprinted to catch up. Moha, Maulid and Joe scampered to join in. From left back, Dek was the first to reach the Lewiston fan section after waiting a moment to make sure no one called a foul. *Damn, we scored!* he thought, looking at the sea of screaming blue-and-white faces. *We are actually going to win this!*

As the rest of the blue swarm neared Lewiston's fan section, Q leaped into the air to greet Zak. They piled on Abdi H., all tumbling to the ground.

That was the most important throw-in ever, Maslah thought. *Now let's take that trophy home.*

An "own goal," meaning a goal scored by a team on itself, has an uncomfortable history in soccer. After scoring one against the United States during the Men's World Cup in 1994, Colombian Andrés Escobar returned to a country furious with him. Days later, three men confronted him in a nightclub parking lot, allegedly yelling "GOOOOOAAAAAL!" Six shots later, he was dead.

For Caron, however, there were no mortal consequences. He knew all too well what could happen with a good throw-in.

"Did we score?" Maulid yelled when he reached his teammates, unsure of what happened. "DID WE SCORE?" he repeated, leaping onto the pile on Abdi H.'s back. "Nice goal," he said to his teammate.

Up in the stands, Negeye, like Maulid, wasn't sure what had happened. Did someone touch it? Did it count? Someone had to touch it for it to count. Negeye saw Abdi H. running—maybe he touched it? Maybe Maslah?

"Own goal!" someone yelled.

"That was ME?" Maulid screamed when he heard the announcer explain the own goal to the crowd and credit it to him. For an entire year, they'd waited for this one goal, and he had done it. He thought for a second about the people making monkey noises. *Take that.*

On the sideline, Moe knew instantly what had happened when he saw Abdi H. and Maslah take off in celebration. He jumped on Gish, so emotional he didn't know what to do. Gish squeezed him, hard, while Henrikson—ponytail flying—jumped into the air, looking more like a rock concert fan than a soccer coach.

Fuller, however, did not celebrate. When the ball went in, he wheeled around to see that Ronda Fournier had mayhem on her hands. She begged the ecstatic students to stay in their seats. While the own goal confused them, as soon as McGraw's arms went up, they knew it was good. Fournier hugged the front rail to keep everything contained. Even Shobow wanted to rush the field, but knew better.

"Yell whatever you want—just don't run onto the field!" Fuller shouted, trying to calm the increasingly rowdy kids around him.

Looking at the 1–0 scoreboard, Shawn Chabot went into high alert. Visitors were always shocked by how quiet Lewiston High School was on any given day. Chabot didn't like chaos there; he didn't want to see it here. He didn't want kids jumping out of seats, tumbling onto the field. He saw Fournier holding them back, talking to them. It was under control for now, but did he dare think forward for a moment? *If we win,* he thought, *what's going to happen?*

One of the people fighting the crowd was Maulid's father, who'd gotten up to buy a drink, albeit keeping his eyes on his son the whole time. Now he couldn't get back to his seat. When he heard the name called after the goal—MAULID ABDOW— he scrambled through the crowd, wanting to be part of the celebration, pushing until he reached friends and family. He couldn't believe it; all these people were cheering his son.

"Don't let them draw the foul!" McGraw yelled to the field, knowing a lot could change with one goal, Scarborough ramping it up to equalize.

Austin, too, was on edge. His experience in big games told him that his teammates would play down for a bit, potentially giving Scarborough more offensive opportunities. He didn't want to go into overtime; he wanted to keep the shutout. But he also wanted them to keep attacking.

From the stands, Denis Wing knew his son's dilemma the second the scoreboard flipped to 1–0. He'd been calm until the ball went into the net. But as soon as he jumped up to celebrate, he felt a hammer hit him—BOOM! His stomach sank, nerves overtaking his entire body. He glanced at the clock to see how long the defense was going to have to hold. The game had just gotten real.

He had no idea how real. Less than a minute later, Caron penetrated Lewiston's backline, leaving just Austin between Scarborough's star and the net. Austin didn't get this kind of challenge very often, but he was ready. He wouldn't hesitate like he had the year before against Cheverus. He and Henrikson reviewed that first Cheverus goal over and over, making corrections to prepare for just this moment. As he dove for the breakaway save, grabbing the ball, he knew it was going to be bad. It was. Caron's knee connected with Austin's jaw, his elbow to his chest, and his foot to his left shoulder. Austin flipped before hitting the ground and descending into brief darkness.

"Is he okay?" Denis Wing yelled to no one, ready to run onto the field.

Zak bolted for his keeper, screaming that he had to get up. Joe and Dek stood, expressions of horror frozen on their faces. Dek was right behind Caron when it happened, giving him a close look. *There's no way he isn't going out,* Dek thought. He looked down at Austin as Zak and Nuri approached.

"Yo, please, please," Dek said to Austin, "just don't go out."

"Take it," Zak yelled at Austin, reaching down to help him. "Take it like a man—get up."

On the sideline, Alex Rivet started to lose his mind. *Get up, get up, get up,* he chanted silently, unsure of whether his concern was for Austin's well-being or his own. He usually only went in when they were ahead, way ahead.

With Zak's help, Austin sat up. He was shaking a little, his knees wobbly. But he didn't want to go out. He reassured the ref he was fine. He noticed a gull flying overhead in the gray. Was the fog in the sky or his head? Dek took Austin's head between his hands and looked into his eyes. It was okay. They'd be okay.

"YOU CAN'T DO THAT!" Lewiston fans chanted at Caron when the ref held up a yellow card, booking Caron for the foul.

Fuller paced anxiously in front of the bleachers, listening to the fans chant, loving how spirited this big crowd was, how they energized the community. But he still worried. *Please don't blow this,* he silently begged. *Please stay put.*

Mouth guard dangling from his lips, Austin took a deep breath before booting the ball downfield as far as he ever had. Inspired by Caron's yellow card, the Blue Devils relentlessly attacked. They knew the dynamic would change when Caron returned to the pitch, and they wanted to make the most of it.

Scarborough's game got messier, more physical. Moha warded off players, Maslah continued to pressure, and Dek and Zak absorbed a lot of abuse. With fourteen minutes left, Scarborough sent a low shot at Austin, who crouched and scooped it up, falling forward but never letting go, never hesitating, never flinching. *He's fine,* Zak thought, running over for a fist-bump while Q and Maulid battled the ball back downfield.

Finally, Lewiston's game was in full force. Maslah patiently toyed with the ball, going one-to-one through Scarborough's midfield before delicately chopping it to Abdi H., who danced through two defenders, weaving and faking, before getting off a gorgeous pass to Maulid. As Moe reentered the game, his ten-minute punishment finally up, he felt like he was playing on a different team. *This,* he thought, *is Lewiston soccer.*

Eager to get back into the game, Moe saw an opportunity as the ball soared overhead, smack in the center of the field, on a high bounce. He wanted to put a head on that ball. He saw Morrissey coming fast as he sprinted toward it, his eyes never leaving the spinning black-and-white hexagons, but never saw Karim coming on the right with the same idea.

"I just remember running for the ball and that's it—I don't know where Moe came from," Karim recalls.

As Moe tore into the air, he hit Karim, who violently crashed down on his back. Moe's legs flew over his head in a complete aerial. He hurtled down on his head, his neck bending back as he landed facedown on the pitch. Darkness.

"OHMYGOD," Moe says recalling the moment, pain visible on his face. "I'm glad I'm alive."

That was a hellacious hit, Fuller thought as the fans went silent.

He waited for some kind of reassurance that they weren't dead. *Move*, Fuller thought. *Just move.*

Karim rolled onto his knees and collapsed, face-first, into the turf. As he sat up, Moha reached down to him while Dek sat, just staring at him. Nearby, Moe clutched his head, flat on his back, moaning. McGraw froze when he saw blood running out of Karim's mouth. *This is bad*, he thought as he walked onto the field, Gish at his side.

"Great," Austin worried, watching from goal, his own head still foggy. "Now we're going to have two people come in."

While two trainers tended to Karim, helping him to stand, another talked to Moe.

"Where am I?" Moe asked Zak, ignoring the trainer.

He didn't want anyone to touch him, didn't want to leave the field. Gish waited patiently while Moe tried to clear his head, throwing down the water bottle Maulid tentatively offered him. As McGraw barked for subs, reconfiguring the field without the two starters, Moe finally walked to the sideline, resigned.

Gish looked at McGraw as they returned to the bench.

"I can't believe you had that all figured out before we walked off the field, no delays," Gish said.

"Expect the unexpected," McGraw snapped, trying to stay focused despite the carnage he'd just witnessed. "I always know exactly who I would put where."

McGraw knew that winning wasn't just about scoring goals. Winning was about having the mentality to see it through until the end, ready for anything to happen, surviving a crash like the one that just happened. No team was deeper than this one. He could bring wave after wave off that bench, and they wouldn't let up. Shaleh. Mwesa. Ian. Yusuf. They could wear down anyone, even Scarborough.

As Karim donned his long-sleeved Blue Devils shirt, finished for the day, Moe kept shaking his head, trying to clear the murkiness.

"I just have to play it out," he kept saying, begging to go back in.

McGraw looked at Moe and then across at Matt Caron warming up behind Scarborough's bench, ready to go back in. He relented, and Moe ran back out.

There was less than a minute to play. In what was likely Scarborough's last chance, Nigro kicked a monster ball downfield, almost to the box, where Caron stood surrounded by Dek, Zak, and Q. Unexpectedly, Austin broke through and grabbed the ball, which bounced off his hands and toward the track. Running, he slid onto it, pouncing as Kacer's feet came near. Fearlessly, Austin held the ball steady.

"Yeah, Austin!" Zak yelled, clenching his fists with delight.

It was Austin's fourth save in the best game of his life. From the sideline, Henrikson wore what McGraw dubbed his "proud papa face," thrilled by his protégé's moves.

"Ten seconds," the announcer called, starting the countdown. Moe threw the ball into play so high, it looked like it was going to bring down one of the airplanes humming overhead. As the announcer called "THREE," the crowd chanting with him, Nigro caught the ball.

After spending the entire game trying to shut everything out, Abdi H. let himself hear the countdown. He glanced at the sideline, where the coaches were restraining everyone—"wait, wait"—from hitting the field too soon. *We play for the last guy on the bench,* Abdi H. thought.

"Oh, my God," Gish whispered to McGraw, the field growing blurry as his eyes filled with tears. "We're really going to do it."

It was no jinx. When the clock hit zero, the bench took flight, hitting the field with arms spread wide. Gish grabbed McGraw, embracing his friend as never before. On the field, Zak fell to his knees, unable to move. It was like a dream.

I gotta wake up, he thought. *I gotta wake up.*

Zak felt a thump as Shaleh landed on the ground beside him after flying across the field from the bench. Like Zak, emotions poured out of Shaleh, an indescribable release of joy. It had been excruciating to stand behind Gish and watch the clock tick more slowly with each second, his teammates defending their one goal. He wanted so badly to be out on the field, contributing. But he knew better than anyone, better than Fuller, even, how important it was to keep it together. He'd only been in eighth grade when his older brother got booked for taunting against Mt. Ararat all those years ago, but it was a lesson learned. Now, they could celebrate.

Austin ran past them, heading straight for Henrikson. He jumped into the coach's arms.

"Good job," Henrikson kept saying. "You did it."

McGraw felt numb. If he was younger, he knew, he would've been jumping up and down, diving on people. Instead, he stood staring at the clock, reassuring himself that all the zeros were there. As he walked to the middle of the field, he saw the team head to the stands, eager to reach their friends, their family, their teachers, their community.

On her phone, Lise Wagner was trying to describe the scene to Eric, but he couldn't hear her, shouting, "WHAT? WHAT?" He didn't care. Hearing the roar, reading texts pouring in from friends, was good enough.

"I gotta go," Lise yelled. "They're coming over to the stands right now!" She raised the phone up so Eric could hear.

Denis Wing saw the team coming as he high-fived anyone who glanced in his direction. There were no strangers in those stands. Everyone was a friend, even the EL player down in front acting like he, too, just won a state championship. Wing looked beyond the mass of blue crawling up the bleachers, Moha leading the way, Q falling, and saw McGraw slowly walking across the field. It seemed like the coach didn't know what to do, as if he was in a daze, wandering here and there.

Fuller jogged over and wrapped his arms around him. He felt McGraw collapse somewhat as emotion poured out.

"Enjoy this," he said to McGraw, tears in his own eyes. "You did it."

Alone again, McGraw turned and slowly raised his arms over his head, taking in the moment, hearing the crowd.

"I wanted to just watch it surround me," he said later.

He looked for his family through wet eyes; saw former players who'd driven hours to be there. He raised his arms higher, just wanting to thank everyone. The din grew louder, something that didn't seem possible, at the sight of McGraw's quiet celebration. Denis Wing knew he wasn't the only one with tears streaming down his face, his heart full.

That, thought Abdikadir Negeye looking at the field, *is a special guy*. McGraw was the heart of Lewiston High School long before the city's latest transformation began, always voted "most school spirit" in the yearbook, always the guy leading the welcome-back-to-school pep rally. The changes he'd made, from his own understanding of the world to the way he coached the game he loved, gave everyone in those stands hope for Lewiston's future. It was no accident it was McGraw standing in the middle of the field, representing everything Lewiston had been and everything it could become.

Watching her friend, Ronda Fournier realized how much everyone around her had sacrificed for that moment. As people clambered around to try to touch the players, she understood that the victory belonged to all of them.

"They could've killed me," she says of being crushed against the railing, "and it would've been fine."

Karim turned from the bleachers and saw McGraw punch the air. Climbing down, he sprinted toward the man he considered a second father. *Get ready,* McGraw thought as he saw Karim approach. *You're going to have to catch this guy.*

Karim ran into McGraw and buried his head in his coach's neck. The rest of the team descended upon them, reaching in to tousle McGraw's white hair. McGraw squeezed his eyes shut as his mouth broke into a huge grin. It was almost too much.

But he was still a coach. He shook off the emotion and got the team ready for the award ceremony. Sitting on the field trying to peel the tape off his socks, Abdi H. watched the Scarborough players, defeat pouring out of every inch of them, step forward as the runners-up. His Mohawk a little worse for wear, Nigro crouched in front of his teammates, elbows on his knees, palms pressed together as if in prayer. Looking at Nigro's face, Abdi H. knew there was no coming in second in this game. There was a winner and a loser.

"If Lewiston coach Mike McGraw and his assistants..." the announcer began, the crowd drowning out the rest. McGraw, flanked by Austin, Abdi H., and an emotional Maslah, finally had the trophy in his hands, a giant gold soccer ball. They stroked it, hardly believing it was theirs. Suddenly, Abdi H. couldn't temper his jubilation any longer. He grabbed the golden ball and sprinted back toward the stands, Maulid at his side, the team falling in behind them. *We have to share it,* he thought, kissing the trophy before offering it up. *These people deserve it as much as we do.*

This is a "we" moment, Shobow thought while looking down at the team. *It's not an "us" versus "them."* The volunteer coaches, the homework workshops, the Boosters, McGraw's "speckled team"—this was all of it coming together. It wasn't black, Somali, immigrant, or white. They were together, chanting, shouting, and drumming. Shobow knew Somalis would always stick out in Lewiston, no matter what their numbers. But here, no one stuck out. Soccer created space, at least at this moment, for them to come together and rejoice. *We are all Blue Devils,* he thought, one community celebrating one goal.

"HEY, HEY, HEY!" McGraw roared, striding over to the stands.

Everyone stopped petting the trophy and froze.

"We have to take a picture!"

Nuri knew how to get them in formation for a photo.

"*YAKULAK!*" they responded as Nuri yelled, their arms around one another, cameras flashing from every angle.

"Now go get your stuff, get the balls," McGraw called. Even champions had things to do.

When McGraw finally walked off the field, equipment check complete, obligatory interviews done, he saw the team taking selfies with the trophy. The photos would hit social media before they even got to the bus. His phone, too, was blowing up with texts and emails. He saw Abdi H. holding the trophy with his mother, who was wearing a dark hijab over a long orange dress, while Nuri and his mom waited for their turn. Q's mother, Suada Osman, stood, congratulating him, a knowing look on her face. *I'm going to have to cut my hair when I get home,* Q thought.

"We did it, baby!" Zak crowed, as his father inspected Karim's face, wondering if his nose was broken from his collision with Moe, asking his son if they should go see a doctor.

"I'm fine," Karim told him. He wanted to ride back on the bus with his team.

As an exhausted Kim Wettlaufer walked to his car with Carolyn to pick up their son at the babysitter's, he decided it was the greatest sporting event he'd ever been part of. Better than being named

All-American runner, better than crossing a finish line first, out-kicking the guy behind him. Nothing compared to this.

Honking cars followed the bus back to Lewiston, players sticking their heads out the windows, yelling, chanting. Doe lost his fedora as they came off the exit ramp into Lewiston, forcing Fuller to pull off the road to find it. Joined by a police escort, they drove down Lisbon Street, Austin and Abdi H. holding the trophy so people could see.

When the bus finally parked, an unprecedented crowd welcomed the team. It was one thing to celebrate at Fitzpatrick Stadium; it was another to really be home.

"It was pretty nice," says Dek of the moment. "Like, we like who we are."

THE DEVILS
THAT YOU KNOW

Early the next morning, Gish heard a knock at his door. He was exhausted. Last night, they'd taken the trophy to the Blue Goose, the quintessential Lewiston dive bar smack in the middle of downtown, to celebrate. McGraw, who'd been drinking inexpensive pitchers of beer at the Goose since his twenty-first birthday in November of 1970, held court at a booth while the golden ball sat on the bar. Alums poured in to pay homage, an old-school showing of Lewiston pride with McGraw at the center. The coach was now a symbol of how to accept change, embrace change, revel in change.

Gish took lots of pictures, figuring he wouldn't see the trophy again for months as it made rounds through the community. But when he answered the door, McGraw stood there, trophy in hand.

"I thought you might want to bring it to your dad," McGraw rasped.

Gish was overcome. His father, who suffered from Alzheimer's, lived at St. Mary's d'Youville Pavilion, a local nursing home. After serving for twenty-eight years in the Air Force, a mechanic on *Air Force One* for two presidents, he no longer recognized his family. McGraw knew that Gish would be having family dinner at the nursing home later that day, and he wanted to make sure he had the trophy with him.

The golden ball took a circuitous route to its home in Fuller's office, causing the athletic director a lot of stress. Every few days, especially after he saw a picture of it on Facebook or Twitter, Fuller called McGraw, but never got the same answer twice as to its whereabouts. Hersi took it for a week, then his dad brought it to the middle school. There was an enormous community celebration at the Ramada Inn, the city's finest hour, according to Negeye, where just about everyone in Lewiston took a photo with it. A high school pep rally celebrating the trophy included a BMX biker who jumped over McGraw's head while students screamed with delight.

Maulid's parents spent hundreds of dollars on a party for the team. Nuri's mother helped with the cooking—*sambusa*, cake, chicken, soda. They wanted to make sure the party matched the achievement.

"I did it because my son was in the final game and I was very happy for him and very happy for the community," Hassan Matan says, clutching his heart at the memory, determined to talk about it in English. "We needed to celebrate. Whenever there is a game, I try to go. I am always there. The team and the people, they know me. They think I am part of the team. They know. I am very proud and happy because it brings people together. More people know now we are together, all people, because of the team."

It wasn't just the community who recognized the achievements of the Blue Devils. The National Soccer Coaches Association of America named McGraw New England Coach of the Year. He told Fuller that he wanted to cut up the plaque and share it with his assistants, honor them in some way.

"Mike," Fuller said with a sigh, "you ain't cuttin' up your plaque."

Many members of the team received regional and state accolades, but no one more than Abdi H. Named player of the year by the Maine *Sunday Telegram*, the Maine Soccer Coaches Association, and Gatorade, in January, Lewiston's all-time leading scorer traveled to Baltimore with McGraw and Gish to receive the ultimate prize. Abdirahman Shariff-Hassan: All-American.

The spotlight was exhausting, including a trip to the Maine State House, where the team posed for photographs with state reps and took turns pounding the gavel of the Senate. Muktar, for one, was unimpressed.

"Get up, clap, sit down," he remembers. "Why do they get up and sit down so many times?"

Everyone wanted a piece of the team. They were, as U.S. Senator Angus King submitted to the *Congressional Record*, "a fine example of Maine citizens from diverse ethnic, religious, and experiential backgrounds coming together to achieve victory, while championing Maine's spirit and America's highest ideals of inclusiveness and unity."

When the Paris terrorist attacks heightened the debate regarding the ongoing Syrian crisis, stories about the team countered the parade of U.S. governors, including Maine's Paul LePage, who proclaimed that Syrian refugees were not welcome in their states.

"To bring Syrian refugees into our country without knowing who they are is to invite an attack on American soil just like the one we saw in Paris last week and in New York City on 9/11," LePage wrote in a statement three days after Paris. "That is why I adamantly oppose any attempt by the federal government to place Syrian refugees in Maine, and will take every lawful measure in my power to prevent it from happening."

The governor, of course, had no such power, as immigration questions are decided at the federal level. President Obama affirmed that the United States would forge ahead with its plan to accept some ten thousand Syrians in the coming year. They were the victims of terrorism, said Obama, not perpetrators.

But LePage, who had a history of unsavory—racist, even—remarks, found momentum in the presidential campaign of Trump, telling a radio show host that he was "Donald Trump before Donald Trump was Donald Trump." In the wake of Paris, Trump followed his promise to build a wall between Mexico and the United States with a call for a "total and complete" ban on Muslim immigration. He even went so far as to have Rosa Hamid, who was dressed in hijab and a shirt saying "Salam, I come in peace," thrown out of a campaign rally in South Carolina. These moments continued to embolden Islamophobic sentiment, evidenced when CBS's *Evening News* visited Lewiston for a segment that included the soccer team. "These filth have no place in the West and should be expelled by any means necessary," wrote one viewer in the comments section of the CBS website about Lewiston's Somalis.

The media hype surrounding the team eventually settled down. Most days, the champions went through the rituals of high school life like everyone else. Some, like Ben and Joe, hit the track for the indoor season, while others, like Alex, won another state championship—against Scarborough, no less—in hockey. Over February break, Zak and Karim traveled to try out for FC Miami City, a Premiere Development League team.

The first day back from break loomed cold but sunny, hinting of spring. Students filed across the frozen grass, avoiding small piles of snow that remained from the relatively light—by Maine's standards—winter. Tunics and colorful dresses peeked below the hems of puffy parkas.

Inside, McGraw stands in his usual spot outside his classroom, his gravelly voice calling out to students as they pass by. He is in his element, catching up with students, asking what they did over break. Yusuf stops by with news: Nuri is moving to Minnesota. He has family there, and his mother wants to join them.

"I won't sleep tonight," McGraw mutters, his eyes losing their twinkle as he sinks deep into thought, already reconfiguring next fall's offense in his head.

McGraw is sad about losing Nuri. He knows there's nothing he can do—family comes first—but he's going to miss the kid, not just the player. Nuri worked so hard, rose to the top. But Muktar's little brother Warsame is coming up, McGraw remembers. Coach Abdi told McGraw the kid is really good, smart, and definitely ready for a four-year varsity run. And Shaleh, quiet, studious, and strong, shows great leadership potential. Captain potential, perhaps.

McGraw heads into his classroom, perked up by the thought of Warsame and Shaleh. The walls are filled with the usual student project posters screaming in neon pink and green about "DEOXYRIBONUCLEIC ACID," words like "replication" and "translation" explaining the intricate patterns of colorful squares and circles. There's a new poster added to the mix, a photograph of the team with CLASS A STATE CHAMPIONS scrawled across the bottom. On another shelf sits a framed photo of McGraw facing the crowd, hands in the air, at Fitzpatrick Stadium. Chabot called the *Sun Journal* the day after the photo ran and asked for a copy, framing it to present to McGraw at a faculty meeting. As always, McGraw was humble, giving credit to the kids and his assistants, wanting to share any spotlight shed upon him. *It isn't an act,* Chabot thought, watching him. There just weren't a lot of Mike McGraws in the world.

McGraw's classroom closet is now filled with the team's backpacks, the fierce devil mascot embroidered at the center. Even though it's February, McGraw is still collecting kits; something akin, he says, to pulling teeth.

"If they don't turn the stuff in," he grumbles, taking a mental count of the bags before him, "they don't get their championship jacket."

The jackets were a gift from Lee Auto Malls, a venerable local family business. On a chilly day in January, the team met with Adam Lee, who presented a $4,000 check to thank them for becoming such an important part of the city's history, "a dramatic example of what we can all accomplish together."

McGraw preps for his first class, which will include a lab about diffusion through a membrane. He writes definitions of *hypotonic, isotonic,* and *hypertonic* on the blackboard, his left hand working in an efficient, neat, script, when Maslah saunters in. Throughout the winter, McGraw has been his anchor, going with him to talk to teachers, helping him keep up with his work.

"Did you see Coach Fuller?" McGraw asks. "Did you talk to him last week about prep school?"

"I was supposed to," Maslah says, looking down, "but I didn't come in."

"Go see him when you're on one of those," McGraw commands, pointing to the hall pass in Maslah's hand, his coach voice creeping in. "Go see him."

McGraw shifts gears and asks Maslah about his team jersey, which he hasn't returned.

"I need number nine," McGraw says.

"I'll pay for it," Maslah counters, shaking his head.

"You can't," declares McGraw. "It's irreplaceable. If you don't give it back, some kid next year isn't going to have a jersey."

He pauses, letting it sink in.

"It's a famous number, you know," McGraw says.

"Yeah," answers Maslah, smiling as he thinks about the twenty-six goals he scored in that shirt. "Well, it is now."

Undeterred, McGraw weaves one of his stories, his expression serious, his gruff voice gentle. He tells Maslah that the number has a history—a "famous" history. He cites past players who wore it. McGraw enjoys his raconteur moments, but also just wants the jersey back. He knows Maslah is having a hard time letting go of more than a shirt. As the dance continues, Maslah's demeanor changes from wayward student flaunting a hall pass to player listening to coach. He agrees to find the shirt and bring it to McGraw.

McGraw never got the jersey back.

In June, Lewiston High School graduated fourteen members of the championship soccer team. These days, immigrant students graduate at a higher rate than native-born Mainers, 78.3 percent to 73.3 percent. In the fall, Maulid would be the only returning varsity starter, flanked by others who logged minutes on the championship team, like Muktar and Joe, Shaleh and Ben, Yusuf and Alex. Maulid was excited to be a captain, but there was a lot to do before the start of the season. Summer games. Ramadan. A trip to Gillette Stadium to be honored by the New England Revolution.

Denis Wing arranged a coach bus to take the team to Gillette, figuring they'd earned padded seats and a little air conditioning. The Revs wanted to honor the Blue Devils as "Heroes of the Match" on the infield before the start of the game. Wing told the players to meet at the high school at 12:30, plenty of time for them to be late. Ben strolled in wearing a turquoise button-down shirt and a black bow tie, ready for the occasion. McGraw arrived dressed in khaki shorts, his blue coach shirt, and a blue baseball hat, already texting those he hadn't heard back from. Zak and Karim were in Minnesota visiting family. Nuri had already moved.

"Where's Yusuf?" McGraw barked. "Where's Khalid?"

A few Booster parents arrived with a giant cooler loaded with water, and dispersed Costco-sized boxes of snacks to the back of the bus. As the players boarded, they were grateful for the blast of cold air that greeted them. The July day loomed hot and humid, and most had been up much of the night before. It was Eid, the end of Ramadan, a day filled with celebration and family, starting with morning prayers at nine at the Lewiston Armory, used on occasions when the city's mosques are not big enough. "*Eid Mubarak!*" players greeted one another.

"There's H!" someone cried, spying Abdi H. walking across the parking lot with a platter of Subway sandwiches provided by Kim Wettlaufer. The sandwiches were gone in minutes.

About halfway into the trip, McGraw strolled back to give them one last speech. The players, many of whom were sleeping, shook themselves to attention. Most of them had graduated. But he was still their coach.

"This is a big deal," McGraw announced. "These people have invited us, and it's a big deal. I don't know what they have in store for you down there, but you are representing a lot while you're there. Your team. Your school. Your families. Our community. I expect you to remember that. This might be it. This might be the last time. So this is a big deal."

The parking lot at Gillette was a sauna, heat radiating from the black pavement. After their initial awe at the stadium, the team was dismayed at the high prices of the restaurants, only a handful having enough money to make any purchases. Before going onto the infield, Revs striker Kei Kamara, who hails from Sierra Leone and came to the United States through a refugee resettlement program, greeted them, taking selfies with each player.

After the game, there were fireworks. The team was tired, but they were used to staying up late from Ramadan, eating far into the night. Joe sat next to McGraw, transfixed, while Maulid never flinched as the colors burst in the sky. He now knew that the loud bangs and booms his parents once ran from, the terrorizing and paralyzing sounds of war, were how some Americans celebrated.

That fall, the Blue Devils would fail to repeat their championship season, going out in the quarterfinals to Camden Hills. After spending the summer teaching soccer in South Africa, Abdi H. headed to the Kent School in Connecticut with Moe for a postgraduate year, while others enrolled in classes at the local community college or at the University of Southern Maine.

Before the season started, a late-summer visit to Maine from then–presidential candidate Donald Trump resurrected some of the myths and stereotypes of Lewiston's past. Trump warned Maine of the criminal and terrorist element housed in its Somali community. He was, of course, wrong. Crime wasn't up in Lewiston since the Somalis came, Lewiston Police Chief Brian O'Malley assured residents. It was down. Way down.

"He's crazy, right?" Maulid asked of Trump. "He doesn't want any of us here."

Maulid's mother woke him early on November 8, 2016, urging him to vote before school, fearful about what a Trump presidency might mean for her family. She knows that as a U.S. citizen she is safe, but still, she worries. Within a few months of Trump's improbable election, thousands would descend on America's airports, including Bangor and Portland, to protest his executive order banning citizens from seven Muslim-majority countries, including Somalia. Yet again, Lewiston's refugee community found itself on high alert, worried that the city's racial divide could crack open. A student wearing a Trump shirt told Maulid that his time in the city was coming to an end, while a driver threatened a Somali woman who was crossing the street, yelling at her to take off her hijab as he sped by.

"You guys are okay," a classmate told one soccer player, reigniting a familiar refrain. "Just no *more* immigrants."

McGraw knows that Androscoggin County voted for Trump. It was the first time in thirty years the region went Republican. Just because a community came together doesn't mean it stays together. But McGraw hopes that if he keeps the team focused on winning, there won't be much space for what he calls "the other stuff." Soccer, he trusts, can continue to lead the way, giving the city something tangible to hang onto as it espouses the benefits of a global community, and does the hard work of keeping its arms open.

Maulid agrees. Gazing at his bedroom wall, clippings and photos from the championship season hanging in a bright mosaic, he dreams of playing soccer professionally. Then he wants to return to Lewiston and build more soccer fields, teaching kids how to play. He loves having little kids walk up to him on the street, asking about the flip throw, and taking selfies with him. Soccer is the beginning, the end, and the middle.

"We brought the community together," he says. "They believed in it, and they believed in us."

LEWISTON HIGH SCHOOL BLUE DEVILS SOCCER
STATE CHAMPIONS 2015

No.	Name	Position	Gr.
1	Abdirizak Ali	Midfield	12
2	Abdiaziz Shaleh	Midfield	11
3	Dek Hassan	Defender	12
4	Hassan Qeyle	Midfield	12
5	Zakariya Abdulle	Defender	12
6	Noralddin Othman	Midfield	10
7	Muktar Ali	Striker	10
8	Mohamed Khalid	Defender	12
9	Maslah Hassan	Striker	12
10	Abdi Shariff-Hassan	Striker	12
11	Maulid Abdow	Midfield	11
12	Mohamed Abdisalan	Midfield	12
13	Yusuf Mohamed	Forward	10
14	Joséph Kalilwa	Midfield	11
15	Hassan Hassan	Midfield	11

No.	Name	Position	Gr.
16	Mwesa Mulonda	Midfield	11
17	Ben Doyle	Defender	12
18	Abdulkarim Abdulle	Striker	12
19	Ian Hussey	Defender	11
20	Benjamin Musese	Defender	11
21	Timo Teckenberg	Midfield	10
22	Ryan Bossie	Defender	10
23	Evan Cox	Defender	10
32	Austin Wing	Goalkeeper	12
GK	Alex Rivet	Goalkeeper	10

Coaches: Mike McGraw, Dan Gish, Abdijabar
 Hersi, Per Henrikson
Athletic Director: Jason Fuller
Principal: Shawn Chabot
Scorer: Doe Mahamud
Mascot: Blue Devil

SOCCER IS LIFE

It was August 2017, and Nuri was back in town. The defensive midfielder missed his friends and former teammates. He'd played soccer his junior year in Minnesota, but the season had ended with a torn ACL and meniscus. Despite the tough road back from surgery, he was determined to play the game again. And he wanted to do it in Lewiston.

Muktar was the only other remaining member of the 2015 championship squad. Young and inexperienced, the Blue Devils needed leaders. A few weeks into the season, they decided Nuri should have a captain's band on his arm. Just as he had once looked up to Karim and Abdi H., these younger players now looked up to him.

Unlike 2015, this season, which saw most of Lewiston's home games played at Bates College while the high school's playing fields were renovated, was not perfect. But McGraw thought something felt very right. It wasn't just the return of Nuri. The next generation was rising.

Muktar's younger brother, Warsame, was coming into his own. Bilal Hersi—one of Coach Abdi's younger sons—looked to be a top scorer. Noor Aden wanted to follow in Shobow's footsteps. Bakar Shariff-Hassan knew how big Abdi H.'s shoes were and wondered if he could ever fill them.

Playing in freezing rain on Bates's Garcelon Field in the regional final against heavily favored Bangor, these players came of age. In a tight game from the start, Lewiston hit halftime in a 1–0 deficit. About five minutes into the second half, Bilal put Lewiston on the board. Then, with twenty minutes to go, he kicked the ball in front of Bakar, who put it into the net. Goalie Dido Lumu, who had stepped up when Alex Rivet left Lewiston for prep school, made two monster saves in the final minutes to keep the Blue Devils on top.

The upset sent them to the state championship game for the third time in four years.

November 4, 2017, broke chilly but clear as Lewiston prepared to play Portland High School. Eric Wagner made the drive from Swarthmore, determined not to miss this one. On the way, Wagner picked up Abdi H. at the University of Massachusetts, Lowell, where he now played Division 1 soccer.

The tense, defensive game was a stalemate. "Overtime," Wagner texted former teammates who couldn't be there. "Fifteen minutes of golden goal."

"You've got this, you've got this," McGraw told the team before sending them back out. "Get the ball into a dangerous place, and we'll see what we see."

With just over five minutes left on the overtime clock, Nuri lined up for an indirect kick about forty-two yards out. He looked at his teammates on the field. No Karim. No Maslah. No Maulid. No Abdi H. No Q. But here he was, doing what he did best, trying to place the ball in front of someone. He called Warsame's name. He knew the sophomore jumped higher than anyone else and would have an advantage for a clean header.

As the ball soared over traffic, Warsame gritted his teeth. He wanted this so badly. A golden goal for a golden trophy that would match his bleached hair and his shiny metallic cleats. He was hungry for his own title, to be sure, but even more, he wanted Muktar to have another one. He knew Portland's goalie was going to come out as soon as Nuri launched the ball—it had been his pattern throughout the game. Warsame leaped and barely flicked the ball toward the corner. It bounced and rolled slowly toward the net. Warsame froze, waiting, hoping.

Goal: 1–0 Lewiston. They were champions again.

The team lifted Warsame toward the sky as fans—including Abdi H. and Moe, who ran out onto the field to tackle McGraw—celebrated. Warsame was overcome. Teachers regularly told him he could be a leader one day. Feeling his teammates hold him up made him think that day had arrived. This wasn't about his one goal, he realized. It was about all of them: the coaches, the players, the fans, and, above all, Muktar.

The 2015 team was, from every angle, every statistic, in every way, a dream team. But now, Warsame knew, they had taken their turn. And there were many more behind them, ready to play this game, for this school, in this city.

"We bleed blue and always will," Warsame says of the moment. "Soccer is life."

ACKNOWLEDGMENTS

As an undergraduate history major at Bates College, I lived in Lewiston for four years. But I never really knew Lewiston. I am grateful I've had this chance to go back, and glad the city obliged my return. So many there helped make this book a reality, starting with Coach Mike McGraw. He thought a bit (as he should have) before saying yes to me, but then I never again had to ask if I could tag along. From postgame chats at the Goose to a very special afternoon visiting with his mother, Florence, our unfolding relationship was constantly reassuring that I might be up to the task of telling this story.

At Lewiston High School, coaches Dan Gish, Abdijabar Hersi, and Per Henrikson answered my questions and became my cheerleaders. A special thanks to Per, and his cameraman Dan Jacques, for providing hours of invaluable game footage. Principal Shawn Chabot and Athletic Director Jason Fuller opened doors and made sure I knew where to go. Gus Le Blanc and Ronda Fournier were wonderful resources.

I am most indebted to the Blue Devils themselves, especially those whose names appear in this book. From the locker room to their homes, practices to games, they were patient, funny, and giving. Whether I was on the sideline of a playoff game, in the middle of a team huddle, at the fence of the venerable Respect Ramadan Tournament, or in their kitchens, they welcomed my camera, my questions, and me. Extra shout-outs to Abdi Shariff-Hassan, Moe Khalid, Karim and Zak Abdulle, Austin Wing, Alex Rivet, Hassan Qeyle, Abdiaziz Shaleh, Dek Hassan, Ian Hussey, Nuri Othman, Ben Musese, Joe Kalilwa, Maslah Hassan, Mwesa Mulonda, Ridwan Ali, Muktar and Warsame Ali, and, especially, Maulid Abdow. Special thanks to all of their parents, but especially Hassan Matan, Shafea Omar, Habibo Farah, Denis and Kathy Wing, and the Booster Club. I wish Suada Osman had lived to see the finished book; she is remembered with love.

Kim Wettlaufer and Carolyn McNamara made sure I didn't always eat by myself in a hotel room, and showed me how to be part of this community. Abdullahi Abdi always greeted my questions with a warm smile in his gentle way. His daughter, Halima, became a trusted friend; his grandchildren became my playmates. Shobow Saban, Abdikadir Negeye, and everyone at Maine Immigrant and Refugee Services, as well as Phil Nadeau at City Hall, and LHS alums Eric Wagner and Lise Wagner honed my perspective on soccer and immigration in Lewiston. The very talented filmmaker Ian Clough was a fellow traveler. I am so grateful for his generosity, good humor, and long talks. Erin Reed's work at Trinity Jubilee is heroic. Thanks to Joel Costigan, Josh Morrissey, and Colleen and Matt Whitaker for showing me what Lewiston looks like from the other side of the field. Thanks, too, to Jake Rosenwasser, Judge George Singal, Audree Burns, Tammy Levesque English, Kirby Bradley, Julia Sleeper, and Mary Carillo.

Cheers to my soccer connoisseurs Greg Lalas, Nate Kalin, Harry Miller, my nephew Max Wojtas, and, especially, Michael

Beattie, my MVP, whose generous feedback kept me in line. Whitney Kassel provided a skilled editorial eye on Somalia and refugee resettlement; Stash Wislocki gave me corresponding photos. Colleagues Nick, Dan, Becca, Roblyn, and Nereida make professional life bearable, while Dr. Nahed Nourreddine offered expert Arabic translation. Catherine Pearlman read my earliest pages and offered wise advice; Beth McGregor, Rodney Bedsole, Emma Bates Zar, Dan Smith, Rebecca Traister, Lisa Genova, Kate Bolick, and Aaron Cohen all pitched in. Sarah Tynan Sullivan read pages far into the night, brainstorming, supporting, and being the dearest friend a person can be. Anne, Gwen, Dierdra, Ashley, Scott, Anna, Sandee, Val, Sally, Beth, Lori, Sam, Ken, Rachel, Julie, Liza, and Limor are my village.

The excellent, insightful scholarship of Kimberly Huisman, Catherine Besteman, Mary Rice-DeFosse, and James Myall provided essential secondary resource material. I am grateful I met Kevin Mills before his untimely passing. His articles about Lewiston soccer deservedly won awards. Thanks to Justin Pelletier at the *Lewiston Sun Journal*; Steve Greenlee at the *Portland Press Herald*; and Jay Burns, Darby Ray, Marianne Nolan Cowan, Bill Hiss, and Phyllis Gerber Jenson at Bates College.

CNN Opinion's Pat Wiedenkeller and Robert Gallant said yes when I first wanted to write about a soccer team in Maine, and then provided support when the ugly, hateful reactions to the piece came in.

I am indebted to my editor, Mauro DiPreta, for wanting to turn that first article into a book. His fine editorial eye and his compassion for the story contributed greatly to making this a better book. Thanks also to his patient assistant, David Lamb, as well as the copyediting, production, and publicity mavens at Hachette.

Dan Strone of Trident Media is not just an agent; he is a connection to one of the most important pieces of my heart. He stepped in and stuck like glue, honoring what he first called "our Miltie pact," brilliantly guiding me through this process while understanding how timing can be bittersweet.

My father, Milton Bass, the quintessential raconteur, would've loved the evolution this book represents for me as a writer. My mother, Ruth, my brother, Michael, and my sister, Elissa, have helped mark what this project means. My husband, Evan, held down the fort so I could be a soccer groupie in Maine, packed me snacks for the road, and spent more time with these pages than he'd care to admit. He and our daughter, Hannah, who had a blast on the sideline, will always be my championship team.

ONE GOAL

BY AMY BASS

1. Consider *One Goal's* epigraph, a statement by Ronaldinho: "When you have a football at your feet, you are free." What might this mean? In what various ways do the many stories throughout the book concern the idea of freedom? What are essential freedoms?

2. What is it about the game of soccer that makes it the most popular sport to play around the world? What might explain why baseball, football, and basketball seem more popular in the United States, while soccer is thought of as "an outlier"? What are important differences between participating in a sport and simply being a spectator?

3. What does Bass mean when she writes that the success of the Lewiston Blue Devils shows what happens "when America works the way it is supposed to"?

4. How is it that mistreated immigrants from only a generation ago, like many of the Québécois in Lewiston, can be so critical of more recent immigrants like the Somali refugees? Why is such "an old story" so enduring?

5. Of the many valuable qualities of Coach Mike McGraw, which seem the most admirable? How is he able to connect so genuinely with students and players coming from such profoundly different experiences? What in his experience might help explain his democratic values? Their consistency? His willingness and ability to evolve and adapt as he ages? How is it that changes in his life and community don't threaten these values but actually strengthen them?

6. Consider Lewiston's "coach of everyone," Abdullahi Abdi. What skills and qualities does he bring to the players and the program? What does he offer that McGraw cannot? Why is it important for him to be at each game? Why does he value "possession" soccer more than "direct" soccer? In what ways outside of soccer is he a mentor?

7. Considering Coach McGraw, Abdullahi Abdi, Abdijabar Hersi, Abdikadir Negeye, and players like Shobow Saban, Abdi H., and others, what are the various qualities of strong and effective leaders?

8. Why is it that "schools became the front line of the many transitions taking place" in Lewiston? How did Gus LeBlanc handle such a complex challenge? What additional skills and value did ZamZam Mohamud contribute?

9. Given the particular geographical, cultural, and familial complexity of their lives, how do the boys and girls cultivate an identity, a sense of who they are? What elements of life create or maintain the cultural identity served by organizations like SBYA/MEIRS and Trinity Jubilee?

10. In what ways does Halima Hersi experience "the pull of life in America"? What does she mean when she says that her daughter and her friends are "making their own identity as Muslim women"?

11. How do various players on the team manifest or alter their unique personalities when on the pitch, in their game? What is particularly special about players like Abdi H., Moe, Maulid, Karim, and others both on and off the field?

12. What in particular does the life of Shobow Saban demonstrate about the immigrant experience, soccer, and immigrants' potential to make a difference in their adoptive Lewiston communities? How is it that, as he learned first with his close friend Jonny McDonough, questions are "an important step in the building of bridges"?

13. Lewiston AD Jason Fuller says that without William "Kim" Wettlaufer the integrated soccer program "doesn't happen," that his "role and influence is monumental." What did Wettlaufer bring to the program and community at large? Why, unlike so many others in Lewiston, couldn't he and his wife Carolyn McNamara "look away" once they started watching Shobow and the others enliven and transform the soccer program?

14. What's the difference between "direct" or "kick and chase" soccer and "possession soccer"? Why was the latter style more appropriate for the new players at Lewiston? What might such a style of play suggest about solving complex personal and social problems in the community? What is "the advantage of the ball"?

15. Essential to the success of the team was the building of trust between the players on the field, and between them and the coaches. How was trust built or earned in these various relationships? How did it manifest during practices and games? What qualities or behaviors were important to building trust with the players' families and within the larger community of Lewiston?

16. What is the significance of the Blue Devil's rallying cry "PAMOJA NDUGU!"? In what various ways, on the field and off, is it demonstrated?

17. What challenges beyond those of normal competition did the Blue Devils face? What responses were suggested or demanded by Coach McGraw, especially regarding unfair and even racist treatment? Is it always best to "ignore ignorance"? When, if ever, is some kind of retaliation necessary? What form should it take?

18. Despite subscribing to Coach McGraw's mantra that players should never retaliate in response to trash talk or physical play, why does Moe Khalid lose his temper when an opposing player says something about his mother? What is the significance of the Somali expression "Hooyadu waa lama huran" (*It's not necessary to live with a mother; it's hard to live without a mother*)? In what ways are the players' mothers a central part of the broader community? What kinds of special responsibilities do these players have in terms of supporting their parents?

19. How does the team evolve over time, especially after its heartbreaking loss to Cheverus? What was necessary to transform them into a championship team?

20. When Maslah returns to the team, Abdi H. offers a powerful insight regarding teamwork when he says, "Trying to do your own thing is not as fun." Why is this? What does group success have or create that individual accomplishment doesn't?

21. Coach McGraw passionately defends the players on the bench, reminding the starters: "Don't you disrespect them...they are our all-stars sitting there." What does he mean? Beyond the players, who are the important all-stars, part of the "good, strong, deep bench" of the community?

22. What does the huge supportive crowd at the state championship game reveal about the evolution of Lewiston? What is it about the team that seems to override animosity or bias in many people? How do sports in general offer an opportunity to gather seemingly disparate people? At what point can team loyalty become divisive?

23. What were particularly important moments in the championship game against Scarborough? How did the Blue Devils have to adapt in ways they hadn't all season? What was the significance of "YAKULAK!"? What effects might such a historic victory have had on each of the players personally?

24. Even in the spotlight as New England Coach of the Year, McGraw is "humble, giving credit to the kids and his assistants." Where does such humility come from? Why is it true that, as Bass states, "there just [aren't] a lot of Mike McGraws in the world"?

25. Despite the powerful and transformative success of the Lewiston Blue Devils, many in the community are still entrenched in racist beliefs and behaviors. Why is this? What are they attached to? Why does it often take decades or generations for such prejudice to fade?

26. After Lewiston's second state championship two years later, Warsame offers the profound and simple statement "Soccer is life." What does this mean?